FAVORITE BRAND NAME

MUFFIN COLLECTION

PUBLICATIONS INTERNATIONAL, LTD.

ISBN: 1-56173-760-7

Library of Congress Catalog Card Number: 92-85258

Pictured on front cover: *Top row, left:* Cranberry Orange Nut Muffins (*page 10*), Carrot-Raisin Bran Muffins (*page 10*), Sweet Potato Pecan Muffins (*page 14*); *Center:* Blueberry Orange Corn Muffins (*page 108*), Apple Nugget Muffins (*page 141*), Raspberry Apple Streusel Muffins (*page 141*); *Right:* Nutty Blueberry Muffins (*page 27*). *Bottom row, left:* Home-Style Blueberry Muffins (*page 149*); *Center:* Chocolate Macadamia Muffins (*page 119*), Mini Crumbcakes (*page 119*), Chocolate Streusel Pecan Muffins (*page 120*); *Right:* Double Oat Muffins (*page 20*).

Pictured on back cover: *Top row, left:* Bacon Brunch Buns (*page 152*); *Center:* Country Biscuits (*page 172*); *Right:* Chocolate Chunk Sour Cream Muffins (*page 140*), Chocolate Chunk Banana Bread (*page 208*). *Bottom row, left:* Sunday Morn Cranberry-Orange Bread (*page 194*), California Date-Nut Muffins (*page 32*), Our Very Best Bran Muffins (*page 32*), Chili-Cheese Corn Muffins (*page 96*), Quick Banana-Bran Bread (*page 192*); *Center:* Deluxe Blueberry Muffins (*page 117*); *Right:* Roasted Red Pepper Biscuits (*page 171*).

8   7   6   5   4   3   2   1

Manufactured in U.S.A.

Microwave ovens vary in wattage and power output; cooking times given with microwave directions in this book may need to be adjusted. Consult manufacturer's instructions for suitable microwave-safe cooking dishes.

Contents

❖

TIPS AND TECHNIQUES

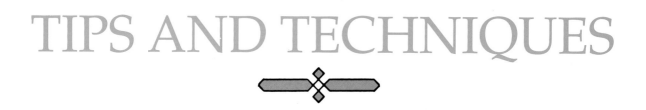

Muffins originated in the mid-1800's when a pan made of iron or tin cups fastened together by a rack was created. This special baking pan was called "gem" cups and even today muffins are still called gems in some areas of the country.

Muffins are especially appealing since they are convenient and wholesome treats. The next time your family asks, "Is there anything to eat?" think of how easy making muffins for a snack can be. Baking powder and/or baking soda are used to make the muffins rise and to give them a light texture enabling you to have old-fashioned freshly baked goods in less than one hour. They're certainly not just for breakfast. Muffins are perfect for packed lunches, coffee breaks at the office, a nutrient booster when hiking and camping, or a simple dessert.

Whether you're new to muffin baking or a whiz in the kitchen, the following tips and techniques will help insure baking success. Besides general guidelines, you'll find hints on preparing batter, storing muffins and gift giving.

GENERAL GUIDELINES
The following techniques lay the foundation for baking skills for great muffins and other baked goodies.

• Read the entire recipe before beginning to make sure you have all the necessary ingredients and baking utensils.

• Remove butter, margarine and cream cheese from the refrigerator to soften, if necessary.

• Toast and chop nuts, peel and slice fruit, and melt chocolate before preparing the batter.

• Measure all the ingredients accurately and assemble them in the order they are called for in the recipe.

• Use the pan size specified in the recipe. Prepare the pans according to the recipe directions. Adjust oven racks and preheat the oven. Check oven temperature for accuracy with an oven thermometer.

• Follow recipe directions and baking times exactly. Check for doneness using the test given in the recipe.

MEASURING INGREDIENTS
Dry Ingredients: Always use standardized measuring spoons and cups. Fill the correct measuring spoon or cup to overflowing and level it off with a metal spatula or knife. When measuring flour, lightly spoon it into a measuring cup and then level it off. Do not tap or bang the measuring cup as this will pack the flour. If a recipe calls for "sifted flour," sift the flour before it is measured. If a recipe calls for "flour, sifted," measure the flour first and then sift it.

Liquid Ingredients: Use a standardized glass or plastic measuring cup with a pouring spout. Place the cup on a flat surface, fill to the desired mark and check the measurement at eye level. When measuring sticky liquids, such as honey and molasses, grease the measuring cup or spray it with vegetable cooking spray before adding the liquid to make their removal easier.

Melting Chocolate

Make sure the utensils you use for melting are completely dry. Moisture will make the chocolate become stiff and grainy. If this happens, add 1/2 teaspoon shortening (not butter) for each ounce of chocolate and stir until smooth. Chocolate scorches easily, and once scorched cannot be used. Follow one of these three methods for successful melting.

Double Boiler: This is the safest method because it prevents scorching. Place the chocolate in the top of a double boiler or in a bowl over hot, not boiling water; stir until smooth. (Make sure that the water remains just below a simmer and is one inch below the top pan.) Be careful that no steam or water gets into the chocolate.

Direct Heat: Place the chocolate in a heavy saucepan and melt over very low heat, stirring constantly. Remove the chocolate from the heat as soon as it is melted. Be sure to watch the chocolate carefully since it is easily scorched with this method.

Microwave Oven: Place an unwrapped 1-ounce square or 1 cup of chips in a small microwavable bowl. Microwave on High (100%) 1 to 1 1/2 minutes, stirring after 1 minute. Stir the chocolate at 30-second intervals until smooth. Be sure to stir microwaved chocolate since it retains its original shape even when melted.

Toasting Nuts

Toasting nuts brings out their flavor and makes them crisp. Spread the nuts in a single layer on a rimmed baking sheet. Bake in a preheated 350°F oven for 8 to 10 minutes or until golden. Shake the pan or stir the nuts occasionally during baking to insure even toasting. The nuts will darken and become crisper as they cool. To toast a small amount of nuts, place them in a dry skillet over low heat. Stir constantly for 2 to 4 minutes, until the nuts darken slightly. Allow nuts to cool before chopping.

PREPARATION

Stirred Muffins: The batter for muffins is usually stirred, but may be creamed. For stirred muffins, first combine the dry ingredients together in a large bowl. This is done to distribute the baking powder and/or baking soda with the flour. If the leavening is unevenly distributed, the muffins may have a bitter taste. Next, combine the liquid ingredients in a separate bowl and add them all at once to a well in the dry ingredients. Stir *just* until the dry ingredients are moistened. The batter should be lumpy; the lumps will disappear during baking. Overstirring the batter develops the gluten in the flour causing the baked muffin to have tunnels, peaked tops and a tough texture. Nuts, fruits, chocolate chips or other ingredients are folded gently into the batter at the end.

Creamed Muffins: Creamed muffins have a cake-like texture. In this type of muffin the shortening and sugar are creamed (beaten) together before adding the other ingredients. They are usually a sweeter muffin.

Quick Loaves: The batter for quick loaves is prepared the same way as muffin batter and can also be stirred or creamed. As with muffins, it is important to combine the dry ingredients well and to avoid overbeating the batter.

Biscuits and Scones: When preparing biscuits, cut the butter or shortening into the dry ingredients with a pastry blender or two knives until the mixture forms *coarse* crumbs. Blending the fat in any further produces mealy biscuits. Mix the dough gently and quickly to achieve light and tender results. Overworking the dough makes the biscuits tough. On a lightly floured surface, roll or pat out the dough to the desired thickness. Press a floured cutter straight down through the dough; twisting produces lopsided biscuits. Use a wide spatula to transfer the cut-out biscuits to the baking sheet. For crusty biscuits, place them at least one inch apart on the baking sheet. For soft, fluffy biscuits, place them close together. Biscuits are best when served hot from the oven. Scones are similar to biscuits, but the dough is richer due to the addition of cream and eggs. While the dough can be cut into any shape, scones are usually cut into wedges or triangles. They are traditionally served with butter, preserves and whipped cream.

Popovers: Before baking powder was invented in the 1850's, popovers were one of the few breads cooks could make quickly. The name popover came about because the batter "popped over" the edge of the pan as it baked. Popovers "pop" because of the steam that forms inside as they bake. To insure popping, use *large* eggs to help the popovers set and don't add more meat, cheese or other ingredients than the recipe directs, since they will become too heavy.

BAKING

Muffins: Begin by preheating the oven to the recommended baking temperature, then prepare the muffin pan. The standard size muffin cups vary in size from manufacturer to manufacturer and are generally 2½ to 2¾ inches in diameter. Mini muffin cups vary from 1¼ to 1¾ inches in diameter. Jumbo muffin cups (often called Texas-size) are about 4 inches in diameter. The muffin cups should be either well greased or paper lined. When making jumbo muffins be sure to grease the top of the pan so that the batter won't stick. If a recipe does not call for foil or paper liners, grease the muffin cups since that particular batter will stick to the liners when baked. For best results with microwave recipes, line the microwavable muffin pan with double paper baking cups so that the outer liner will absorb the moisture and the inner liner will stick to the baked muffin.

Unless otherwise stated, muffin cups should be filled ⅔ to ¾ full with batter. When adding muffin batter to the pan, a ¼ cup measure or a soup ladle is less messy than a spoon and makes it easier to place an equal amount of batter in each cup. If there is not enough batter to fill all the cups, fill empty cups half full with water to prevent the pan from scorching or warping in the oven. The water also allows for even baking.

Begin checking for doneness at the minimum time given in the recipe. Muffins are done when the center springs back when lightly touched and generally when a wooden pick inserted in the center comes out clean. Check recipes for other indications of doneness.

When the muffins test done, immediately remove from cups and cool on a wire rack. If the muffins stick to the pan, let them sit about 5 minutes. The steam from the pan should loosen them. If they still stick, loosen muffins from the pan by running a knife around the edge of the cup. Most muffins are best if they are served warm.

Quick Loaves: Fill greased loaf pans ½ to ⅔ full unless otherwise indicated. The loaf is done when it pulls away slightly from the sides of the pan and generally when a wooden pick inserted in the center comes out clean. Check recipes for other doneness indicators. It is normal for the loaf to crack across the top during baking. Let the loaf cool in the pan for about 10 minutes, then remove it to a wire rack. Quick loaves are easier to slice if completely cooled.

Biscuits and Scones: These baked goods are done when the bottom and top crusts are evenly and lightly browned. Slightly lift biscuits or scones from the baking sheet with a spatula to check the bottoms.

Popovers: Popover pan or custard cups should be greased generously to insure easy removal and popping of popovers. When filling the cups, stir the batter since it will settle after mixing. To prevent overbrowning, lower the oven shelf so the *tops* of the popover pan cups or custard cups are in the center of the oven. Popovers are done when they are firm to the touch and tops are golden brown. To prevent popovers from becoming soggy, prick them with a fork to let steam escape immediately after removing from oven. For crisp popovers, turn off the oven and bake for 5 minutes longer or to desired crispness. Remove popovers from pans while still warm. Since popovers will fall if they are underdone, follow baking times carefully and bake until they are firm. Also, don't open the oven while baking since the rush of cool air can make them fall.

STORAGE

Muffins: Store cooled muffins at room temperature in a sealed plastic bag up to three days. For longer storage, muffins may be frozen. Wrap cooled muffins in heavy-duty foil. Seal, label and date package. For best flavor, use within one month. To reheat, warm in preheated 350°F oven about 20 minutes. Or unwrap and microwave on High (100%) about 45 seconds per muffin.

You can store muffin batter in the refrigerator and bake as needed up to one week. However, the longer the batter is stored, the lower the volume will be of the baked muffin. Baking powder and baking soda work best if baked immediately after mixing. When stored, they begin to lose their leavening power.

Quick Loaves: After the loaves have cooled, wrap well and store at room temperature overnight to let the flavors develop. Quick loaves will stay fresh about one week at room temperature or up to three months in the freezer. Thaw loaves unwrapped at room temperature. To reheat, cover with foil and heat in preheated 350°F oven about 10 minutes.

Biscuits and Scones: Stored in an airtight container or sealed plastic bag, they will keep at room temperature two to three days. To reheat, wrap in foil and heat in preheated 300°F oven 10 to 12 minutes. Wrapped in heavy-duty foil, they can be frozen up to three months. To reheat, place frozen, wrapped biscuits or scones in preheated 300°F oven 20 to 25 minutes.

Popovers: Popovers are best when served hot. But they can be frozen in a freezer bag up to three months. To reheat frozen popovers, place on baking sheet and bake in preheated 400°F oven 10 to 15 minutes.

GIFT GIVING IDEAS

Wrap cooled muffins individually in clear plastic wrap. Place in a new muffin pan and send the pan as a gift with the muffins. Or, wrap loaves tightly with plastic wrap. Tie a ribbon around each loaf as you would a gift box. For a beautiful housewarming gift, give a basket filled with tea-time goodies. Place colored cotton napkins in a basket and fill with your favorite tea and preserves. Then add cooled scones and mini muffins sealed in a decorative bag. When the treats are gone, they'll still have a basket.

To send baked goods, fill the bottom of the shipping container with an even layer of packing material. Do not use popped popcorn or puffed cereal as it may attract insects. Crumpled waxed paper, newspaper or paper toweling works well. Fill any crevices with packing material and add a final layer at the top of the box.

WEIGHTS AND MEASURES

Dash = less than ⅛ teaspoon

½ tablespoon = 1½ teaspoons

1 tablespoon = 3 teaspoons

2 tablespoons = ⅛ cup

¼ cup = 4 tablespoons

⅓ cup = 5 tablespoons plus 1 teaspoon

½ cup = 8 tablespoons

¾ cup = 12 tablespoons

1 cup = 16 tablespoons

½ pint = 1 cup or 8 fluid ounces

1 pint = 2 cups or 16 fluid ounces

1 quart = 4 cups or 2 pints or 32 fluid ounces

1 gallon = 16 cups or 4 quarts

1 pound = 16 ounces

SUBSTITUTION LIST

If you don't have:	Use:
1 teaspoon baking powder	¼ teaspoon baking soda + ½ teaspoon cream of tartar
½ cup firmly packed brown sugar	½ cup granulated sugar mixed with 2 tablespoons molasses
1 cup buttermilk	1 tablespoon lemon juice or vinegar plus milk to equal 1 cup (Stir; let mixture stand 5 minutes.)
1 ounce (1 square) unsweetened baking chocolate	3 tablespoons unsweetened cocoa + 1 tablespoon shortening
3 ounces (3 squares) semi-sweet baking chocolate	3 ounces (½ cup) semi-sweet chocolate morsels
½ cup corn syrup	½ cup granulated sugar + 2 tablespoons liquid
1 whole egg	2 egg yolks + 1 tablespoon water
1 cup honey	1¼ cups granulated sugar + ¼ cup water
1 teaspoon freshly grated orange or lemon peel	½ teaspoon dried peel
1 teaspoon pumpkin pie spice	Combine: ½ teaspoon cinnamon, ¼ teaspoon nutmeg and ⅛ teaspoon *each* allspice and cardamom

SOLUTIONS TO QUICK BREAD PROBLEMS

Problems:

Solutions:

MUFFINS AND QUICK LOAVES

Problems	Solutions
Tunnels, peaked tops, crumbly texture	Avoid overstirring; batter should be lumpy.
Tough texture	Thoroughly mix egg with liquid ingredients before adding to dry ingredients.
Uneven tops with ledges	Grease muffin cups or baking pans only on the bottoms and half way up the sides.
Flat tops, batter doesn't rise	Bake immediately after filling muffin cups in *preheated* oven so that the leavening power of the baking powder and/or baking soda is not lost.
Soggy bottoms	Cool in pans only as long as recipe indicates, then remove to cooling rack.
Raisins or other dried fruit sink	Toss fruit lightly with flour before adding to batter.

BISCUITS AND SCONES

Problems	Solutions
Mealy not flaky texture	Avoid overblending the shortening with the flour. Blend only to *coarse* crumbs. Use chilled butter or margarine to make it easier to cut into coarse crumbs.
Dry or tough texture	Avoid overkneading dough. Knead to distribute moisture only. Cut out as many biscuits or scones in a single rolling since rerolling and adding more flour makes them tough.
Heavy, not light	Avoid overmixing dough. Stir only until dry ingredients are just moistened.
Yellow specks on the top crust	Combine dry ingredients well to evenly distribute the baking powder and/or baking soda.
Hard crust	Check oven temperature with oven thermometer since it may be too high. Check for doneness at the minimum baking time.

POPOVERS

Problems	Solutions
Overbrowned	Lower the oven shelf so the *tops* of the popover pan or custard cups are in the center of the oven.
Popovers are soggy	Prick with a fork to let steam escape immediately after removing. Turn off oven; return popovers for 5 minutes.
Don't "pop"	Generously grease popover pan or custard cups. Use large eggs to insure they set. Don't add more meat, cheese or other ingredients than recipe directs.
Popovers fall	Popovers may be underdone. Follow baking time carefully; bake until firm. Also, don't open the oven while baking.

RISE 'N' SHINE MUFFINS

Carrot-Raisin Bran Muffins

MAZOLA® No Stick cooking spray
2 cups bran flake cereal with raisins
⅔ cup buttermilk
½ cup KARO® Dark Corn Syrup
1 cup flour
2 teaspoons baking soda
1 teaspoon cinnamon
¼ teaspoon salt
1 egg, slightly beaten
¼ cup sugar
¼ cup MAZOLA® Corn Oil
1 cup shredded carrots

Preheat oven to 400°F. Spray 12 (2½-inch) muffin pan cups with cooking spray.

In large bowl mix cereal, buttermilk and corn syrup; let stand 5 minutes. In medium bowl combine flour, baking soda, cinnamon and salt; set aside. Add egg, sugar and corn oil to cereal mixture; mix until blended. Stir in flour mixture until well blended. Stir in carrots. Spoon into prepared muffin pan cups.

Bake 20 minutes or until lightly browned and firm to touch. Cool in pan on wire rack 5 minutes; remove from pan.
Makes 12 muffins

Cranberry Orange Nut Muffins

MAZOLA® No Stick cooking spray
1½ cups flour
½ cup sugar
2 teaspoons baking powder
½ teaspoon salt
2 eggs
½ cup KARO® Light Corn Syrup
½ cup orange juice
¼ cup MAZOLA® Corn Oil
1 teaspoon grated orange peel
1 cup fresh or frozen cranberries, chopped
½ cup chopped walnuts

Preheat oven to 400°F. Spray 12 (2½-inch) muffin pan cups with cooking spray.

In medium bowl combine flour, sugar, baking powder and salt. In large bowl combine eggs, corn syrup, orange juice, corn oil and orange peel. Stir in flour mixture until well blended. Stir in cranberries and walnuts. Spoon into prepared muffin pan cups.

Bake 18 to 20 minutes or until lightly browned and firm to touch. Cool in pan on wire rack 5 minutes; remove from pan.
Makes 12 muffins

In basket from left to right: Cranberry Orange Nut Muffins, Carrot-Raisin Bran Muffins and Sweet Potato Pecan Muffins (page 14)

Nutty Banana Jam Muffins

1¼ cups ground walnuts, divided
1½ cups sugar, divided
¾ cup margarine, softened
2 extra-ripe, medium DOLE® Bananas, peeled
1 egg
2 cups all-purpose flour
2 teaspoons baking powder
1½ teaspoons ground cinnamon
½ teaspoon ground nutmeg
¼ teaspoon salt
1 ripe, small DOLE® Banana, peeled
3 tablespoons raspberry jam

Preheat oven to 400°F. Line 18 (2½-inch) muffin cups with paper liners. In shallow dish, combine ¾ cup walnuts and ½ cup sugar; set aside.

Beat remaining ½ cup walnuts, 1 cup sugar and margarine in large bowl until light and fluffy. Purée 2 medium bananas in blender (1 cup). Beat puréed bananas and egg into sugar-margarine mixture. Combine flour, baking powder, cinnamon, nutmeg and salt in medium bowl. Beat dry ingredients into banana mixture until well mixed.

Mash small banana in small bowl; stir in raspberry jam. For each muffin, roll 1 heaping tablespoon dough in walnut-sugar mixture to coat. Place in prepared muffin cup. Make a dimple in center of dough with back of spoon. Spoon 1 teaspoon jam mixture into center. Roll 1 more heaping tablespoon dough in walnut-sugar mixture. Drop over jam mixture. Repeat with remaining dough and jam mixture.

Bake 15 to 20 minutes or until lightly browned. Cool slightly in pan; remove to wire rack. Serve warm.

Makes 18 muffins

Left to right: Nutty Banana Jam Muffins and Peanut Orange Breakfast Puff

Peanut Orange Breakfast Puffs

2 cups sifted all-purpose flour
1 tablespoon baking powder
1 teaspoon salt
1/4 cup sugar
1 cup milk
1 egg, beaten
1/4 cup peanut oil
1/2 cup chopped salted peanuts

Topping:

1/4 cup sugar
1 teaspoon grated orange peel
1/4 cup butter or margarine, melted

Preheat oven to 425°F.

Sift together flour, baking powder, salt and 1/4 cup sugar in large bowl. Combine milk, egg and peanut oil in small bowl. Add milk mixture all at once to flour mixture, stirring only until moistened. Fold in peanuts. Fill 12 oiled 2½-inch muffin cups, filling 2/3 full.

Bake 15 to 20 minutes or until tops are lightly browned. Meanwhile, blend 1/4 cup sugar and orange peel in small bowl until crumbly. When muffins are baked, remove from muffin cups and immediately dip tops in melted butter, then in orange-sugar mixture. Serve warm.   *Makes 12 muffins*

*Favorite recipe from **Oklahoma Peanut Commission***

Apple Spice Muffins

1½ cups all-purpose flour
1/2 cup KRETSCHMER® Original Wheat Germ
1/2 cup granulated sugar
1 tablespoon baking powder
1¼ teaspoons ground cinnamon
1/2 teaspoon salt (optional)
1 cup peeled, chopped apple
1 cup 2% low-fat milk
1/4 cup vegetable oil
1 egg, slightly beaten
1/3 cup chopped nuts
2 tablespoons margarine or butter, melted

Heat oven to 400°F. Line 12 (2½-inch) muffin cups with paper baking cups or grease lightly.

In large bowl, combine flour, wheat germ, 1/4 cup of the sugar, the baking powder, 3/4 teaspoon of the cinnamon and the salt. Stir in apple. In small bowl, combine milk, oil and egg. Add to flour mixture, stirring just until moistened. Fill muffin cups almost full. In small bowl, combine remaining 1/4 cup sugar, 1/2 teaspoon cinnamon, the nuts and margarine. Sprinkle over muffins.

Bake 20 to 25 minutes or until golden brown and wooden pick inserted in center comes out clean. Remove from pan.   *Makes 12 muffins*

Tip: To freeze muffins, wrap securely in foil or place in freezer bag. Seal, label and freeze. To reheat frozen muffins, unwrap muffins. Microwave at HIGH (100%) about 30 seconds per muffin.

Raisin Rice Bran Muffins

1¼ cups whole-wheat flour
¾ cup rice bran
¾ cup raisins
½ cup sugar
2 teaspoons baking powder
1 teaspoon ground cinnamon
½ teaspoon salt
1¼ cups buttermilk
3 tablespoons vegetable oil
2 egg whites, lightly beaten
   Vegetable cooking spray

Combine flour, bran, raisins, sugar, baking powder, cinnamon, and salt in large bowl. Combine buttermilk, oil, and egg whites in small bowl; add to dry ingredients. Stir just until dry ingredients are moistened. Spoon batter into 12 (2½-inch) muffin cups coated with cooking spray.

Bake at 400°F. for 15 to 17 minutes. Cool slightly on wire rack. Serve warm.

Makes 12 muffins

Tip: Muffins may be stored in the freezer in freezer bag or tightly sealed container. To reheat frozen muffins, microwave each muffin on HIGH 30 to 40 seconds or heat at 350°F. for 12 to 15 minutes.

Favorite recipe from **USA Rice Council**

Raisin Rice Bran Muffin

Sweet Potato Pecan Muffins

MAZOLA® No Stick cooking spray
1¾ cups flour
⅓ cup sugar
2 teaspoons baking powder
1 teaspoon cinnamon
½ teaspoon salt
⅛ teaspoon nutmeg
¾ cup cooked, mashed sweet potatoes
¾ cup KARO® Dark Corn Syrup
⅓ cup MAZOLA® Corn Oil
2 eggs
1 teaspoon vanilla
1 cup chopped pecans

Preheat oven to 400°F. Spray 12 (2½-inch) muffin pan cups with cooking spray.

In medium bowl combine flour, sugar, baking powder, cinnamon, salt and nutmeg. In large bowl with mixer at medium speed, beat sweet potatoes, corn syrup, corn oil, eggs and vanilla until blended. Stir in flour mixture until well blended. Stir in pecans. Spoon into prepared muffin pan cups.

Bake 20 minutes or until lightly browned and firm to the touch. Cool in pan on wire rack 5 minutes; remove from pan.

Makes 12 muffins

Pear Yogurt Muffins

2 cups all-purpose flour
¼ cup sugar
1½ teaspoons baking powder
1 teaspoon baking soda
½ teaspoon salt
1 egg, slightly beaten
1 cup plain yogurt
¼ cup vegetable oil
2 tablespoons lemon juice
1 teaspoon grated lemon peel
1 (16-ounce) can Bartlett pears, drained and diced

Preheat oven to 400°F.

Combine flour, sugar, baking powder, baking soda and salt in large bowl. Blend egg, yogurt, oil, lemon juice and peel in small bowl; add to dry ingredients. Stir in pears, mixing just until moistened. Spoon evenly into greased 2½-inch muffin cups.

Bake 20 to 25 minutes or until golden brown and wooden pick inserted near center comes out clean.

Makes 12 to 18 muffins

Favorite recipe from **Canned Fruit Promotion Service**

Pineapple Carrot Raisin Muffins

Golden Oatmeal Muffins

1 package DUNCAN HINES® Moist Deluxe Butter Recipe Golden Cake Mix
1 cup quick-cooking oats (not instant or old-fashioned)
¼ teaspoon salt
¾ cup milk
2 eggs, slightly beaten
2 tablespoons butter or margarine, melted

1. Preheat oven to 400°F. Grease 24 (2½-inch) muffin cups (or use paper liners).

2. Combine cake mix, oats and salt in large bowl. Add milk, eggs and melted butter; stir until moistened. Fill muffin cups two-thirds full. Bake at 400°F for 13 minutes or until golden brown. Cool in pans 5 to 10 minutes. Loosen carefully before removing from pans. Serve with honey or your favorite jam.

Makes 2 dozen muffins

Tip: For a slight variation, try adding 1 teaspoon ground cinnamon with the dry ingredients.

Pineapple Carrot Raisin Muffins

2 cups all-purpose flour
1 cup sugar
2 teaspoons baking powder
½ teaspoon ground cinnamon
¼ teaspoon ground ginger
½ cup shredded DOLE® Carrots
½ cup DOLE® Raisins
½ cup chopped walnuts
1 can (8 ounces) DOLE® Crushed Pineapple in Juice
2 eggs
½ cup margarine, melted
1 teaspoon vanilla extract

Preheat oven to 375°F. Grease 12 (2½-inch) muffin cups.

Combine flour, sugar, baking powder, cinnamon and ginger in large bowl. Stir in carrots, raisins and walnuts. Combine undrained pineapple, eggs, margarine and vanilla in small bowl. Stir into dry ingredients until just blended. Spoon into prepared muffin cups.

Bake 20 to 25 minutes. Remove from pan; cool on wire rack. *Makes 12 muffins*

Refrigerator Applesauce Wheat Muffins

¾ cup all-purpose flour
½ cup whole wheat flour
1 cup uncooked quick-cooking rolled oats
½ cup packed brown sugar
1 teaspoon baking powder
½ teaspoon baking soda
½ teaspoon ground cinnamon
¼ teaspoon salt
¾ cup buttermilk
¼ cup applesauce
¼ cup vegetable oil
1 egg, beaten
¼ cup raisins

Microwave Directions: Combine flours, oats, brown sugar, baking powder, baking soda, cinnamon and salt in large bowl. Combine buttermilk, applesauce, oil and egg in small bowl until blended. Stir into flour mixture just until moistened. Fold in raisins. Cover and refrigerate overnight or up to 1 week.

Line 6 microwavable muffin cups with double paper liners. Spoon batter into prepared muffin cups, filling ½ full. Microwave at HIGH 3 to 3½ minutes or until wooden pick inserted in center comes out clean. Rotate dish ½ turn halfway through cooking. Let stand 5 minutes. Remove from pan. Repeat procedure. For last 3 muffins, line 3 muffin cups with double paper liners. Microwave at HIGH 1½ to 2 minutes. Let stand 5 minutes. Remove from pan.

Makes about 15 muffins

Conventional Directions: Preheat oven to 400°F. Grease or paper-line 12 (2½-inch) muffin cups. Prepare batter as directed. Spoon into prepared muffin cups. Bake 16 minutes or until wooden pick inserted in center comes out clean. Remove from pan. *Makes 12 muffins*

Tip: Mix up this batter and refrigerate tightly covered in a plastic bowl. If you cook for one, you can scoop out batter for one muffin at a time. Bake in the microwave oven at HIGH 30 to 50 seconds.

Molasses Muffins

1⅔ cups unsifted all-purpose flour
3 tablespoons sugar
2 teaspoons baking powder
1 teaspoon ground ginger
½ teaspoon salt
½ cup dark molasses
2 eggs, slightly beaten
¼ cup CRISCO® Oil
¼ cup milk

Preheat oven to 400°F. Place paper liners in 12 (2½-inch) muffin cups.

Mix flour, sugar, baking powder, ginger and salt in medium mixing bowl. Make a well in center of mixture. Blend remaining ingredients in small mixing bowl. Pour into well in dry ingredients. Stir just until ingredients are moistened. Pour into prepared cups, filling each about two-thirds full.

Bake at 400°F, about 15 minutes, or until centers spring back when touched lightly.

Makes 1 dozen muffins

Orange Raisin Muffins: Follow recipe above, omitting ginger. Add ½ cup raisins and 2 teaspoons grated orange peel to dry ingredients.

Refrigerator Applesauce Wheat Muffins

Carrot Bran Muffins

2 cups finely shredded carrots
1 cup 40% wheat bran flakes
¾ cup skim milk
2 tablespoons vegetable oil
1 tablespoon lemon juice
1 egg, slightly beaten
1 cup whole wheat flour
2 tablespoons packed brown sugar
1 teaspoon baking powder
½ teaspoon baking soda
½ teaspoon pumpkin pie spice
¼ teaspoon salt

Microwave Directions: Line 6 microwavable muffin cups with double paper liners.

Combine carrots, bran and milk in large bowl. Let stand 5 minutes. Stir in oil, lemon juice and egg. Combine flour, sugar, baking powder, baking soda, spice and salt in medium bowl. Stir into bran mixture just until moistened. (Batter will be lumpy.) Spoon batter into prepared muffin cups, filling ½ full.

Microwave at HIGH 2 to 4½ minutes or until top springs back when touched. Rotate dish ½ turn halfway through cooking. Let stand 5 minutes. Remove from pan. Repeat procedure with remaining batter.   *Makes about 12 muffins*

Date-Nut Muffins

MAZOLA® No Stick cooking spray
1 package (8 ounces) pitted dates, coarsely chopped
¾ cup boiling water
¼ cup MAZOLA® Corn Oil
½ teaspoon vanilla
1 cup all-purpose flour
½ cup whole wheat flour
½ cup sugar
⅓ cup coarsely chopped walnuts
½ teaspoon baking soda

Preheat oven to 375°F. Spray 12 (2½-inch) muffin pan cups with cooking spray.

In large bowl combine dates, water, oil and vanilla; stir to mix. In medium bowl combine flours, sugar, walnuts and baking soda. Add to date mixture, stirring just until moistened. Spoon into prepared muffin pan cups.

Bake 25 minutes or until wooden pick inserted into center comes out clean. Remove from pan. Serve warm or cool on wire rack.   *Makes 12 muffins*

Morning Muffins

2¾ cups QUAKER® Crunchy Bran Cereal, finely crushed to 1 cup
1½ cups all-purpose flour
⅓ cup firmly packed brown sugar
4 teaspoons baking powder
1 teaspoon ground cinnamon
1 cup chopped pitted prunes
1¼ cups 2% low-fat milk
⅓ cup vegetable oil
1 egg, slightly beaten

Heat oven to 400°F. Line 12 (2½-inch) muffin cups with paper baking cups or grease lightly.

In large bowl, combine cereal, flour, brown sugar, baking powder and cinnamon. Stir in prunes. In small bowl, combine milk, oil and egg. Add to flour mixture, stirring just until moistened. Fill muffin cups almost full.

Bake 25 minutes or until wooden pick inserted in center comes out clean. Cool in pan on wire rack 5 minutes. Remove from pan. Serve warm.

Makes 12 muffins

Tip: To freeze muffins, wrap securely in foil or place in freezer bag. Seal, label and freeze. To reheat frozen muffins, unwrap muffins; wrap in paper towel. Microwave at HIGH (100%) about 45 seconds per muffin.

Banana Breakfast Muffins

Banana Breakfast Muffins

1½ cups NABISCO® 100% Bran™
 1 cup milk
 ¼ cup FLEISCHMANN'S® Margarine,
  melted
 1 egg, slightly beaten
 1 cup all-purpose flour
 ⅓ cup firmly packed light brown sugar
 2 teaspoons DAVIS® Baking Powder
 1 teaspoon ground cinnamon
 ½ cup mashed banana
 ½ cup seedless raisins

Mix bran, milk, margarine and egg; let
stand 5 minutes.

In bowl, blend flour, brown sugar, baking
powder and cinnamon; stir in bran
mixture just until blended. (Batter will be
lumpy.) Stir in banana and raisins. Spoon
batter into 12 greased 2½-inch muffin-
pan cups.

Bake at 400°F for 20 to 25 minutes or until
toothpick inserted in center comes out
clean. Serve warm.

Makes 1 dozen muffins

Microwave Directions: Prepare batter as
above. In each of 6 microwavable muffin-
pan cups, place 2 paper liners. Spoon
batter into cups, filling ⅔ full. Microwave
on HIGH (100% power) for 3 to 3½
minutes or until toothpick inserted in
center comes out clean, rotating pan ½
turn after 2 minutes. Let stand in pan 5
minutes. Repeat with remaining batter.
Serve warm.

Apple Sauce Bran Muffins

1½ cups NABISCO® 100% Bran™
1½ cups MOTT'S® Regular or Natural
  Apple Sauce
 1 egg, slightly beaten
 ¼ cup FLEISCHMANN'S® Margarine,
  melted
 ½ cup firmly packed light brown sugar
1½ cups all-purpose flour
 1 tablespoon DAVIS® Baking Powder
 1 teaspoon ground cinnamon
 ½ cup seedless raisins, optional
  Apple Sauce Glaze (recipe follows)

In large bowl, mix bran, apple sauce, egg,
margarine and brown sugar; let stand 5
minutes. In separate large bowl, blend
flour, baking powder and cinnamon; stir
in bran mixture just until blended. (Batter
will be lumpy.) Stir in raisins if desired.
Spoon batter into 12 greased 2½-inch
muffin-pan cups.

Bake at 400°F for 15 to 18 minutes or until
toothpick inserted in center comes out
clean. Remove from pan. Cool slightly.
Drizzle with Apple Sauce Glaze; serve
warm.   *Makes 1 dozen muffins*

Apple Sauce Glaze: Blend ½ cup
confectioners' sugar into 1 tablespoon
MOTT'S® Regular or Natural Apple
Sauce until smooth.

Double Oat Muffins

2 cups QUAKER® OAT BRAN™ Hot
   Cereal, uncooked
1/3 cup firmly packed brown sugar
1/4 cup all-purpose flour
2 teaspoons baking powder
1/4 teaspoon salt (optional)
1/4 teaspoon ground nutmeg (optional)
1 cup skim milk
2 egg whites, slightly beaten
3 tablespoons vegetable oil
1 1/2 teaspoons vanilla
1/4 cup QUAKER® Oats (quick or old
   fashioned, uncooked)
1 tablespoon firmly packed brown
   sugar

Heat oven to 400°F. Line 12 (2 1/2-inch)
muffin cups with paper baking cups or
grease lightly.

In large bowl, combine oat bran, 1/3 cup
brown sugar, flour, baking powder, salt
and nutmeg. In small bowl, combine
milk, egg whites, oil and vanilla. Pour
into oat bran mixture, mixing just until
moistened. Fill muffin cups almost full. In
small bowl, combine oats and remaining
1 tablespoon brown sugar; sprinkle
evenly over batter.

Double Oat Muffins

Bake 20 to 22 minutes or until golden
brown. Remove to wire rack. Cool
completely.   *Makes 12 muffins*

Microwave Directions: Line 6
microwavable muffin cups with double
paper baking cups. Prepare batter as
directed above. Fill muffin cups almost
full. In small bowl, combine oats and
remaining 1 tablespoon brown sugar;
sprinkle evenly over batter. Microwave at
HIGH (100%) 2 minutes 30 seconds to 3
minutes or until wooden pick inserted in
center comes out clean. Remove from
pan; cool 5 minutes before serving. Line
muffin cups with additional double
paper baking cups. Repeat procedure
with remaining batter.

Blueberry Bran Muffins

1 1/2 cups all-purpose flour
1/4 cup sugar
1 tablespoon baking powder
1/4 teaspoon salt
1 1/2 cups KELLOGG'S® COMPLETE®
   BRAN FLAKES cereal
1 cup skim milk
1 egg
1/4 cup vegetable oil
1/2 cup fresh or frozen blueberries
   Vegetable cooking spray

Stir together flour, sugar, baking powder
and salt. Set aside.

In large mixing bowl, combine Kellogg's®
Complete® Bran Flakes cereal and milk.
Let stand about 3 minutes or until cereal
softens. Add egg and oil; mix well. Add
flour mixture, stirring only until
combined. Stir in blueberries. Portion
batter evenly into 12 (2 1/2-inch) muffin-
pan cups coated with cooking spray.

Bake in 400°F oven about 20 minutes or
until golden brown. Serve warm.
   Makes 12 muffins

Tropical Raisin Muffins

2½ cups unprocessed bran
1⅓ cups whole wheat flour
2½ teaspoons baking soda
½ teaspoon salt
1½ cups SUN-MAID® Raisins
1 cup shredded coconut
2 eggs
1 cup mashed ripe bananas
½ cup buttermilk
½ cup vegetable oil
½ cup honey

Preheat oven to 375°F. Grease or paper-line 18 (2¾-inch) muffin cups.

Combine bran, flour, baking soda, salt, raisins and coconut in large bowl. Mix to blend thoroughly. Beat eggs in medium bowl. Add bananas, buttermilk, oil and honey. Beat to blend thoroughly. Stir into dry ingredients, mixing just until blended. Spoon evenly into prepared muffin cups.

Bake 20 to 25 minutes or until springy to the touch and lightly browned. Serve warm. *Makes 18 muffins*

Honey-Lemon Muffins

¾ cup ROMAN MEAL® Original
    Wheat, Rye, Bran, Flax Cereal
1½ cups all-purpose flour
1 tablespoon baking powder
½ teaspoon salt
1 egg, slightly beaten
1 cup plain yogurt
½ cup vegetable oil
½ cup honey
2 teaspoons grated lemon peel
1 to 2 tablespoons lemon juice

Preheat oven to 375°F. Grease 12 (2½-inch) muffin cups.

Combine cereal, flour, baking powder and salt in large bowl. Mix egg, yogurt, oil, honey, lemon peel and juice in small bowl. Add liquid mixture to flour mixture, stirring just until moistened. (Batter will be lumpy.) Spoon evenly into prepared muffin cups.

Bake 20 to 25 minutes or until golden brown. Remove from pan; cool on wire rack. *Makes 12 muffins*

Grape Oat Bran Muffins

1½ cups oat bran cereal
¾ cup all-purpose flour
2 teaspoons baking powder
¼ teaspoon salt
1 cup buttermilk
2 eggs
¼ cup packed brown sugar
2 tablespoons vegetable oil
1 teaspoon grated lemon peel
1⅓ cups California seedless grapes

Preheat oven to 400°F. Grease 12 (2½-inch) muffin cups.

Combine oat bran cereal, flour, baking powder and salt in large bowl. Beat together buttermilk, eggs, brown sugar, oil and lemon peel in medium bowl. Quickly stir liquid mixture and grapes into dry ingredients, mixing only until moistened. Spoon evenly into prepared muffin cups.

Bake 17 to 20 minutes or until golden.
Makes 12 muffins

Tip: To maintain freshness, freeze muffins and thaw as needed.

*Favorite recipe from **California Table Grape Commission***

Coffee Cake Muffins

Topping (recipe follows)
1½ cups all-purpose flour
½ cup granulated sugar
2 teaspoons baking powder
½ teaspoon salt
½ cup butter or margarine, melted
1 egg
⅓ cup milk
Icing (recipe follows)

Microwave Directions: Line 6 microwavable muffin cups with double paper liners. Prepare Topping; set aside.

Combine flour, granulated sugar, baking powder and salt in large bowl. Pour in butter; add egg and milk. Stir until ingredients are blended. (Batter will be soft.) Spoon 1 tablespoon batter into each prepared muffin cup. Sprinkle 1 teaspoon Topping evnly over batter. Spoon 1 tablespoon batter over Topping, filling about ½ full. Sprinkle 1 teaspoon Topping evenly over batter; press lightly into batter.

Microwave at HIGH 2½ to 4½ minutes or until wooden pick inserted in center comes out clean. Rotate dish ½ turn halfway through cooking. Let stand 5 minutes. Remove from pan. Repeat procedure using remaining batter and Topping. Prepare Icing and drizzle over warm muffins.　　*Makes 10 muffins*

Topping: Combine ¼ cup packed brown sugar, ¼ cup chopped walnuts, 3 tablespoons all-purpose flour and 1 teaspoon ground cinnamon in small bowl. Add 1 tablespoon melted butter or margarine, stirring until mixture resembles moist crumbs.

Icing: Combine ½ cup powdered sugar, 1 tablespoon milk and 1 teaspoon vanilla extract in small bowl, stirring until smooth.

Banana Corn Muffins

1 cup all-purpose flour
¾ cup QUAKER® or AUNT JEMIMA®
　　Enriched Corn Meal
¼ cup granulated sugar
1 tablespoon baking powder
½ teaspoon salt (optional)
¾ cup mashed ripe banana
½ cup milk
⅓ cup vegetable oil
1 egg, slightly beaten

Heat oven to 425°F. Line 12 (2½-inch) muffin cups with paper baking cups or grease lightly.

In medium bowl, combine flour, corn meal, sugar, baking powder and salt. In small bowl, combine banana, milk, oil and egg. Add to flour mixture, stirring just until moistened. Fill muffin cups ¾ full.

Bake 15 to 18 minutes or until golden brown. Remove from pan. Serve warm.
Makes 12 muffins

Microwave Directions: Line 6 microwavable muffin cups with double paper baking cups. Prepare batter as directed, only increase the vegetable oil to ½ cup. Fill muffin cups ⅔ full. Microwave at HIGH (100%) about 1 minute: 30 seconds or until wooden pick inserted in center comes out clean. Rotate dish ½ turn after 1 minute of cooking. Remove from pan. Repeat procedure with remaining batter. Serve warm.
Makes about 15 muffins

Coffee Cake Muffins

Good-For-You Muffins

1 cup whole wheat flour
1 cup all-purpose flour
½ cup granulated sugar
½ cup chopped dates
½ cup chopped walnuts
1 tablespoon baking powder
1 teaspoon ground cinnamon
½ teaspoon ground nutmeg
¼ teaspoon salt
1 egg, lightly beaten
1 cup LIBBY'S® Solid Pack Pumpkin
1 cup *undiluted* CARNATION®
    Evaporated Milk
¼ cup butter or margarine, melted
¼ cup honey
2 teaspoons grated orange zest

In large bowl, combine flours, sugar, dates, walnuts, baking powder, cinnamon, nutmeg, and salt; set aside. In medium bowl, whisk together egg, pumpkin, evaporated milk, butter, honey, and orange zest; blend well. Add liquid ingredients to dry ingredients; stir until dry ingredients are moistened. Spoon into greased or paper-lined muffin cups, filling ½ full.

Bake in preheated 375°F. oven for 20 to 25 minutes, or until wooden pick inserted in center comes out clean. Cool 3 to 4 minutes. Remove from pan; cool on wire rack.   *Makes 18 muffins*

Cranberry Banana Muffins

Cranberry Banana Muffins

2 cups QUAKER® OAT BRAN™ Hot
    Cereal, uncooked
½ cup firmly packed brown sugar
¼ cup all-purpose flour
2 teaspoons baking powder
½ teaspoon salt (optional)
½ teaspoon ground cinnamon
½ cup finely chopped cranberries
⅔ cup cranberry juice cocktail
½ cup mashed ripe banana (about
    1 medium)
2 egg whites, lightly beaten
3 tablespoons vegetable oil

Preheat oven to 400°F. Line 12 (2½-inch) muffin cups with paper baking cups or grease lightly.

In large bowl, combine oat bran, brown sugar, flour, baking powder, salt and cinnamon. Gently stir in cranberries. In small bowl, combine cranberry juice, banana, egg whites and oil. Stir into flour mixture, mixing just until moistened. Fill muffin cups almost full.

Bake 20 to 22 minutes or until golden brown and wooden pick inserted in center comes out clean. Remove to wire rack. Cool completely.

Makes 12 muffins

Tip: To freeze muffins, wrap securely in foil or place in freezer bag. Seal, label and freeze. To reheat frozen muffins, unwrap muffins. Microwave at HIGH (100%) about 30 seconds per muffin.

Blueberry Yogurt Muffins

2 cups QUAKER® OAT BRAN™ Hot Cereal, uncooked
¼ cup firmly packed brown sugar
2 teaspoons baking powder
1 carton (8 ounces) plain low-fat yogurt
2 egg whites, lightly beaten
¼ cup skim milk
¼ cup honey
2 tablespoons vegetable oil
1 teaspoon grated lemon peel
½ cup fresh or frozen blueberries

Heat oven to 425°F. Line 12 (2½-inch) muffin cups with paper baking cups or grease lightly.

In large bowl, combine oat bran, brown sugar and baking powder. In small bowl, combine yogurt, egg whites, milk, honey, oil and lemon peel. Stir into oat bran mixture, mixing just until moistened. Fold in blueberries. Fill muffin cups almost full.

Bake 18 to 20 minutes or until golden brown and wooden pick inserted in center comes out clean. Remove to wire rack. Cool completely.

Makes 12 muffins

Honey Fig Whole Wheat Muffins

1 cup whole wheat flour
½ cup all-purpose flour
½ cup wheat germ
2 teaspoons baking powder
1 teaspoon ground cinnamon
½ teaspoon salt
½ teaspoon ground nutmeg
½ cup milk
½ cup honey
¼ cup butter or margarine, melted
1 egg
1 cup chopped dried figs
½ cup chopped walnuts

Preheat oven to 375°F. Grease or paper-line 12 (2½-inch) muffin cups.

Combine flours, wheat germ, baking powder, cinnamon, salt and nutmeg in large bowl. Combine milk, honey, butter and egg in small bowl until well blended. Stir into flour mixture just until moistened. Fold in figs and walnuts. Spoon evenly into prepared muffin cups.

Bake 20 minutes or until lightly browned on edges and wooden pick inserted in center comes out clean. Remove from pan.

Makes 12 muffins

Honey Fig Whole Wheat Muffins

Special Bran Muffins

3 cups bran flakes or other bran cereal
2 cups BORDEN® or MEADOW
   GOLD® Buttermilk
1 cup water
1¼ cups sugar
1 (9 ounce) package NONE SUCH®
   Condensed Mincemeat, crumbled
½ cup margarine or butter, melted
2 eggs
2½ cups all-purpose flour
2½ teaspoons baking soda

Preheat oven to 425°F.

In large bowl, combine bran cereal, buttermilk and water; mix well. Stir in sugar, mincemeat, margarine and eggs. Combine flour and baking soda; add to mincemeat mixture in small amounts just until blended and moistened. Let stand 20 minutes to soften cereal. Fill greased or paper-lined 2½-inch muffin cups ¾ full.

Bake 15 to 20 minutes or until golden brown. Immediately turn out of pans. Serve warm.

Makes about 3 dozen muffins

Oatmeal Raisin Muffins

1 can (8 ounces) DOLE® Crushed
   Pineapple in Juice
1 cup dairy sour cream
1 egg
¼ cup margarine, melted
1½ cups all-purpose flour
1 cup old-fashioned oats
½ cup sugar
1 tablespoon baking powder
1 teaspoon ground cinnamon
½ teaspoon ground nutmeg
½ teaspoon salt
1 cup DOLE® Raisins

Preheat oven to 350°F. Grease 12 (2½-inch) muffin cups.

Combine undrained pineapple, sour cream, egg and margarine in small bowl until well blended. Combine remaining ingredients in large bowl; make well in center. Pour in pineapple mixture. Stir just until mixed. Spoon evenly into prepared muffin cups.

Bake 30 to 35 minutes or until lightly browned and wooden pick inserted in center comes out clean. Remove from pan. Serve warm.   *Makes 12 muffins*

Ginger Peach Muffins

2 cups NABISCO® 100% Bran™
1 cup plain nonfat yogurt
½ cup skim milk
¼ cup FLEISCHMANN'S® Margarine,
   melted
¼ cup EGG BEATERS® 99% Real Egg
   Product
1 cup all-purpose flour
⅓ cup firmly packed light brown sugar
1 tablespoon DAVIS® Baking Powder
1 teaspoon ground ginger
½ cup chopped canned or fresh
   peaches

Mix bran, yogurt, milk, margarine and Egg Beaters®; let stand 5 minutes.

In bowl, blend flour, brown sugar, baking powder and ginger; stir in bran mixture just until blended. (Batter will be lumpy.) Stir in peaches. Spoon batter into 12 greased 2½-inch muffin-pan cups.

Bake at 400°F for 18 to 20 minutes or until toothpick inserted in center comes out clean. Serve warm.

Makes 1 dozen muffins

Nutty Blueberry Muffins

Nutty Blueberry Muffins

**1 package DUNCAN HINES®
    Blueberry Muffin Mix**
2 egg whites
½ cup water
⅓ cup chopped pecans

1. Preheat oven to 400°F. Grease 2½-inch muffin cups (or use paper liners).

2. Rinse blueberries from Mix with cold water and drain.

3. Empty muffin mix into bowl. Break up any lumps. Add egg whites and water.

Stir until moistened, about 50 strokes. Stir in pecans; fold in blueberries.

4. For large muffins, fill cups two-thirds full. Bake at 400°F for 17 to 22 minutes or until toothpick inserted in center comes out clean. (For medium muffins, fill cups half full. Bake at 400°F for 15 to 20 minutes.) Cool in pan 5 to 10 minutes. Loosen carefully before removing from pan.

Makes 8 large or 12 medium muffins

Tip: To reheat leftover muffins, wrap muffins tightly in foil. Place in 400°F oven for 10 to 15 minutes.

Spicy Sweet Potato Muffins

2 tablespoons packed brown sugar
1 teaspoon ground cinnamon
1½ cups all-purpose flour
2 teaspoons baking powder
1 teaspoon ground cinnamon
½ teaspoon salt
½ teaspoon baking soda
½ teaspoon ground allspice
⅓ cup packed brown sugar
1 cup mashed cooked or canned sweet potatoes
¾ cup buttermilk
¼ cup vegetable oil
1 egg, beaten

Preheat oven to 425°F. Grease 12 (2½-inch) muffin cups.

Combine 2 tablespoons brown sugar and cinnamon in small bowl; set aside. Combine flour, baking powder, cinnamon, salt, baking soda and allspice in large bowl. Stir in ⅓ cup brown sugar. Combine sweet potatoes, buttermilk, oil and egg in medium bowl. Stir buttermilk mixture into dry ingredients just until combined. Spoon batter into prepared muffin cups, filling each ⅔ full. Sprinkle each muffin with ½ teaspoon of sugar-cinnamon mixture.

Bake about 14 to 16 minutes or until wooden pick inserted in center comes out clean.   *Makes 12 muffins*

Muffin Surprise

1½ cups all-purpose flour
2½ teaspoons baking powder
¼ teaspoon salt
1 cup oat bran
½ cup packed light brown sugar
1 cup milk
⅓ cup vegetable oil
2 eggs, lightly beaten
1 teaspoon vanilla extract
1 package (3 ounces) cream cheese
¾ cup apricot-pineapple jam

Preheat oven to 425°F. Grease 12 (2½-inch) muffin cups.

Combine flour, baking powder and salt in medium bowl. Stir in oat bran and brown sugar. Combine milk, oil, eggs and vanilla in small bowl. Stir milk mixture into dry ingredients just until moistened. Cut cream cheese into 12 equal pieces. Spoon about ½ of batter into prepared muffin cups, filling about ⅓ full. Spoon about 1 tablespoon jam on top of batter. Top with 1 piece of cream cheese. Spoon remaining batter over jam and cheese, filling each muffin cup ⅔ full.

Bake about 14 to 16 minutes or until browned.   *Makes 12 muffins*

Tip: These muffins need no butter or jam; they are perfect for a buffet.

Top to bottom: Spicy Sweet Potato Muffins and Muffin Surprise

Noel Bran Muffins

1¼ cups whole bran cereal
1 cup milk
1½ cups flour
½ cup firmly packed brown sugar
½ cup shredded carrots
2 teaspoons baking powder
¼ teaspoon salt
¼ teaspoon nutmeg
¼ cup butter or margarine, melted
2 eggs
1 cup chopped DEL MONTE® Dried
   Apricots or Seedless Raisins

Soften bran in milk. In large bowl, blend together flour, brown sugar, carrots, baking powder, salt and nutmeg. Combine bran mixture, butter and eggs; add to dry ingredients. Stir until flour mixture is moistened. Fold in chopped apricots or raisins. Fill 12 paper-lined or greased 2½-inch muffin cups with batter.

Bake in 375°F oven 25 to 30 minutes or until golden. Serve warm.

Makes 12 muffins

Carrot Wheat Germ Muffins

Topping (recipe follows)
1 cup all-purpose flour
⅔ cup sugar
¼ cup wheat germ
½ teaspoon baking powder
½ teaspoon baking soda
½ teaspoon ground cinnamon
⅛ teaspoon salt
1 cup shredded carrots
½ cup vegetable oil
¼ cup buttermilk
2 eggs
½ cup chopped pecans or walnuts

Microwave Directions: Line 6 microwavable muffin cups with double paper liners. Prepare Topping; set aside.

Combine flour, sugar, wheat germ, baking powder, baking soda, cinnamon, salt and carrots in large bowl. Combine oil, buttermilk and eggs in small bowl. Add to flour mixture, stirring just until moistened. Fold in pecans. Spoon into prepared muffin cups, filling ½ full. Sprinkle Topping over batter.

Microwave at HIGH 2½ to 4½ minutes or until wooden pick inserted in center comes out clean. Rotate dish ½ turn halfway through cooking. Let stand 5 minutes. Remove from pan. Repeat procedure. For last 3 muffins, line 3 muffin cups with double paper liners. Microwave at HIGH 1½ to 2 minutes. Let stand 5 minutes. Remove from pan.

Makes about 15 muffins

Topping: Combine 1 tablespoon wheat germ, 2 teaspoons sugar and 1 teaspoon ground cinnamon in small bowl.

Carrot Wheat Germ Muffins

Banana-Honey Muffins

1½ cups oat bran flakes cereal
1 cup mashed bananas (about
    2 medium)
¾ cup milk
1 egg, beaten
¼ cup butter, melted
2 tablespoons honey
1¼ cups all-purpose flour
1 tablespoon baking powder
¼ teaspoon salt

Preheat oven to 400°F. Spray 12 (2½-inch) muffin cups with nonstick cooking spray or paper-line.

Combine cereal, bananas, milk, egg, butter and honey in medium bowl. Let stand 5 minutes. Combine flour, baking powder and salt in large bowl. Add cereal mixture to flour mixture all at once, stirring just until moistened. Spoon evenly into prepared muffin cups.

Bake 20 to 25 minutes or until wooden pick inserted in center comes out clean. Remove from pan. *Makes 12 muffins*

Almond Citrus Muffins

½ cup whole natural almonds
1¼ cups all-purpose flour
2 teaspoons baking powder
¼ teaspoon salt
1 cup shreds of wheat bran cereal
¼ cup packed brown sugar
¾ cup milk
¼ cup orange juice
1 teaspoon grated orange peel
1 egg
¼ cup vegetable or almond oil

Preheat oven to 350°F. Grease 12 (2½-inch) muffin cups. Spread almonds in single layer on baking sheet. Bake 12 to

Almond Citrus Muffins

15 minutes, stirring occasionally, until lightly toasted. Cool and chop; set aside. *Increase oven temperature to 400°F.*

Combine flour, baking powder and salt in large bowl. Combine cereal, brown sugar, milk, orange juice and peel in medium bowl. Let stand 2 minutes or until cereal is softened. Add egg and oil; beat well. Stir in almonds. Add liquid mixture to flour mixture; stir just until moistened. (Batter will be lumpy; do not overmix.) Spoon evenly into prepared muffin cups.

Bake in preheated 400°F oven 20 minutes or until lightly browned. Remove to wire rack to cool. *Makes 12 muffins*

*Favorite Recipe from **Almond Board of California***

California Date-Nut Muffins

MAZOLA® No Stick cooking spray
1 cup all-purpose flour
1/3 cup sugar
1/4 cup whole wheat flour
1 1/2 teaspoons baking powder
1/8 teaspoon salt
1 cup chopped pitted dates
1 egg, lightly beaten
1/3 cup HELLMANN'S® or BEST
   FOODS® Real Mayonnaise or
   Light Reduced Calorie
   Mayonnaise Dressing
1/3 cup water
1/2 teaspoon vanilla
1/2 cup coarsely chopped walnuts

Preheat oven to 375°F. Spray 10 (2 1/2-inch) muffin pan cups with cooking spray.

In large bowl combine all-purpose flour, sugar, whole wheat flour, baking powder and salt. Stir in dates. In small bowl combine egg, mayonnaise, water and vanilla until smooth. Stir into flour mixture just until moistened. Spoon into prepared muffin pan cups. Sprinkle with chopped walnuts.

Bake 30 minutes or until golden. Immediately remove from pan. Cool on wire rack or serve warm.

Makes 10 muffins

Prune Yogurt Muffins

1 1/2 cups DEL MONTE® Bite Size Prunes
1 3/4 cups whole wheat flour
2 teaspoons baking powder
1/2 teaspoon salt
2 eggs, beaten
3/4 cup plain yogurt
1/2 cup sugar
1/4 cup butter or margarine, melted
1/4 teaspoon grated orange peel

Place prunes in saucepan; add water to 1/2 inch above fruit. Bring to a boil. Cover; simmer gently, 10 to 15 minutes. Drain, pit and chop prunes. Combine flour, baking powder and salt. Combine eggs, yogurt, sugar, butter and orange peel. Add to dry ingredients; stir until all flour is moistened. Fold in prunes. Fill 12 greased 2 1/2-inch muffin cups 2/3 full.

Bake in 400°F oven 25 minutes or until wooden pick inserted in center comes out clean. *Makes 12 muffins*

Our Very Best Bran Muffins

MAZOLA® No Stick cooking spray
1 1/4 cups flour
1 tablespoon baking powder
1/4 teaspoon salt
1 1/2 cups whole or flake bran cereal
1 1/4 cups milk
3 tablespoons firmly packed light
   brown sugar
1/3 cup HELLMANN'S® or BEST
   FOODS® Real Mayonnaise or
   Light Reduced Calorie
   Mayonnaise Dressing
1 egg, lightly beaten
1/2 cup raisins

Preheat oven to 400°F. Spray 12 (2 1/2-inch) muffin pan cups with cooking spray.

In small bowl combine flour, baking powder and salt. In large bowl combine bran cereal, milk and brown sugar; let stand 1 to 2 minutes or until bran is softened. Stir in mayonnaise and egg until well blended. Add raisins. Stir in flour mixture just until moistened. Spoon into prepared muffin pan cups.

Bake 25 minutes or until lightly browned. Immediately remove from pan. Serve warm. *Makes 12 muffins*

Top to bottom: Sunday Morn Cranberry-Orange Bread (page 194), California Date-Nut Muffins, Our Very Best Bran Muffins, Chili-Cheese Corn Muffins (page 96) and Quick Banana-Bran Bread (page 192)

Honey Muffins

1 can (8 ounces) DOLE® Crushed
      Pineapple in Juice
1½ cups wheat bran cereal (not flakes)
⅔ cup buttermilk
1 egg, slightly beaten
⅓ cup chopped pecans or walnuts
3 tablespoons vegetable oil
½ cup honey, divided
⅔ cup whole wheat flour
½ teaspoon baking soda
⅛ teaspoon salt

Microwave Directions: Line six microwavable muffin cups or six 6-ounce microwavable custard cups with double thickness paper baking cups. (Outer cup will absorb moisture so inner cup sticks to cooked muffin.)

Combine undrained pineapple, cereal and buttermilk in large bowl. Let stand 10 minutes until cereal has absorbed liquid. Stir in egg, pecans, oil and ¼ cup honey. Combine flour, baking soda and salt in small bowl. Stir into bran mixture until just moistened. Spoon batter into prepared cups, filling to the top.

Honey Muffins

Microwave at HIGH (100%) for 3½ to 4 minutes, rotating pan ½ turn after 1½ minutes. Muffins are done when they look dry and set on top. Remove from oven; immediately spoon 1 teaspoon of remaining honey over each muffin. Remove to cooling rack after honey has been absorbed. Repeat procedure with remaining batter and honey. Serve warm.
Makes 12 muffins

Hi-Fiber Date Muffins

½ cup all-purpose flour
½ cup whole wheat flour
½ cup wheat germ or unprocessed bran
½ cup whole bran cereal (not flakes)
1 tablespoon baking powder
¼ teaspoon salt
¼ cup vegetable oil
½ cup firmly packed brown sugar
1 egg
¼ cup milk
1 can SOLO® *or* 1 jar BAKER® Date
      Filling

Preheat oven to 375°F. Grease 12 (2½-inch) muffin cups.

Stir flours, wheat germ, bran cereal, baking powder and salt in medium bowl until blended. Beat oil, brown sugar, egg, milk and date filling in medium bowl with electric mixer until well blended. Make well in center of dry ingredients and add date mixture. Stir with wooden spoon until thoroughly combined. Spoon into prepared muffin cups, filling about ⅔ full.

Bake 18 to 22 minutes or until wooden pick inserted in center comes out clean. Cool in pan on wire rack 5 minutes. Remove from pan; serve warm or cool completely on rack. *Makes 12 muffins*

Papaya Muffin

Papaya Muffins

1½ cups whole wheat flour
 1 tablespoon baking powder
 ½ teaspoon salt
1½ cups KELLOGG'S® ALL-BRAN®
    cereal
1¼ cups skim milk
 ¼ cup honey
 ¼ cup vegetable oil
 1 tablespoon dark molasses
 1 egg
 ¾ cup chopped fresh papaya
 2 teaspoons finely chopped
    crystallized ginger

Stir together flour, baking powder and salt. Set aside.

Measure Kellogg's® All-Bran® cereal and milk into large mixing bowl. Let stand 2 minutes or until cereal is softened. Add honey, oil, molasses and egg. Beat well. Stir in papaya and ginger. Add flour mixture, stirring only until combined. Portion batter evenly into 12 greased 2½-inch muffin-pan cups.

Bake in 400°F oven about 25 minutes or until muffins are golden brown. Serve warm. *Makes 12 muffins*

Golden Oat Muffins

1¼ cups all-purpose flour
 1 tablespoon baking powder
 1 cup uncooked rolled oats
 1 container (8 ounces) MOUNTAIN
    HIGH® or BORDEN® LITE-LINE®
    Plain Yogurt
 ¾ cup CARY'S®, MAPLE ORCHARDS®
    or MACDONALD'S™ Pure Maple
    Syrup
 ¼ cup butter or margarine, melted
 1 egg, lightly beaten
 ½ cup raisins
    Pecan halves

Preheat oven to 400°F. Grease or paper-line 12 (2½-inch) muffin cups.

In large bowl, combine flour and baking powder. Make well in center. In medium bowl, combine oats and yogurt; let stand 5 minutes. Stir in syrup, butter, egg and raisins; mix well. Pour into flour mixture, stirring just until flour mixture is moistened. (Batter will be lumpy.) Spoon into prepared muffin cups, filling each about ⅔ full. Top with pecan halves.

Bake 20 to 25 minutes or until golden brown and toothpick inserted in centers comes out clean. Cool 5 minutes in pan on wire rack. Remove from pan; serve warm. *Makes 12 muffins*

Raisin Orange Muffins

1 cup whole wheat flour
½ cup uncooked rolled oats
¼ cup sugar
2 teaspoons baking powder
¼ teaspoon salt
¼ teaspoon ground allspice
⅔ cup skim milk
2 eggs, slightly beaten
2 tablespoons vegetable oil
1 teaspoon grated orange peel
¼ cup raisins

Microwave Directions: Line 6 microwavable muffin cups with double paper liners.

Combine flour, oats, sugar, baking powder, salt and allspice in large bowl. Make well in center. Combine milk, eggs, oil and orange peel in small bowl. Pour into flour mixture, stirring just until moistened. (Batter will be lumpy.) Fold in raisins. Spoon into prepared cups, filling ½ full.

Microwave at HIGH 2 to 4½ minutes or until top springs back when touched. Rotate dish ½ turn halfway through cooking. Let stand 5 minutes. Remove from pan. Repeat procedure with remaining batter.   *Makes 12 muffins*

Raisin Orange Muffin

Hawaiian Muffins

1 (8-ounce) can crushed pineapple, undrained
2 cups NABISCO® 100% Bran™
¼ cup FLEISCHMANN'S® Margarine, melted
¼ cup EGG BEATERS® 99% Real Egg Product
½ teaspoon almond extract
1¼ cups all-purpose flour
⅓ cup sugar
2 teaspoons DAVIS® Baking Powder
½ teaspoon baking soda
¼ cup chopped almonds

Drain pineapple, reserving juice. Add enough water to juice to equal 1 cup. Mix bran, juice mixture, margarine, Egg Beaters® and extract; let stand 5 minutes.

In bowl, blend flour, sugar, baking powder and baking soda; stir in bran mixture just until blended. (Batter will be lumpy.) Stir in pineapple. Spoon batter into 12 greased 2½-inch muffin-pan cups; sprinkle each with 1 teaspoon almonds, pressing lightly.

Bake at 400°F for 20 to 25 minutes or until toothpick inserted in center comes out clean. Serve warm.

Makes 1 dozen muffins

Graham Muffins

2 Stay Fresh Packs HONEY MAID® Grahams, finely rolled (about 3 cups crumbs)
¼ cup sugar
1 tablespoon DAVIS® Baking Powder
2 eggs, well beaten
1½ cups milk
⅓ cup BLUE BONNET® Margarine, melted

In medium bowl, combine crumbs, sugar and baking powder; set aside.

In small bowl, combine eggs, milk and margarine; stir into crumb mixture just until moistened. Spoon batter into 12 greased 2½-inch muffin-pan cups.

Bake at 400°F for 18 to 20 minutes or until toothpick inserted in center comes out clean. Serve warm.

Makes 1 dozen muffins

Breakfast Muffins

1¾ cups sifted all-purpose flour
2 tablespoons sugar
1 teaspoon baking powder
½ teaspoon ARM & HAMMER®
   Baking Soda
½ teaspoon salt
1 cup buttermilk
1 egg, slightly beaten
3 tablespoons butter or margarine,
   melted

Preheat oven to 400°F.

Sift together flour, sugar, baking powder, baking soda and salt in large bowl. Combine buttermilk, egg and butter in medium bowl; pour into flour mixture, stirring just until moistened. Spoon into greased 2½-inch muffin cups, filling ⅔ full.

Bake 20 to 25 minutes or until wooden pick inserted in center comes out clean. Remove from pan. Serve warm with butter or preserves.

Makes about 12 muffins

Healthy Banana-Walnut Muffins

2 cups oat bran flakes cereal
1½ cups mashed bananas (about
   3 medium)
1 egg
½ cup buttermilk
¼ cup butter, melted
1½ cups all-purpose flour
¼ cup packed brown sugar
1 tablespoon baking powder
½ teaspoon ground cinnamon
¼ teaspoon baking soda
¼ cup chopped walnuts

Preheat oven to 400°F. Spray 12 (2½-inch) muffin cups with nonstick cooking spray or paper-line.

Combine cereal, bananas, egg, buttermilk and butter in medium bowl. Let stand 5 minutes. Combine flour, brown sugar, baking powder, cinnamon and baking soda in large bowl. Add cereal mixture to flour mixture, stirring just until moistened. Spoon evenly into prepared muffin cups. Sprinkle with walnuts.

Bake 20 to 22 minutes or until wooden pick inserted in center comes out clean. Remove from pan. *Makes 12 muffins*

Note: To freeze muffins, wrap tightly or place in airtight container.

Blueberry Buttermilk Muffins

1 cup buttermilk
½ cup butter or margarine, melted
2 eggs, beaten
2½ cups all-purpose flour
1 cup sugar
2½ teaspoons baking powder
¼ teaspoon salt
1½ cups fresh or dry-pack frozen
    blueberries

Preheat oven to 400°F. Grease 12 (2½-inch) muffin cups.

Combine buttermilk, butter and eggs in small bowl until blended. Combine flour, sugar, baking powder and salt in large bowl. Make well in center. Add buttermilk mixture, stirring until flour mixture is just moistened. Fold in blueberries. Spoon into prepared muffin cups, filling ⅔ full.

Bake 20 minutes or until tops are golden and wooden pick inserted in center comes out clean. Remove from pan. Serve warm or cool on wire rack.

Makes about 12 muffins

Favorite recipe from MBG Marketing™

Bountiful Breakfast Muffins

1 cup all-purpose flour
1 teaspoon baking powder
¼ teaspoon pumpkin pie spice
1 cup (4 ounces) diced mixed dried
    fruit bits
½ cup butter, softened
⅔ cup sugar
6 eggs
1 teaspoon vanilla extract
⅓ cup rolled oats

Preheat oven to 350°F. Paper-line 12 (2½-inch) muffin cups.

Stir together flour, baking powder and spice in small bowl. Toss fruit with 1 tablespoon flour mixture. Set both mixtures aside. Beat butter and sugar in large bowl with electric mixer at medium speed until light and fluffy. Beat in eggs until well blended. Beat in vanilla. At low speed, gradually beat in reserved flour mixture just until blended. Stir in reserved fruit mixture and oats. Pour scant ⅓ cup batter into each prepared muffin cup.

Bake 20 minutes or until wooden pick inserted in center comes out clean. Remove from pan. Cool on wire rack.

Makes 12 muffins

Favorite recipe from American Egg Board

Cran-Apple Muffins

1 can (8 ounces) DEL MONTE®
    Crushed Pineapple In Its Own
    Juice
1 egg, beaten
¼ cup milk
⅓ cup sugar
2 cups biscuit mix
2 tablespoons butter or margarine,
    melted
½ cup chopped fresh or frozen
    cranberries

Drain pineapple, reserving ¼ cup juice. Combine reserved juice, egg, milk, sugar, biscuit mix and butter; beat vigorously 30 seconds. Fold in pineapple and cranberries. Fill greased 2½-inch muffin cups ⅔ full.

Bake in 400°F oven 15 to 20 minutes or until wooden pick inserted in center comes out clean. Serve warm.

Makes 12 muffins

Blueberry Buttermilk Muffins

Always Ready Prune Bran Muffins

1 cup boiling water
3 cups bran cereal
2½ cups flour
2½ teaspoons baking soda
½ teaspoon salt
½ cup butter or margarine, softened
1¼ cups sugar
2 eggs
2 cups buttermilk
1 cup chopped DEL MONTE® Pitted Prunes

Pour water over 1 cup cereal; mix well. Set aside to cool. Combine flour, baking soda and salt. Cream butter, sugar and eggs until light and fluffy. Stir in buttermilk, soaked bran, remaining 2 cups cereal and dry ingredients; mix well. Fold in prunes. Cover tightly and store in refrigerator for minimum of 12 hours (up to maximum of 3 weeks). Fill paper-lined or greased 2½-inch muffin cups ⅔ full.

Bake in 375°F oven 20 minutes or until wooden pick inserted in center comes out clean. *Makes 2½ dozen muffins*

Always Ready Prune Bran Muffins

Microwave Directions: Prepare batter as directed above. Fill double-paper-lined microwavable muffin cups ⅔ full. Cook on High as follows: 1 muffin, 35 to 40 seconds; 2 muffins, 45 to 60 seconds; 4 muffins, 60 to 90 seconds; or 6 muffins, 1 minute 45 seconds to 2 minutes 15 seconds.

Backpack Banana Muffins

2 extra-ripe, large DOLE® Bananas, peeled
1 cup whole bran cereal (not flakes)
¼ cup milk
2 eggs
1 cup packed brown sugar
½ cup margarine, melted
1 teaspoon vanilla extract
1¼ cups all-purpose flour
2 teaspoons baking powder
1 teaspoon ground cinnamon
½ teaspoon salt

Preheat oven to 350°F. Grease 12 (2½-inch) muffin cups.

Purée bananas in blender (1¼ cups). Mix bran and milk in small bowl to soften slightly. Add cereal mixture to blender along with eggs, brown sugar, margarine and vanilla. Blend and stir until well mixed. Combine remaining ingredients in large bowl; pour in banana mixture. Stir until just blended. Spoon evenly into prepared muffin cups.

Bake 25 to 30 minutes or until wooden pick inserted in center comes out clean. Remove from pan. *Makes 12 muffins*

Cranberry Walnut Bran Muffins

1 cup NABISCO® 100% Bran™
½ cup milk
1 egg, beaten
2 tablespoons FLEISCHMANN'S® Margarine, melted
½ cup all-purpose flour
3 tablespoons firmly packed light brown sugar
1 teaspoon DAVIS® Baking Powder
¼ cup chopped cranberries
¼ cup chopped walnuts
Crumb Topping (recipe follows)

Mix bran, milk, egg and margarine; let stand 5 minutes.

In bowl, blend flour, brown sugar and baking powder; stir in bran mixture just until blended. (Batter will be lumpy.) Stir in cranberries and walnuts. Spoon batter into 6 greased 2½-inch muffin-pan cups; top with Crumb Topping.

Bake at 400°F for 18 to 20 minutes or until toothpick inserted in center comes out clean. Serve warm. *Makes 6 muffins*

Crumb Topping: Mix 3 tablespoons *each* Nabisco® 100% Bran™, all-purpose flour and firmly packed light brown sugar with 1 tablespoon melted margarine until crumbly.

Tips: Recipe may be doubled to make 12 muffins.

To reduce cholesterol, substitute ¼ cup Egg Beaters® 99% Real Egg Product for whole egg.

For variety, substitute an equal amount of chopped apple or peaches, shredded carrot or seedless raisins for chopped cranberries.

Peach Oat Muffins

1 (16-ounce) can California peach halves in juice or extra light syrup, drained
1 egg, beaten
¼ cup vegetable oil
1 teaspoon vanilla extract
½ teaspoon grated orange peel
¼ teaspoon almond extract
1 cup all-purpose flour
1 cup old-fashioned rolled oats
¾ cup packed brown sugar
2 teaspoons baking powder
1 teaspoon ground cinnamon
½ cup raisins

Preheat oven to 400°F. Grease or paper-line 12 (2½-inch) muffin cups. Chop 2 peach halves; set aside. Purée remaining peach halves to equal 1 cup.

Combine peach purée, egg, oil, vanilla, orange peel and almond extract in small bowl. Combine flour, oats, brown sugar, baking powder and cinnamon in large bowl; mix well. Pour liquid ingredients into dry ingredients; mix just until moistened. Fold in chopped peaches and raisins. Spoon evenly into prepared muffin cups.

Bake 20 minutes or until wooden pick inserted near center comes out clean. *Makes 12 muffins*

*Favorite recipe from **Canned Fruit Promotion Service***

Treasure Bran Muffins

1¼ cups wheat bran cereal
1 cup milk
¼ cup vegetable oil
1 egg, beaten
1¼ cups all-purpose flour
½ cup sugar
1 tablespoon baking powder
½ teaspoon salt
½ cup raisins
1 (8-ounce) package PHILADELPHIA
  BRAND® Cream Cheese,* softened
¼ cup sugar
1 egg, beaten

In large bowl, combine cereal and milk. Let stand 2 minutes. In small bowl, combine oil and 1 egg; stir into cereal mixture. In medium bowl, combine flour, ½ cup sugar, baking powder and salt. Add to cereal mixture, stirring just until moistened. Fold in raisins. Spoon into greased and floured 2½-inch muffin cups, filling each ⅔ full.

In small bowl, combine cream cheese, ¼ cup sugar and 1 egg, mixing until well blended. Drop rounded measuring tablespoonfuls of cream cheese mixture onto batter. Bake at 375°F 25 minutes. Remove from pan.   *Makes 12 muffins*

*Light Philadelphia Brand® Neufchatel Cheese may be substituted.

Fruit Juice Muffins

1½ cups NABISCO® 100% Bran™
1 cup apple, cranberry or orange juice
¼ cup EGG BEATERS® 99% Real Egg
  Product
¼ cup FLEISCHMANN'S® Margarine,
  melted
½ cup firmly packed light brown sugar
1½ cups all-purpose flour
1 tablespoon DAVIS® Baking Powder
1 teaspoon ground cinnamon

Mix bran, juice, Egg Beaters®, margarine and brown sugar; let stand 5 minutes.

In large bowl, blend flour, baking powder and cinnamon; stir in bran mixture just until blended. (Batter will be lumpy.) Spoon batter into 12 greased 2½-inch muffin-pan cups.

Bake at 400°F for 15 to 18 minutes or until toothpick inserted in center comes out clean. Serve warm.

Makes 1 dozen muffins

Peachy Drop Muffins

2 cups NABISCO® 100% Bran™
1 cup skim milk
1 cup all-purpose flour
⅓ cup firmly packed light brown sugar
2 teaspoons DAVIS® Baking Powder
½ teaspoon baking soda
¼ cup FLEISCHMANN'S® Margarine,
  melted
¼ cup EGG BEATERS® 99% Real Egg
  Product
½ cup chopped canned peaches
½ cup dark seedless raisins

Mix bran and milk; let stand 5 minutes.

In bowl, blend flour, brown sugar, baking powder and baking soda; set aside. Blend margarine and Egg Beaters® into bran mixture. Stir in flour mixture just until blended. (Batter will be lumpy.) Stir in peaches and raisins. Drop batter by ¼ cupfuls, 2 inches apart, onto greased baking sheet, or spoon batter into 12 greased 2½-inch muffin-pan cups.

Bake at 400°F for 18 to 20 minutes or until toothpick inserted in center comes out clean. Serve warm.

Makes 1 dozen muffins

Pineapple Citrus Muffins

Bran Muffins

   1 cup boiling water
   3 cups bran cereal
   ½ cup (1 stick) butter, softened
   ¾ cup sugar
   2 eggs
   2 cups buttermilk
   2½ cups all-purpose flour
   2½ teaspoons baking soda
   1½ teaspoons salt

Combine boiling water and 1 cup bran cereal; let stand, uncovered, 5 minutes. Cream butter and sugar in a large mixing bowl until light and fluffy. Beat in eggs. Stir in bran-water mixture and buttermilk. Combine dry ingredients. Gradually add to batter. Stir in remaining 2 cups bran cereal. Store batter in covered container in refrigerator up to 1 month.

To bake, fill buttered muffin cups ⅔ full. Bake in preheated 400°F oven 20 to 22 minutes. Serve warm with butter. (Bake only as many as needed; keep remaining batter refrigerated for convenience.)

Makes 2 dozen muffins

Variation: Sprinkle 1 tablespoon of any of the following in each buttered muffin cup: chopped dates, raisins or chopped nuts. Fill and bake as directed above.

Favorite recipe from **American Dairy Association**

Pineapple Citrus Muffins

   ⅓ cup honey
   ¼ cup margarine, softened
   1 egg
   1 can (8 ounces) DOLE® Crushed
      Pineapple in Juice
   1 tablespoon grated orange peel
   1 cup all-purpose flour
   1 cup whole wheat flour
   1½ teaspoons baking powder
   ¼ teaspoon salt
   ¼ teaspoon ground nutmeg
   1 cup DOLE® Chopped Dates
   ½ cup DOLE® Chopped Natural
      Almonds, toasted

Preheat oven to 375°F. Grease 12 (2½-inch) muffin cups.

Beat honey and margarine in large bowl 1 minute. Beat in egg, then undrained pineapple and orange peel. Combine flours, baking powder, salt, nutmeg, dates and almonds in medium bowl. Stir into pineapple mixture until just moistened. Spoon evenly into prepared muffin cups.

Bake 25 minutes or until wooden pick inserted in center comes out clean. Remove from pan. Cool on wire rack.

Makes 12 muffins

Apple Date Nut Muffins

1½ cups all-purpose flour
⅔ cup packed brown sugar
½ cup uncooked rolled oats
1 tablespoon baking powder
1 teaspoon ground cinnamon
½ teaspoon salt
⅛ teaspoon ground nutmeg
⅛ teaspoon ground ginger
  Dash ground cloves
1 cup coarsely chopped peeled apples
½ cup chopped walnuts
½ cup chopped pitted dates
½ cup butter or margarine, melted
¼ cup milk
2 eggs

Preheat oven to 400°F. Grease well or paper-line 12 (2½-inch) muffin cups.

Combine flour, brown sugar, oats, baking powder, cinnamon, salt, nutmeg, ginger and cloves in large bowl. Mix in apples, nuts and dates. Combine butter, milk and eggs in small bowl until blended. Pour into flour mixture, stirring just until moistened. Spoon evenly into prepared muffin cups.

Bake 20 to 25 minutes or until wooden pick inserted in center comes out clean. Remove from pan.   *Makes 12 muffins*

Old-Fashioned Bran Muffins

  MAZOLA® No Stick cooking spray
⅓ cup boiling water
1 cup natural high-fiber bran cereal shreds
1 cup flour
1 teaspoon baking soda
¼ teaspoon salt
½ cup buttermilk*
1 egg
½ cup KARO® Light or Dark Corn Syrup
¼ cup sugar
¼ cup MAZOLA® Corn Oil

Preheat oven to 400°F. Spray 12 (2½-inch) muffin pan cups with cooking spray.

In large bowl pour boiling water over cereal; let stand 2 minutes. In medium bowl combine flour, baking soda and salt; set aside. Add buttermilk, egg, corn syrup, sugar and corn oil to cereal mixture; mix until blended. Stir in flour mixture until well blended. Spoon into prepared muffin pan cups.

Bake 25 minutes or until lightly browned and firm to touch. Cool in pan on wire rack 5 minutes; remove from pan.
Makes 12 muffins

*When there's no buttermilk on hand, use a homemade substitute. Combine 1½ teaspoons vinegar with enough milk to equal ½ cup; let stand 5 minutes.

Apple Date Nut Muffins

Four-Grain Pear Muffins

Vegetable cooking spray
2 fresh California Bartlett pears, cored and chopped (2⅓ cups)
½ cup packed brown sugar
½ cup low-fat milk
½ cup vegetable oil
1 egg
¾ cup all-purpose flour
¾ cup yellow cornmeal
½ cup buckwheat or whole wheat flour
½ cup oat bran
¼ cup raisins
1 tablespoon baking powder

Preheat oven to 375°F. Coat 12 (2½-inch) muffin cups with vegetable cooking spray.

Beat pears, brown sugar, milk, oil and egg in large bowl until brown sugar is dissolved. Combine remaining ingredients in medium bowl; stir into pear mixture until just combined. Spoon evenly into prepared muffin cups.

Bake 25 minutes or until wooden pick inserted in center comes out clean. Remove from oven and let cool 5 minutes. Turn out onto wire rack to cool completely. *Makes 12 muffins*

Tip: Recipe can be doubled. Make one batch for now and freeze the other batch for later.

Favorite recipe from **California Tree Fruit Agreement**

High Fiber Bran Muffins

2 cups NABISCO® 100% Bran™
1¼ cups milk
1 cup all-purpose flour
⅓ cup firmly packed light brown sugar
2 teaspoons DAVIS® Baking Powder
½ teaspoon baking soda
¼ cup BLUE BONNET® Margarine, melted
1 egg, beaten

In medium bowl, combine bran and milk; let stand 5 minutes.

In small bowl, combine flour, brown sugar, baking powder and baking soda; set aside. Mix margarine and egg into bran mixture. Stir in flour mixture just until blended. (Batter will be lumpy.) Spoon batter into 12 greased 2½-inch muffin-pan cups.

Bake at 400°F for 18 to 20 minutes or until toothpick inserted in center comes out clean. *Makes 1 dozen muffins*

Low Cholesterol Variation: Substitute skim milk for whole milk, Fleischmann's® Margarine for Blue Bonnet® Margarine and ¼ cup Egg Beaters® 99% Real Egg Product for egg.

Microwave Directions: Prepare batter as above. In each of 6 microwavable muffin-pan cups, place 2 paper liners. Spoon batter into cups, filling ⅔ full. Microwave on HIGH (100% power) for 2 to 2½ minutes or until toothpick inserted in center comes out clean, rotating pan ½ turn after 1 minute. Let stand in pan 1 minute; remove from pan. Repeat with remaining batter.

Banana Blueberry Muffins

Banana Blueberry Muffins

  2 extra-ripe, medium DOLE® Bananas,
    peeled
  2 eggs
  1 cup packed brown sugar
  ½ cup margarine, melted and cooled
  1 cup blueberries
  1 teaspoon vanilla extract
2¼ cups all-purpose flour
  2 teaspoons baking powder
  ½ teaspoon ground cinnamon
  ½ teaspoon salt

Preheat oven to 350°F. Grease 12
(2½-inch) muffin cups.

Purée bananas in blender (1 cup).
Combine puréed bananas, eggs, brown
sugar and margarine in medium bowl
until well blended. Stir in blueberries and
vanilla. Combine flour, baking powder,
cinnamon and salt in large bowl. Stir
banana mixture into flour mixture until
evenly moistened. Spoon evenly into
prepared muffin cups.

Bake 25 to 30 minutes or until wooden
pick inserted in center comes out clean.
Remove from pan; serve warm.

Makes 12 muffins

Cranberry All-Bran® Muffins

1¼ cups all-purpose flour
  ½ cup sugar
  ¼ teaspoon salt
  1 tablespoon baking powder
  ½ teaspoon pumpkin pie spice
1½ cups KELLOGG'S® ALL-BRAN®
    cereal
1¼ cups skim milk
  2 egg whites
  ¼ cup vegetable oil
  1 cup coarsely chopped cranberries
  ½ cup raisins
  1 teaspoon grated orange peel

Stir together flour, sugar, salt, baking
powder and pumpkin pie spice. Set aside.

Measure Kellogg's® All-Bran® cereal and
milk into large mixing bowl; stir until
cereal is softened. Add egg whites and
oil; beat well. Stir in cranberries, raisins
and orange peel. Add dry ingredients to
cereal mixture, stirring only until
combined. Divide batter evenly among 12
greased 2½-inch muffin-pan cups.

Bake in 400°F oven about 22 minutes or
until lightly browned. Serve hot.

Makes 12 muffins

MUFFINS OF A DIFFERENT SIZE

Strawberry Banana Muffins

1²/₃ cups all-purpose flour
 ¹/₂ cup firmly packed light brown sugar
2¹/₂ teaspoons baking powder
 ¹/₂ teaspoon salt
 1 cup mashed bananas
    (about 2 medium)
 ¹/₃ cup milk
 ¹/₄ cup butter or margarine, melted
 1 teaspoon vanilla extract
 2 tablespoons strawberry preserves

Preheat oven to 400°F. Grease or paper-line 24 (1³/₄-inch) mini-muffin cups.

Combine flour, brown sugar, baking powder and salt in large bowl. Combine bananas, milk, butter and vanilla in small bowl until blended; stir into flour mixture just until moistened. Spoon into prepared muffin cups, filling almost full. Break up any large strawberry pieces in preserves with spoon. Spoon ¹/₄ teaspoon preserves onto top of each muffin, pressing into surface gently.

Bake 15 to 17 minutes or until wooden pick inserted in center comes out clean. Let rest in pans 5 minutes. Remove from pans. Cool on wire racks.

Makes 24 mini muffins

Apricot Lemon Muffins

1³/₄ cups all-purpose flour
 ¹/₂ cup sugar
 2 teaspoons baking powder
 ¹/₂ teaspoon baking soda
 ¹/₂ teaspoon salt
 ¹/₃ cup milk
 ¹/₃ cup fresh lemon juice
 ¹/₄ cup butter or margarine, melted
 1 teaspoon vanilla extract
 ¹/₂ cup chopped dried apricots
 2 teaspoons grated lemon peel

Preheat oven to 400°F. Grease or paper-line 24 (1³/₄-inch) mini-muffin cups.

Combine flour, sugar, baking powder, baking soda and salt in large bowl. Combine milk, lemon juice, butter and vanilla in small bowl until blended; stir into flour mixture just until moistened. Fold in apricots and lemon peel. Spoon into prepared muffin cups, filling almost full.

Bake 14 to 16 minutes or until wooden pick inserted in center comes out clean. Remove from pans. Cool on wire racks.

Makes 24 mini muffins

Strawberry Banana Muffins and
Apricot Lemon Muffins

Spiced Brown Bread Muffins

2 cups whole wheat flour
²/₃ cup all-purpose flour
²/₃ cup packed brown sugar
2 teaspoons baking soda
1 teaspoon pumpkin pie spice
2 cups buttermilk
³/₄ cup raisins

Preheat oven to 350°F. Grease 6 (4-inch) large muffin cups.

Combine flours, brown sugar, baking soda and spice in large bowl. Stir in buttermilk just until flour mixture is moistened. Fold in raisins. Spoon evenly into prepared muffin cups.

Bake 35 to 40 minutes or until wooden pick inserted in center comes out clean. Remove from pan.

Makes 6 jumbo muffins

Tip: Quick to make, serve these with a hearty stew.

Spiced Brown Bread Muffin

Blueberry Cornmeal Muffins

Lemon-Sugar Topping
(recipe follows)
1²/₃ cups all-purpose flour
²/₃ cup yellow cornmeal
²/₃ cup sugar
1 tablespoon baking powder
1 teaspoon baking soda
¹/₂ teaspoon salt
²/₃ cup dairy sour cream
²/₃ cup milk
6 tablespoons butter or margarine, melted
3 eggs, beaten
1 cup fresh blueberries

Preheat oven to 425°F. Grease 12 (3¹/₂-inch) large muffin cups. Prepare Lemon-Sugar Topping; set aside.

Combine flour, cornmeal, sugar, baking powder, baking soda and salt in large bowl. Combine sour cream, milk, butter and eggs in small bowl until blended; stir into flour mixture just until moistened. Fold in blueberries. Spoon into prepared muffin cups, filling ¹/₂ full. Sprinkle Lemon-Sugar Topping evenly over tops of muffins.

Place muffins in preheated oven. *Reduce oven temperature to 400°F.* Bake 25 to 30 minutes or until wooden pick inserted in center comes out clean. Cool in pans on wire rack 5 minutes. Remove from pans. Cool on wire rack.

Makes 12 jumbo muffins

Lemon-Sugar Topping: Combine ¹/₄ cup sugar and 1 teaspoon grated lemon peel in small bowl.

Date-Pecan Muffins

  Cinnamon-Sugar Topping
    (recipe follows)
  2 cups all-purpose flour
  1/4 cup firmly packed light brown sugar
  2 teaspoons baking powder
  1/4 teaspoon salt
  1 cup milk
  1/4 cup butter or margarine, melted
  1 egg, beaten
  1 teaspoon vanilla extract
  1/2 cup diced pitted dates
  1/4 cup chopped pecans
  1 teaspoon grated orange peel

Preheat oven to 400°F. Grease or paper-line 24 (1¾-inch) mini-muffin cups. Prepare Cinnamon-Sugar Topping; set aside.

Combine flour, brown sugar, baking powder and salt in large bowl. Combine milk, butter, egg and vanilla in small bowl until blended; stir into flour mixture just until moistened. Fold in dates, pecans and orange peel. Spoon into prepared muffin cups, filling almost full. Sprinkle about 1/4 teaspoon Cinnamon-Sugar Topping over top of each muffin.

Bake 14 to 16 minutes or until wooden pick inserted in center comes out clean. Remove from pans. Cool on wire racks.

Makes 24 mini muffins

Cinnamon-Sugar Topping: Combine 2 tablespoons granulated sugar and 1/2 teaspoon ground cinnamon in small bowl.

Tomato Spice Muffins

  1 package (18.25 ounces) pudding-included spice cake mix
  1 can (10¾ ounces) condensed tomato soup
  1/4 cup water
  1 cup chopped pitted dates

Preheat oven to 400°F. Grease 12 (3½-inch) large muffin cups.

Prepare cake mix according to package directions, substituting soup and water for the liquid. (Add eggs, if package directs.) Fold in dates. Spoon into prepared muffin cups, filling 1/2 full.

Bake 20 to 25 minutes or until wooden pick inserted in center comes out clean. Cool in pans on wire rack 5 minutes. Remove from pans. Cool on wire rack.

Makes 12 jumbo muffins

Easy Fruited Gingerbread Muffins

  1 package (14 to 14.5 ounces) gingerbread mix
  1 cup diced dried mixed fruit
  1 tablespoon grated lemon peel

Preheat oven to 400°F. Grease 12 (3½-inch) large muffin cups.

Prepare gingerbread mix according to package directions, *reducing* water by 1/4 cup. Fold in fruit and lemon peel. Spoon into prepared muffin cups, filling 1/2 full.

Bake 20 to 25 minutes or until wooden pick inserted in center comes out clean. Cool in pans on wire rack 5 minutes. Remove from pans. Cool on wire rack.

Makes 12 jumbo muffins

Pepper Cheese Muffins

1¼ cups all-purpose flour
1¼ cups yellow cornmeal
 3 tablespoons sugar
 4 teaspoons baking powder
 ½ teaspoon salt
 ¾ cup milk
 ½ cup mild or hot salsa
 ⅓ cup vegetable oil
 2 eggs, beaten
 ¾ cup (3 ounces) shredded jalapeño
   Monterey Jack cheese

Preheat oven to 400°F. Grease 6 (3½-inch) large muffin cups.

Combine flour, cornmeal, sugar, baking powder and salt in large bowl. Combine milk, salsa, oil and eggs in small bowl until blended; stir into flour mixture just until moistened. Fold in cheese. Spoon into prepared muffin cups, filling ¾ full.

Bake 25 to 30 minutes or until wooden pick inserted in center comes out clean. Cool in pan on wire rack 5 minutes. Remove from pan. Cool on wire rack.

Makes 6 jumbo muffins

Banana Pecan Muffins

1¾ cups all-purpose flour
 ½ cup firmly packed light brown sugar
2½ teaspoons baking powder
 ½ teaspoon salt
 1 cup mashed ripe bananas
   (about 2 medium)
 ⅓ cup milk
 ¼ cup butter or margarine, melted
 1 egg, beaten
 1 teaspoon vanilla extract
 ½ cup chopped pecans

Preheat oven to 425°F. Grease or paper-line 24 (1¾-inch) mini-muffin cups.

Combine flour, brown sugar, baking powder and salt in large bowl. Combine bananas, milk, butter, egg and vanilla in small bowl until blended; stir into flour mixture just until moistened. Fold in pecans. Spoon into prepared muffin cups, filling almost full.

Bake 14 to 16 minutes or until wooden pick inserted in center comes out clean. Remove from pans. Cool on wire racks.

Makes 24 mini muffins

Oatmeal Raisin Spice Muffins

 1 cup quick-cooking or old-fashioned
   oats, uncooked
 ⅔ cup all-purpose flour
 ⅓ cup firmly packed light brown sugar
 2 teaspoons baking powder
 ¾ teaspoon ground cinnamon
 ¾ teaspoon ground nutmeg
 ½ teaspoon salt
 ¼ teaspoon ground cloves
 ¾ cup milk
 3 tablespoons vegetable oil
 1 egg, beaten
 1 teaspoon vanilla extract
 ½ cup raisins

Preheat oven to 400°F. Grease or paper-line 24 (1¾-inch) mini-muffin cups.

Combine oats, flour, brown sugar, baking powder, cinnamon, nutmeg, salt and cloves in large bowl. Combine milk, oil, egg and vanilla in small bowl until blended; stir into flour mixture just until moistened. Fold in raisins. Spoon into prepared muffin cups, filling ¾ full.

Bake 14 to 16 minutes or until wooden pick inserted in center comes out clean. Remove from pans. Cool on wire racks.

Makes 24 mini muffins

Five-Day Pumpkin Gems

2½ cups all-purpose flour
2 teaspoons baking soda
1 teaspoon baking powder
½ teaspoon salt
2 teaspoons ground cinnamon
1 teaspoon ground nutmeg
2 eggs
1 cup LIBBY'S® Solid Pack Pumpkin
1 cup buttermilk
½ cup vegetable oil
⅓ cup light molasses
¾ cup packed dark brown sugar
3 cups fruit and fiber cereal

In medium bowl, combine flour, baking soda, baking powder, salt, cinnamon, and nutmeg; set aside. In large bowl, beat eggs, pumpkin, buttermilk, oil, molasses, and brown sugar. Mix in dry ingredients and cereal just until moistened. Batter can be baked immediately, or stored in refrigerator for up to 5 days in tightly sealed container.

To bake, spoon batter into greased or paper-lined 1¾-inch mini-muffin cups, filling ⅔ full. Bake in preheated 375°F. oven for 11 to 13 minutes or until wooden pick inserted in center comes out clean. Serve warm.

Makes about 55 mini muffins

Variations: Top muffins with any of the following: uncooked quick rolled oats, wheat germ, wheat bran, or crumbled fruit and fiber cereal.

Toffee Crunch Muffins

Toffee Crunch Muffins

1½ cups all-purpose flour
⅓ cup firmly packed light brown sugar
2 teaspoons baking powder
½ teaspoon baking soda
½ teaspoon salt
½ cup milk
½ cup dairy sour cream
3 tablespoons butter or margarine, melted
1 egg, beaten
1 teaspoon vanilla extract
3 bars (1.4 ounces each) chocolate covered toffee, chopped and divided

Preheat oven to 400°F. Grease or paper-line 36 (1¾-inch) mini-muffin cups.

Combine flour, brown sugar, baking powder, baking soda and salt in large bowl. Combine milk, sour cream, butter, egg and vanilla in small bowl until blended; stir into flour mixture just until moistened. Fold in ⅔ of candy. Spoon into prepared muffin cups, filling almost full. Sprinkle remaining candy evenly over tops of muffins.

Bake 16 to 18 minutes or until wooden pick inserted in center comes out clean. Remove from pans. Cool on wire racks.

Makes 36 mini muffins

Cheesy Ham and Pepper Muffins

2½ cups all-purpose flour
3 tablespoons sugar
1 tablespoon baking powder
¼ teaspoon black pepper
1 cup milk
6 tablespoons vegetable oil
2 eggs, beaten
2 tablespoons Dijon-style prepared
    mustard
¾ cup diced cooked ham
¾ cup (3 ounces) shredded Swiss
    cheese
3 tablespoons chopped red or green
    bell pepper

Preheat oven to 400°F. Grease 6 (3½-inch)
large muffin cups.

Combine flour, sugar, baking powder and
black pepper in large bowl. Combine
milk, oil, eggs and mustard in small bowl
until blended; stir into flour mixture
just until moistened. Fold in ham, cheese
and bell pepper. Spoon into prepared
muffin cups, filling ¾ full.

Bake 25 to 30 minutes or until wooden
pick inserted in center comes out clean.
Cool in pan on wire rack 5 minutes.
Remove from pan. Cool on wire rack.
Makes 6 jumbo muffins

Quick Nutty Carrot Raisin Muffins

1 package (18 ounces) pudding-
    included carrot cake mix
1 cup chopped walnuts, divided
½ cup seedless raisins

Preheat oven to 400°F. Grease 12
(3½-inch) large muffin cups.

Prepare cake mix according to package
directions, *reducing* water by ⅓ cup. Fold
in ½ cup walnuts and raisins. Spoon into
prepared cups, filling ½ full. Sprinkle
remaining ½ cup walnuts evenly over
tops of muffins.

Bake 20 to 25 minutes or until wooden
pick inserted in center comes out clean.
Cool in pans on wire rack 5 minutes.
Remove from pans. Cool on wire rack.
Makes 12 jumbo muffins

Savory Pumpkin Bacon Muffins

1¾ cups all-purpose flour
¼ cup sugar
2 teaspoons baking powder
¾ teaspoon ground nutmeg
½ teaspoon salt
⅔ cup canned solid pack pumpkin
    (not pumpkin pie filling)
⅔ cup milk
¼ cup vegetable oil
1 egg, beaten
½ cup cooked crumbled bacon

Preheat oven to 425°F. Grease or paper-
line 24 (1¾-inch) mini-muffin cups.

Combine flour, sugar, baking powder,
nutmeg and salt in large bowl. Combine
pumpkin, milk, oil and egg in small bowl
until blended; stir into flour mixture just
until moistened. Fold in bacon. Spoon
into prepared muffin cups, filling almost
full.

Bake 16 to 18 minutes or until wooden
pick inserted in center comes out clean.
Remove from pans. Cool on wire racks.
Makes 24 mini muffins

Cheesy Ham and Pepper Muffins

Clockwise from top right: Taffy Apple Muffins, Pineapple Carrot Raisin Muffins (page 15) and Crunch Top Blueberry Muffins

Taffy Apple Muffins

　2 cups all-purpose flour
　1/2 cup granulated sugar
　1 tablespoon baking powder
　1/2 teaspoon salt
　1/4 teaspoon ground nutmeg
　1/2 cup milk
　1/4 cup butter or margarine, melted
　2 eggs
　1 teaspoon vanilla extract
　1 cup chopped apple
　1/2 cup honey
　1/2 cup packed dark brown sugar
　3/4 cup finely chopped walnuts

Preheat oven to 400°F. Grease 36 (1 3/4-inch) mini-muffin cups.

Combine flour, granulated sugar, baking powder, salt and nutmeg in large bowl. Combine milk, butter, eggs and vanilla in small bowl until blended; stir into flour mixture just until moistened. Fold in apple. Spoon evenly into prepared muffin cups.

Bake 10 to 12 minutes or until lightly browned and wooden pick inserted in center comes out clean. Remove from pan.

Meanwhile, heat honey and brown sugar in small saucepan over medium-high heat to a boil; stir to dissolve sugar. Remove from heat. Dip warm muffins into hot glaze, then into walnuts. Spear with popsicle sticks or wooden skewers, if desired. *Makes 36 mini muffins*

Crunch Top Blueberry Muffins

　Crunch Topping (recipe follows)
　2 cups all-purpose flour
　2/3 cup sugar
　1 tablespoon baking powder
　1/2 teaspoon salt
　1/2 teaspoon ground nutmeg
1 1/2 cups fresh or frozen blueberries*
　3/4 cup milk
　1/2 cup butter or margarine, melted
　2 eggs, beaten

Preheat oven to 400°F. Grease or paper-line 6 (4-inch) large muffin cups. Prepare Crunch Topping; set aside.

Combine flour, sugar, baking powder, salt and nutmeg in large bowl. Add 1 tablespoon flour mixture to the blueberries; toss to coat. Combine milk, butter and eggs in small bowl until blended; stir into flour mixture just until moistened. Fold in blueberries. Spoon evenly into prepared muffin cups. Sprinkle Crunch Topping over tops of muffins.

Bake 30 to 35 minutes or until wooden pick inserted in center comes out clean. Remove from pan. Cool on wire rack.
Makes 6 jumbo muffins

*If you are using frozen blueberries, do not thaw. Baking time may need to be increased by up to 10 minutes.

Crunch Topping: Combine ¹/₂ cup uncooked rolled oats, ¹/₂ cup all-purpose flour, ¹/₄ cup packed brown sugar and 1 teaspoon ground cinnamon in medium bowl. Cut in ¹/₄ cup softened butter or margarine with fork until mixture resembles coarse crumbs.

Chocolate Peanut Butter Muffins

6 tablespoons butter or margarine, softened
1¹/₄ cups sugar
2 eggs
1¹/₂ teaspoons vanilla extract
2¹/₂ cups all-purpose flour
¹/₃ cup unsweetened cocoa
2 teaspoons baking soda
¹/₂ teaspoon salt
1¹/₃ cups buttermilk
1 cup peanut butter chips

Preheat oven to 400°F. Grease 12 (3¹/₂-inch) large muffin cups.

Beat butter and sugar in large bowl with electric mixer at medium speed until light and fluffy. Beat in eggs until well blended. Beat in vanilla. Combine flour, cocoa, baking soda and salt in medium bowl; gradually stir into butter mixture alternately with buttermilk at low speed until well blended. Fold in peanut butter chips. Spoon into prepared muffin cups, filling ¹/₂ full.

Bake 25 to 30 minutes or until wooden pick inserted in center comes out clean. Cool in pans on wire rack 5 minutes. Remove from pans. Cool on wire rack.
Makes 12 jumbo muffins

Pumpkin Raisin Nut Muffins

2¹/₂ cups all-purpose flour
³/₄ cup firmly packed light brown sugar
1 tablespoon baking powder
1¹/₂ teaspoons pumpkin pie spice
¹/₂ teaspoon salt
1 cup canned solid pack pumpkin (not pumpkin pie filling)
³/₄ cup milk
6 tablespoons butter or margarine, melted
2 eggs, beaten
¹/₂ cup seedless raisins
¹/₂ cup chopped pecans

Preheat oven to 400°F. Grease 6 (3¹/₂-inch) large muffin cups.

Combine flour, brown sugar, baking powder, spice and salt in large bowl. Combine pumpkin, milk, butter and eggs in small bowl until blended; stir into flour mixture just until moistened. Fold in raisins and pecans. Spoon into prepared muffin cups, filling ³/₄ full.

Bake 30 to 35 minutes or until wooden pick inserted in center comes out clean. Cool in pan on wire rack 5 minutes. Remove from pan. Cool on wire rack.
Makes 6 jumbo muffins

Swiss Almond Muffins

Almond Topping (recipe follows)
1¾ cups all-purpose flour
3 tablespoons sugar
1 tablespoon baking powder
1 cup milk
3 tablespoons butter or margarine, melted
1 egg, beaten
1 teaspoon Worcestershire sauce
¾ cup (3 ounces) shredded Swiss cheese

Preheat oven to 400°F. Grease or paper-line 24 (1¾-inch) mini-muffin cups. Prepare Almond Topping; set aside.

Combine flour, sugar and baking powder in large bowl. Combine milk, butter, egg and Worcestershire in small bowl until blended; stir into flour mixture just until moistened. Fold in cheese. Spoon into prepared muffin cups, filling almost full. Sprinkle Almond Topping evenly over tops of muffins.

Bake 16 to 18 minutes or until wooden pick inserted in center comes out clean. Remove from pans. Cool on wire racks.

Makes 24 mini muffins

Almond Topping: Combine ⅓ cup chopped blanched almonds, 2 tablespoons melted butter or margarine and ½ teaspoon seasoned salt in small bowl.

Cinnamon Chocolate Nut Muffins

¼ cup butter or margarine, softened
⅔ cup sugar
2 eggs
1⅓ cups all-purpose flour
3 tablespoons unsweetened cocoa
1½ teaspoons baking soda
1¼ teaspoons ground cinnamon
¼ teaspoon salt
1 container (8 ounces) low-fat vanilla yogurt
1 cup chopped walnuts, divided

Preheat oven to 400°F. Grease or paper-line 24 (1¾-inch) mini-muffin cups.

Beat butter and sugar in large bowl with electric mixer at medium speed until light and fluffy. Beat in eggs until well blended. Combine flour, cocoa, baking soda, cinnamon and salt in small bowl; gradually beat into butter mixture at low speed. Mix in yogurt until mixture is smooth. Fold in ⅔ cup walnuts with wooden spoon. Spoon into prepared muffin cups, filling almost full. Sprinkle remaining ⅓ cup walnuts evenly over tops of muffins.

Bake 14 to 16 minutes or until wooden pick inserted in center comes out clean. Remove from pans. Cool on wire racks.

Makes 24 mini muffins

Swiss Almond Muffins

Mocha Macadamia Nut Muffins

2½ cups all-purpose flour
1¼ cups sugar
⅓ cup unsweetened cocoa
2 teaspoons baking soda
½ teaspoon salt
1⅓ cups buttermilk
6 tablespoons butter or margarine, melted
2 eggs, beaten
2 tablespoons instant coffee, dissolved in 2 tablespoons hot water
1½ teaspoons vanilla extract
1 cup coarsely chopped macadamia nuts

Preheat oven to 400°F. Grease 12 (3½-inch) large muffin cups.

Combine flour, sugar, cocoa, baking soda and salt in large bowl. Combine buttermilk, butter, eggs, instant coffee mixture and vanilla in small bowl until blended; stir into flour mixture just until moistened. Fold in macadamia nuts. Spoon into prepared muffin cups, filling ½ full.

Bake 25 to 30 minutes or until wooden pick inserted in center comes out clean. Cool in pans on wire rack 5 minutes. Remove from pans. Cool on wire rack.

Makes 12 jumbo muffins

White Chocolate Chunk Muffins

2½ cups all-purpose flour
1 cup firmly packed light brown sugar
⅓ cup unsweetened cocoa
2 teaspoons baking soda
½ teaspoon salt
1⅓ cups buttermilk
6 tablespoons butter or margarine, melted
2 eggs, beaten
1½ teaspoons vanilla extract
1½ cups chopped white chocolate

Preheat oven to 400°F. Grease 12 (3½-inch) large muffin cups.

Combine flour, brown sugar, cocoa, baking soda and salt in large bowl. Combine buttermilk, butter, eggs and vanilla in small bowl until blended; stir into flour mixture just until moistened. Fold in white chocolate. Spoon into prepared muffin cups, filling ½ full.

White Chocolate Chunk Muffins

Bake 25 to 30 minutes or until wooden pick inserted in center comes out clean. Cool in pans on wire rack 5 minutes. Remove from pans. Cool on wire rack.

Makes 12 jumbo muffins

Double Peanut Butter Muffins

1⅓ cups buttermilk baking mix
½ cup firmly packed light brown sugar
½ cup milk
½ cup creamy peanut butter
2 tablespoons vegetable oil
1 egg, beaten
1 teaspoon vanilla extract
½ cup peanut butter chips

Preheat oven to 400°F. Grease or paper-line 24 (1¾-inch) mini-muffin cups.

Combine baking mix and brown sugar in large bowl. Combine milk, peanut butter, oil, egg and vanilla in small bowl until blended; stir into baking mix mixture just until moistened. Fold in peanut butter chips. Spoon into prepared muffin cups, filling ¾ full.

Bake 15 to 17 minutes or until wooden pick inserted in center comes out clean. Remove from pans. Cool on wire racks.

Makes 24 mini muffins

Butterscotch Nut Muffins

2½ cups all-purpose flour
⅔ cup firmly packed light brown sugar
1 tablespoon baking powder
½ teaspoon salt
1 cup milk
6 tablespoons vegetable oil
2 eggs, beaten
1 cup butterscotch chips
½ cup chopped pecans

Preheat oven to 400°F. Grease 6 (3½-inch) large muffin cups.

Combine flour, brown sugar, baking powder and salt in large bowl. Combine milk, oil and eggs in small bowl until blended; stir into flour mixture just until moistened. Fold in butterscotch chips and pecans. Spoon into prepared muffin cups, filling ⅔ full.

Bake 25 to 30 minutes or until wooden pick inserted in center comes out clean. Cool in pan on wire rack 5 minutes. Remove from pan. Cool on wire rack.

Makes 6 jumbo muffins

Cherry Vanilla Muffins

1⅔ cups all-purpose flour
⅓ cup sugar
2 teaspoons baking powder
1 teaspoon ground cinnamon
½ teaspoon baking soda
¼ teaspoon salt
1 container (8 ounces) low-fat vanilla yogurt
¼ cup butter or margarine, melted
1 egg, beaten
1 teaspoon vanilla extract
½ cup chopped maraschino cherries, drained

Preheat oven to 400°F. Grease or paper-line 24 (1¾-inch) mini-muffin cups.

Combine flour, sugar, baking powder, cinnamon, baking soda and salt in large bowl. Combine yogurt, butter, egg and vanilla in small bowl until blended; stir into flour mixture just until moistened. Fold in cherries. Spoon into prepared muffin cups, filling almost full.

Bake 14 to 16 minutes or until wooden pick inserted in center comes out clean. Remove from pans. Cool on wire racks.

Makes 24 mini muffins

Brown Sugar Maple Muffins

¾ cup all-purpose flour
¾ cup quick-cooking or old-fashioned
   oats, uncooked
½ cup firmly packed light brown sugar
1½ teaspoons baking powder
½ teaspoon baking soda
½ teaspoon salt
 1 cup whipping cream
 1 egg, beaten
 2 teaspoons maple extract
¾ cup chopped walnuts, divided

Preheat oven to 400°F. Grease or paper-line 24 (1¾-inch) mini-muffin cups.

Combine flour, oats, brown sugar, baking powder, baking soda and salt in large bowl. Combine whipping cream, egg and maple extract in small bowl until blended; stir into flour mixture just until moistened. Fold in ½ cup walnuts. Spoon into prepared muffin cups, filling ¾ full. Sprinkle remaining ¼ cup walnuts evenly over tops of muffins.

Bake 16 to 18 minutes or until wooden pick inserted in center comes out clean. Remove from pans. Cool on wire racks.
Makes 24 mini muffins

Molasses Bran Muffins

 1 cup oat bran
⅔ cup all-purpose flour
 1 teaspoon baking powder
 1 teaspoon baking soda
¼ teaspoon salt
½ cup buttermilk
½ cup light molasses
 1 egg, beaten
 2 tablespoons vegetable oil
½ cup chopped pitted dates

Preheat oven to 400°F. Grease or paper-line 24 (1¾-inch) mini-muffin cups.

Combine oat bran, flour, baking powder, baking soda and salt in large bowl. Combine buttermilk, molasses, egg and oil in small bowl until blended; stir into oat bran mixture just until moistened. Fold in dates. Let mixture stand 2 minutes. Spoon into prepared muffin cups, filling ⅔ full.

Bake 14 to 16 minutes or until wooden pick inserted in center comes out clean. Remove from pans. Cool on wire racks.
Makes 24 mini muffins

Hawaiian Mini Muffins

 1 can (8 ounces) crushed pineapple in
   unsweetened juice, undrained
1¾ cups buttermilk baking mix
⅓ cup sugar
¾ teaspoon ground cinnamon
 1 egg, beaten
 2 tablespoons butter or margarine,
   melted
 1 teaspoon vanilla extract
½ cup shredded coconut
 1 tablespoon grated orange peel

Preheat oven to 400°F. Grease or paper-line 24 (1¾-inch) mini-muffin cups.

Drain pineapple, reserving ½ cup juice; set aside. Combine baking mix, sugar and cinnamon in large bowl. Combine reserved pineapple juice, egg, butter and vanilla in small bowl until blended; stir into baking mix mixture just until moistened. Fold in pineapple, coconut and orange peel. Spoon into prepared muffin cups, filling almost full.

Bake 14 to 16 minutes or until wooden pick inserted in center comes out clean. Remove from pans. Cool on wire racks.
Makes 24 mini muffins

Cranberry Pecan Muffins

1¾ cups all-purpose flour
½ cup firmly packed light brown sugar
2½ teaspoons baking powder
½ teaspoon salt
¾ cup milk
¼ cup butter or margarine, melted
1 egg, beaten
1 cup chopped fresh cranberries
⅓ cup chopped pecans
1 teaspoon grated lemon peel

Preheat oven to 400°F. Grease or paper-line 36 (1¾-inch) mini-muffin cups.

Combine flour, brown sugar, baking powder and salt in large bowl. Combine milk, butter and egg in small bowl until blended; stir into flour mixture just until moistened. Fold in cranberries, pecans and lemon peel. Spoon into prepared muffin cups, filling almost full.

Bake 15 to 17 minutes or until wooden pick inserted in center comes out clean. Remove from pans. Cool on wire racks.

Makes 36 mini muffins

Cranberry Pecan Muffins

German Chocolate Muffins

German Chocolate Topping
(recipe follows)
1 package (18.25 ounces) pudding-
    included German chocolate
    cake mix

Preheat oven to 400°F. Grease 12
(3½-inch) large muffin cups. Prepare
German Chocolate Topping; set aside.

Prepare cake mix according to package
directions, *reducing* water by ¼ cup.
Spoon into prepared muffin cups, filling
½ full. Sprinkle German Chocolate
Topping evenly over tops of muffins.

Bake 20 to 25 minutes or until wooden
pick inserted in center comes out clean.
Cool in pans on wire rack 5 minutes.
Remove from pans. Cool on wire rack.

Makes 12 jumbo muffins

German Chocolate Topping: Combine 3
tablespoons *each* chopped pecans, flaked
coconut and firmly packed light brown
sugar in small bowl.

Double Chocolate Nut Muffins

2⅓ cups all-purpose flour
1¼ cups sugar
  ⅓ cup unsweetened cocoa
2½ teaspoons baking powder
  1 teaspoon baking soda
  ½ teaspoon salt
  1 container (16 ounces) plain yogurt
  ⅓ cup butter or margarine, melted
  2 eggs, beaten
1½ teaspoons vanilla extract
  1 cup semi-sweet mini chocolate chips
  ⅔ cup chopped pecans

Preheat oven to 400°F. Grease 12
(3½-inch) large muffin cups.

Combine flour, sugar, cocoa, baking
powder, baking soda and salt in large
bowl. Combine yogurt, butter, eggs and
vanilla in small bowl until blended; stir
into flour mixture just until moistened.
Stir in chocolate chips and pecans. Spoon
into prepared muffin cups, filling ⅔ full.

Bake 25 to 30 minutes or until wooden
pick inserted in center comes out clean.
Cool in pans on wire rack 5 minutes.
Remove from pans. Cool on wire rack.

Makes 12 jumbo muffins

Mexican Corn Muffins

1¼ cups all-purpose flour
1¼ cups yellow cornmeal
  ⅓ cup sugar
  4 teaspoons baking powder
1½ teaspoons chili powder
  ½ teaspoon salt
1¼ cups milk
  ⅓ cup vegetable oil
  2 eggs, beaten
  ½ cup (2 ounces) shredded Cheddar
      cheese
  ½ cup canned or thawed frozen kernel
      corn, drained
  2 tablespoons chopped mild chilies,
      drained

Preheat oven to 400°F. Grease 6 (3½-inch)
large muffin cups.

Combine flour, cornmeal, sugar, baking
powder, chili powder and salt in large
bowl. Combine milk, oil and eggs in
small bowl until blended; stir into flour
mixture just until moistened. Fold in
cheese, corn and chilies. Spoon into
prepared muffin cups, filling ¾ full.

Bake 25 to 30 minutes or until wooden
pick inserted in center comes out clean.
Cool in pan on wire rack 5 minutes.
Remove from pan. Cool on wire rack.

Makes 6 jumbo muffins

German Chocolate Muffins

Cinnamon Spiced Muffins

1½ cups all-purpose flour
¾ cup sugar, divided
2 teaspoons baking powder
½ teaspoon salt
½ teaspoon ground nutmeg
½ teaspoon ground coriander
½ teaspoon ground allspice
½ cup milk
⅓ cup butter or margarine, melted
1 egg
1 teaspoon ground cinnamon
¼ cup butter or margarine, melted

Preheat oven to 400°F. Grease 36 (1¾-inch) mini-muffin cups.

Combine flour, ½ cup sugar, baking powder, salt, nutmeg, coriander and allspice in large bowl. Combine milk, butter and egg in small bowl; stir into flour mixture just until moistened. Spoon evenly into prepared muffin cups.

Bake 10 to 13 minutes or until edges are lightly browned and wooden pick inserted in center comes out clean. Remove from pan.

Meanwhile, combine remaining ¼ cup sugar and cinnamon in a shallow dish. Dip warm muffin tops in remaining ¼ cup melted butter, then in sugar-cinnamon mixture. Serve warm.

Makes 36 mini muffins

Cinnamon Spiced Muffins

Microwave Directions: Line 6 microwavable muffin cups with double paper liners. Prepare batter as directed. Spoon batter into prepared muffin cups, filling ½ full. Microwave at HIGH 2½ to 4½ minutes or until wooden pick inserted in center comes out clean. Rotate dish ½ turn halfway through cooking. Let stand 5 minutes. Remove from pan. Dip warm muffin tops as directed above. Repeat procedure with remaining batter.

Makes about 12 muffins

Blue Cheese Walnut Muffins

1¾ cups all-purpose flour
3 tablespoons sugar
1 tablespoon baking powder
¾ teaspoon Italian seasoning
¼ teaspoon salt
1 cup milk
¼ cup butter or margarine, melted
1 egg, beaten
3 ounces blue cheese, crumbled
⅓ cup chopped walnuts

Preheat oven to 400°F. Grease or paper-line 24 (1¾-inch) mini-muffin cups.

Combine flour, sugar, baking powder, Italian seasoning and salt in large bowl. Combine milk, butter and egg in small bowl until blended; stir into flour mixture just until moistened. Fold in blue cheese and walnuts. Spoon into prepared muffin cups, filling almost full.

Bake 16 to 18 minutes or until wooden pick inserted in center comes out clean. Remove from pans. Cool slightly on wire racks. Serve warm. (Muffins may be reheated. Wrap in foil; bake in 325°F oven about 10 minutes.)

Makes 24 mini muffins

Chocolate Applesauce Muffins

2½ cups all-purpose flour
1 cup sugar
⅓ cup unsweetened cocoa
1½ teaspoons baking soda
1 teaspoon ground cinnamon
½ teaspoon salt
1½ cups applesauce
½ cup butter or margarine, melted
2 eggs, beaten
1 cup chopped pecans

Preheat oven to 400°F. Grease 6 (3½-inch) large muffin cups.

Combine flour, sugar, cocoa, baking soda, cinnamon and salt in large bowl. Combine applesauce, butter and eggs in small bowl until blended; stir into flour mixture just until moistened. Fold in pecans. Spoon evenly into prepared muffin cups.

Bake 25 to 30 minutes or until wooden pick inserted in center comes out clean. Cool in pan on wire rack 5 minutes. Remove from pan. Cool on wire rack.

Makes 6 jumbo muffins

Currant Spice Muffins

1½ cups all-purpose flour
⅓ cup sugar
2 teaspoons baking powder
1½ teaspoons pumpkin pie spice
½ teaspoon baking soda
½ teaspoon salt
½ cup milk
½ cup dairy sour cream
3 tablespoons butter or margarine, melted
1 egg, beaten
½ teaspoon maple extract
½ cup currants

Preheat oven to 400°F. Grease or paper-line 24 (1¾-inch) mini-muffin cups.

Combine flour, sugar, baking powder, spice, baking soda and salt in large bowl. Combine milk, sour cream, butter, egg and maple extract in small bowl until blended; stir into flour mixture just until moistened. Fold in currants. Spoon into prepared muffin cups, filling almost full.

Bake 14 to 16 minutes or until wooden pick inserted in center comes out clean. Remove from pans. Cool on wire racks.

Makes 24 mini muffins

Nutty Corn Muffins

1 cup all-purpose flour
1 cup yellow cornmeal
1 tablespoon baking powder
1 teaspoon chili powder
½ teaspoon salt
1 cup milk
¼ cup honey
¼ cup vegetable oil
1 egg, beaten
½ cup chopped toasted pecans

Preheat oven to 400°F. Grease or paper-line 24 (1¾-inch) mini-muffin cups.

Combine flour, cornmeal, baking powder, chili powder and salt in large bowl. Combine milk, honey, oil and egg in small bowl until blended; stir into flour mixture just until moistened. Fold in pecans. Spoon into prepared muffin cups, filling almost full.

Bake 14 to 16 minutes or until wooden pick inserted in center comes out clean. Remove from pans. Cool on wire racks.

Makes 24 mini muffins

Cheesy Raisin Muffins

1²/₃ cups all-purpose flour
 ¹/₃ cup sugar
  1 tablespoon baking powder
 ³/₄ teaspoon ground cinnamon
 ¹/₂ teaspoon salt
  1 cup milk
  3 tablespoons butter or margarine,
     melted
  1 egg, beaten
 ³/₄ cup (3 ounces) shredded Cheddar
     cheese
 ¹/₂ cup seedless raisins
 ¹/₄ cup chopped pecans

Preheat oven to 400°F. Grease or paper-line 24 (1³/₄-inch) mini-muffin cups.

Combine flour, sugar, baking powder, cinnamon and salt in large bowl. Combine milk, butter and egg in small bowl until blended; stir into flour mixture just until moistened. Fold in cheese, raisins and pecans. Spoon into prepared muffin cups, filling almost full.

Bake 16 to 18 minutes or until wooden pick inserted in center comes out clean. Remove from pans. Cool on wire racks.

Makes 24 mini muffins

Mint Chocolate Chip Muffins

2¹/₃ cups all-purpose flour
1¹/₄ cups sugar
 ¹/₃ cup unsweetened cocoa
  2 teaspoons baking powder
  1 teaspoon baking soda
 ¹/₂ teaspoon salt
  1 cup dairy sour cream
 ¹/₃ cup butter or margarine, melted
  2 eggs, beaten
 ¹/₄ cup milk
  1 cup mint flavored semi-sweet
     chocolate chips

Preheat oven to 400°F. Grease 12 (3¹/₂-inch) large muffin cups.

Combine flour, sugar, cocoa, baking powder, baking soda and salt in large bowl. Combine sour cream, butter, eggs and milk in small bowl until blended; stir into flour mixture just until moistened. Fold in mint chips. Spoon into prepared muffin cups, filling ¹/₂ full.

Bake 25 to 30 minutes or until wooden pick inserted in center comes out clean. Cool in pans on wire rack 5 minutes. Remove from pans. Cool on wire rack.

Makes 12 jumbo muffins

Lemon Poppy Seed Muffins

  3 cups all-purpose flour
  1 cup sugar
  3 tablespoons poppy seed
  1 tablespoon grated lemon peel
  2 teaspoons baking powder
  1 teaspoon baking soda
 ¹/₂ teaspoon salt
  1 container (16 ounces) low-fat plain
     yogurt
 ¹/₂ cup fresh lemon juice
 ¹/₄ cup vegetable oil
  2 eggs, beaten
1¹/₂ teaspoons vanilla extract

Preheat oven to 400°F. Grease 12 (3¹/₂-inch) large muffin cups.

Combine flour, sugar, poppy seed, lemon peel, baking powder, baking soda and salt in large bowl. Combine yogurt, lemon juice, oil, eggs and vanilla in small bowl until blended; stir into flour mixture just until moistened. Spoon into prepared muffin cups, filling ²/₃ full.

Bake 25 to 30 minutes or until wooden pick inserted in center comes out clean. Cool in pans on wire rack 5 minutes. Remove from pans. Cool on wire rack.

Makes 12 jumbo muffins

Lemon Poppy Seed Muffins

Almond Chocolate Cherry Muffins

Almond Chocolate Cherry Muffins

1¼ cups all-purpose flour
½ cup sugar
3 tablespoons unsweetened cocoa
1½ teaspoons baking soda
¼ teaspoon salt
⅔ cup buttermilk
3 tablespoons butter or margarine, melted
1 egg, beaten
1 teaspoon almond extract
½ cup chopped maraschino cherries, drained
¼ cup sliced natural almonds, chopped

Preheat oven to 400°F. Grease or paper-line 36 (1¾-inch) mini-muffin cups.

Combine flour, sugar, cocoa, baking soda and salt in large bowl. Combine buttermilk, butter, egg and almond extract in small bowl until blended; stir into flour mixture just until moistened. Fold in cherries. Spoon into prepared muffin cups, filling ¾ full. Sprinkle almonds evenly over tops of muffins.

Bake 14 to 16 minutes or until wooden pick inserted in center comes out clean. Remove from pans. Cool on wire racks.

Makes 36 mini muffins

Chocolate Chip Banana Muffins

2½ cups all-purpose flour
¾ cup firmly packed light brown sugar
1 tablespoon baking powder
½ teaspoon salt
1 cup mashed ripe bananas
    (about 2 medium)
½ cup milk
6 tablespoons butter or margarine,
    melted
2 eggs, beaten
1 teaspoon vanilla extract
¾ cup semi-sweet mini chocolate chips

Preheat oven to 400°F. Grease 6 (3½-inch) large muffin cups.

Combine flour, brown sugar, baking powder and salt in large bowl. Combine bananas, milk, butter, eggs and vanilla in small bowl until blended; stir into flour mixture just until moistened. Fold in chocolate chips. Spoon into prepared muffin cups, filling almost full.

Bake 25 to 30 minutes or until wooden pick inserted in center comes out clean. Cool in pan on wire rack 5 minutes. Remove from pan. Cool on wire rack.

Makes 6 jumbo muffins

Double Cheese Apple Muffins

1¾ cups all-purpose flour
¾ cup yellow cornmeal
½ cup sugar
1 tablespoon baking powder
1 teaspoon ground cinnamon
1 cup milk
½ cup small curd cream cottage cheese
⅓ cup butter or margarine, melted
2 eggs, beaten
¾ cup chopped dried apples
½ cup (2 ounces) shredded Cheddar
    cheese

Preheat oven to 400°F. Grease 6 (3½-inch) large muffin cups.

Combine flour, cornmeal, sugar, baking powder and cinnamon in large bowl. Combine milk, cottage cheese, butter and eggs in small bowl until blended; stir into flour mixture just until moistened. Fold in apples and Cheddar cheese. Spoon evenly into prepared muffin cups.

Bake 30 to 35 minutes or until wooden pick inserted in center comes out clean. Cool in pan on wire rack 5 minutes. Remove from pan. Cool on wire rack.

Makes 6 jumbo muffins

Rich Nutmeg Muffins

½ cup plus 2 tablespoons sugar,
    divided
1¾ teaspoons ground nutmeg, divided
1½ cups all-purpose flour
2½ teaspoons baking powder
½ teaspoon salt
⅔ cup whipping cream
3 tablespoons butter or margarine,
    melted
1 egg, beaten
1 teaspoon vanilla extract

Preheat oven to 400°F. Grease or paper-line 24 (1¾-inch) mini-muffin cups. Combine 2 tablespoons sugar and ¼ teaspoon nutmeg in small bowl; set aside.

Combine flour, remaining ½ cup sugar, baking powder, remaining 1½ teaspoons nutmeg and salt in large bowl. Combine whipping cream, butter, egg and vanilla in small bowl until blended; stir into flour mixture just until moistened. Spoon into prepared muffin cups, filling ⅔ full. Sprinkle ¼ teaspoon of nutmeg-sugar mixture over top of each muffin.

Bake 14 to 16 minutes or until wooden pick inserted in center comes out clean. Remove from pans. Cool on wire racks.

Makes 24 mini muffins

Cheesy Bacon Muffins

1¾ cups all-purpose flour
3 tablespoons sugar
1 tablespoon baking powder
¾ teaspoon garlic salt
1 cup milk
3 tablespoons vegetable oil
1 egg, beaten
¾ cup (3 ounces) shredded Cheddar
    cheese
⅓ cup cooked crumbled bacon

Preheat oven to 400°F. Grease or paper-line 24 (1¾-inch) mini-muffin cups.

Combine flour, sugar, baking powder and garlic salt in large bowl. Combine milk, oil and egg in small bowl until blended; stir into flour mixture just until moistened. Fold in cheese and bacon. Spoon into prepared muffin cups, filling almost full.

Bake 18 to 20 minutes or until wooden pick inserted in center comes out clean. Remove from pans. Cool on wire racks.
Makes 24 mini muffins

Double Corn Muffins

1 cup all-purpose flour
1 cup yellow cornmeal
¼ cup sugar
1 tablespoon baking powder
½ teaspoon salt
1 cup milk
¼ cup vegetable oil
1 egg, beaten
⅔ cup canned or thawed frozen kernel
    corn, drained

Preheat oven to 400°F. Grease or paper-line 24 (1¾-inch) mini-muffin cups.

Combine flour, cornmeal, sugar, baking powder and salt in large bowl. Combine milk, oil and egg in small bowl until blended; stir into flour mixture just until moistened. Fold in corn. Spoon into prepared muffin cups, filling almost full.

Bake 14 to 16 minutes or until wooden pick inserted in center comes out clean. Remove from pans. Cool on wire racks.
Makes 24 mini muffins

Honey Apple Nut Muffins

2½ cups all-purpose flour
⅓ cup firmly packed light brown sugar
1¼ teaspoons ground cinnamon
1 teaspoon baking powder
1 teaspoon baking soda
¾ teaspoon ground allspice
⅔ cup honey
½ cup milk
6 tablespoons butter or margarine,
    melted
2 eggs, beaten
2 medium cooking apples, peeled,
    cored and chopped
½ cup chopped pecans

Preheat oven to 400°F. Grease 6 (3½-inch) large muffin cups.

Combine flour, brown sugar, cinnamon, baking powder, baking soda and allspice in large bowl. Combine honey, milk, butter and eggs in small bowl until blended; stir into flour mixture just until moistened. Fold in apples and pecans. Spoon into prepared muffin cups, filling ¾ full.

Bake 25 to 30 minutes or until wooden pick inserted in center comes out clean. Cool in pan on wire rack 5 minutes. Remove from pan. Cool on wire rack.
Makes 6 jumbo muffins

Tomato Basil Cheese Muffins

Tomato Basil Cheese Muffins

2¹/₂ cups all-purpose flour
  3 tablespoons sugar
  1 tablespoon baking powder
  2 teaspoons dried basil leaves, crushed
¹/₂ teaspoon salt
  1 cup milk
  6 tablespoons vegetable oil
  2 eggs, beaten
  1 cup (4 ounces) shredded mozzarella
    or provolone cheese
¹/₂ cup chopped sun-dried tomatoes*

Preheat oven to 400°F. Grease 6 (3¹/₂-inch) large muffin cups.

*If using dried tomatoes, soak in hot water a few minutes. Drain on paper towels; chop. If using oil-packed tomatoes, drain on paper towels; chop.

Combine flour, sugar, baking powder, basil and salt in large bowl. Combine milk, oil and eggs in small bowl until blended; stir into flour mixture just until moistened. Fold in cheese and tomatoes. Spoon evenly into prepared muffin cups.

Bake 25 to 30 minutes or until wooden pick inserted in center comes out clean. Cool in pan on wire rack 5 minutes. Remove from pan. Cool on wire rack.
Makes 6 jumbo muffins

Berries 'n' Cream Muffins

¹/₄ cup butter or margarine, softened
²/₃ cup sugar
  2 eggs
¹/₂ teaspoon almond extract
1¹/₂ cups all-purpose flour
1¹/₂ teaspoons baking powder
¹/₄ teaspoon salt
¹/₂ cup whipping cream
¹/₄ cup chopped fresh strawberries
¹/₄ cup chopped fresh raspberries
  1 teaspoon grated lemon peel

Preheat oven to 375°F. Grease or paper-line 24 (1³/₄-inch) mini-muffin cups.

Beat butter and sugar in large bowl with electric mixer at medium speed until light and fluffy. Beat in eggs until well blended. Beat in almond extract. Combine flour, baking powder and salt in small bowl; gradually beat into butter mixture at low speed just until blended. Beat in whipping cream until mixture is smooth. Fold in strawberries, raspberries and lemon peel with wooden spoon. Spoon into prepared muffin cups, filling almost full.

Bake 18 to 20 minutes or until wooden pick inserted in center comes out clean. Remove from pans. Cool on wire racks.
Makes 24 mini muffins

Fresh Strawberry Muffins

3 cups all-purpose flour
1 cup sugar
2 teaspoons baking powder
1 teaspoon baking soda
¼ teaspoon salt
1 container (16 ounces) dairy sour
   cream
½ cup milk
¼ cup vegetable oil
2 eggs, beaten
1 teaspoon almond extract
1 cup chopped fresh strawberries
¼ cup sliced natural almonds

Preheat oven to 400°F. Grease 12
(3½-inch) large muffin cups.

Combine flour, sugar, baking powder,
baking soda and salt in large bowl.
Combine sour cream, milk, oil, eggs and
almond extract in small bowl until
blended; stir into flour mixture just until
moistened. Fold in strawberries. Spoon
into prepared muffin cups, filling ⅔ full.
Sprinkle almonds evenly over muffins.

Bake 30 to 35 minutes or until golden
brown. Cool in pans on wire rack 5
minutes. Remove from pans. Cool on
wire rack.   *Makes 12 jumbo muffins*

Double Chocolate Muffins

1⅓ cups all-purpose flour
½ cup firmly packed light brown sugar
3 tablespoons unsweetened cocoa
1½ teaspoons baking powder
½ teaspoon baking soda
½ teaspoon salt
1 container (8 ounces) low-fat plain
   yogurt
3 tablespoons butter or margarine,
   melted
2 eggs, beaten
1 teaspoon vanilla extract
½ cup semi-sweet mini chocolate chips

Fresh Strawberry Muffins

Preheat oven to 425°F. Grease or paper-
line 24 (1¾-inch) mini-muffin cups.

Combine flour, brown sugar, cocoa,
baking powder, baking soda and salt in
large bowl. Combine yogurt, butter, eggs
and vanilla in small bowl until blended;
stir into flour mixture just until
moistened. Fold in chocolate chips. Spoon
evenly into prepared muffin cups.

Bake 16 to 18 minutes or until wooden
pick inserted in center comes out clean.
Remove from pans. Cool on wire racks.
   Makes 24 mini muffins

Sun-Dried Tomato Muffins

½ cup all-purpose flour
¼ cup whole wheat flour
1 teaspoon baking powder
1 teaspoon sugar
¼ teaspoon pepper
⅛ teaspoon salt
½ cup milk
2 tablespoons vegetable oil
2 to 3 tablespoons chopped pimiento-
   stuffed green olives
1 tablespoon chopped sun-dried
   tomatoes*

Preheat oven to 425°F. Grease 12
(1¼-inch) mini-muffin cups.

Combine all-purpose flour, whole wheat
flour, baking powder, sugar, pepper and
salt in medium bowl. Whisk together
milk and oil in small bowl; stir into flour
mixture, mixing just until moistened.
Fold in olives and tomatoes. Spoon
evenly into prepared muffin cups.

Bake 15 minutes or until lightly browned.
Serve warm.   *Makes 12 mini muffins*

*If using dried tomatoes, soak in hot
water a few minutes. Drain on paper
towels; chop. If using oil-packed
tomatoes, drain on paper towels; chop.

Cheesy Peperoni Bites

½ pound SWIFT PREMIUM® or
    MARGHERITA® Deli Sandwich
    Peperoni, unsliced
1 cup all-purpose flour
1 cup yellow cornmeal
4 teaspoons baking powder
¼ teaspoon salt
⅛ teaspoon ground red pepper
2 eggs, slightly beaten
1 cup milk
¼ cup vegetable oil
½ cup (2 ounces) shredded Monterey
    Jack cheese
¼ cup canned drained diced green
    chilies

Preheat oven to 400°F. Cut five ⅛-inch-thick slices from peperoni; cut each slice into 8 wedges. Set aside. Cut remaining peperoni into ¼-inch cubes.

Combine flour, cornmeal, baking powder, salt and pepper in large mixing bowl. Combine eggs, milk and oil in small bowl; add to flour mixture, stirring just until dry ingredients are moistened. Fold in cheese, chilies and cubed peperoni. Spoon batter into greased 1¾-inch mini-muffin cups, filling almost full. Top each muffin with 1 wedge of reserved peperoni, pressing halfway into batter.

Bake 10 to 12 minutes or until golden brown. Remove from pans immediately and serve warm or at room temperature.

Makes about 3½ dozen mini muffins

Double Chocolate Zucchini Muffins

2⅓ cups all-purpose flour
1¼ cups sugar
⅓ cup unsweetened cocoa
2 teaspoons baking powder
1½ teaspoons ground cinnamon
1 teaspoon baking soda
½ teaspoon salt
1 cup dairy sour cream
½ cup vegetable oil
2 eggs, beaten
¼ cup milk
1 cup milk chocolate chips
1 cup shredded zucchini

Preheat oven to 400°F. Grease 12 (3½-inch) large muffin cups.

Combine flour, sugar, cocoa, baking powder, cinnamon, baking soda and salt in large bowl. Combine sour cream, oil, eggs and milk in small bowl until blended; stir into flour mixture just until moistened. Fold in chocolate chips and zucchini. Spoon into prepared muffin cups, filling ½ full.

Bake 25 to 30 minutes or until wooden pick inserted in center comes out clean. Cool in pans on wire rack 5 minutes. Remove from pans. Cool on wire rack.

Makes 12 jumbo muffins

Tropical Treat Muffins

Tropical Treat Muffins

  2 cups all-purpose flour
⅓ cup plus 1 tablespoon sugar, divided
  1 tablespoon baking powder
  1 teaspoon grated lemon peel
½ teaspoon salt
¾ cup (4 ounces) dried papaya, finely diced
½ cup coarsely chopped banana chips
½ cup chopped macadamia nuts
¼ cup flaked coconut
½ cup milk
½ cup butter or margarine, melted
¼ cup sour cream
  1 egg, beaten

Preheat oven to 400°F. Grease or paper-line 12 (2½-inch) or 6 (4-inch) large muffins cups.

Combine flour, ⅓ cup sugar, baking powder, lemon peel and salt in large bowl. Combine papaya, banana chips, macadamia nuts and coconut in small bowl; stir in 1 tablespoon flour mixture until well coated. Combine milk, butter, sour cream and egg in another small bowl until blended; stir into flour mixture just until moistened. Fold in fruit mixture. Spoon evenly into prepared muffin cups. Sprinkle remaining 1 tablespoon sugar over tops of muffins.

Bake 15 to 20 minutes for regular-size muffins, 25 to 30 minutes for jumbo muffins, or until wooden pick inserted in center comes out clean. Remove from pan. Cool on wire rack.

Makes 12 regular-size or 6 jumbo muffins

Honey Vanilla Bran Muffins

1¼ cups oat bran
  1 cup all-purpose flour
  2 teaspoons baking powder
  1 teaspoon baking soda
  1 teaspoon ground cinnamon
½ teaspoon ground nutmeg
  1 container (8 ounces) low-fat vanilla yogurt
  6 tablespoons honey
  2 eggs, beaten
  3 tablespoons vegetable oil
  1 teaspoon vanilla extract
½ cup seedless raisins

Preheat oven to 400°F. Grease 6 (3½-inch) large muffin cups.

Combine oat bran, flour, baking powder, baking soda, cinnamon and nutmeg in large bowl. Combine yogurt, honey, eggs, oil and vanilla in small bowl until blended; stir into flour mixture just until moistened. Fold in raisins. Let stand 5 minutes. Spoon into prepared muffin cups, filling ⅔ full.

Bake 20 to 25 minutes or until wooden pick inserted in center comes out clean. Cool in pan on wire rack 5 minutes. Remove from pan. Cool on wire rack.

Makes 6 jumbo muffins

MEALTIME ACCOMPANIMENTS

Caraway Cheese Muffins

1¼ cups all-purpose flour
½ cup rye flour
2 tablespoons sugar
2½ teaspoons baking powder
½ teaspoon salt
1 cup (4 ounces) shredded sharp
    Cheddar or Swiss cheese
1½ teaspoons caraway seed
1 cup milk
¼ cup vegetable oil
1 egg

Preheat oven to 400°F. Paper-line 12 (2½-inch) muffin cups.

Combine flours, sugar, baking powder and salt in large bowl. Add cheese and caraway seed; toss to coat. Combine milk, oil and egg in small bowl until blended; stir into flour mixture just until moistened. Spoon evenly into prepared muffin cups.

Bake 20 to 25 minutes or until golden brown and wooden pick inserted in center comes out clean. Remove from pan. Cool on wire rack 10 minutes. Serve warm.   *Makes 12 muffins*

Ranch Muffins

¾ cup solid vegetable shortening
¼ cup sugar
2 eggs, beaten
1⅔ cups all-purpose flour
1 cup quick-cooking oats, uncooked
1½ teaspoons baking powder
1 teaspoon baking soda
1 package (.4 ounce) HIDDEN
    VALLEY RANCH® Buttermilk
    Recipe Original Ranch® salad
    dressing mix
½ cup chopped walnuts or pecans
1½ cups buttermilk

Preheat oven to 350°F. Grease or paper-line 12 (2½-inch) muffin cups.

Combine shortening and sugar in large bowl. Add eggs; mix well and set aside. Stir together flour, oats, baking powder, baking soda, salad dressing mix and walnuts in medium bowl. Add dry ingredients alternately with buttermilk to egg mixture. Stir until just combined. Spoon batter into prepared muffin cups, filling ⅔ full.

Bake 15 to 20 minutes or until wooden pick inserted in center comes out clean.
Makes 12 muffins

Caraway Cheese Muffins

Gougère Muffin Puffs

1 cup water
½ cup butter or margarine
2 teaspoons Dijon-style prepared
   mustard
1 cup all-purpose flour
⅛ teaspoon ground red pepper
4 eggs
½ cup shredded Gruyère or Swiss
   cheese

Preheat oven to 350°F. Generously grease 12 (2½-inch) muffin cups.

Bring water, butter and mustard to a boil in 2-quart saucepan over medium heat. Remove from heat. Add flour and red pepper; stir vigorously. Return to heat. Cook and stir until mixture forms a ball that leaves side of pan. Remove from heat; let stand 5 minutes. Add eggs, one at a time, beating until smooth after each addition. Stir in cheese. Spoon evenly into prepared muffin cups.

Bake 45 to 50 minutes or until golden brown. Remove from pan. Cool on wire rack 5 minutes. Serve warm.

Makes 12 muffins

Gougère Muffin Puff

Bacon-Topped Chili Corn Bread Muffins

4 slices uncooked bacon, diced
1½ cups stone ground yellow cornmeal
½ cup all-purpose flour
¼ cup instant minced onion
1 tablespoon sugar
2 teaspoons baking powder
1 teaspoon baking soda
½ teaspoon salt
1 cup buttermilk
1 can (4 ounces) chopped green chilies,
   drained
2 eggs
3 tablespoons bacon drippings or oil
4 ounces Monterey Jack cheese, cut
   into ½-inch cubes

Preheat oven to 400°F. Grease 12 (2½-inch) muffin cups. Cook bacon over medium-high heat in heavy skillet until crisp. Drain and reserve drippings; set aside bacon bits.

Combine cornmeal, flour, minced onion, sugar, baking powder, baking soda and salt in large bowl. Combine buttermilk, chilies, eggs and bacon drippings in small bowl until blended; stir into flour mixture just until moistened. Fold in cheese. Spoon evenly into prepared muffin cups. Sprinkle bacon bits evenly over tops of muffins.

Bake 15 to 20 minutes or until lightly browned. Remove from pan. Serve warm.

Makes 12 muffins

Tip: Serve these muffins with a "Tex-Mex" style meal; they would be great with a taco salad.

Cracked Wheat Applesauce Muffins

½ cup boiling water
½ cup cracked wheat (bulgur)
3 cups all-purpose flour
⅔ cup packed light brown sugar
5 teaspoons baking powder
2 teaspoons ground cinnamon
½ teaspoon salt
½ teaspoon ground nutmeg
1 cup applesauce
¾ cup milk
½ cup vegetable oil
2 eggs

Pour boiling water over cracked wheat in small bowl. Let stand 30 minutes until water is absorbed, stirring occasionally.

Preheat oven to 400°F. Grease or paper-line 18 (2½-inch) muffin cups.

Combine flour, brown sugar, baking powder, cinnamon, salt and nutmeg in large bowl. Combine applesauce, milk, oil and eggs in small bowl until blended; stir in soaked wheat. Stir applesauce mixture into flour mixture just until moistened.* Spoon evenly into prepared muffin cups.

Bake 25 to 30 minutes or until golden brown and wooden pick inserted in center comes out clean. Remove from pans. Cool on wire racks. Serve warm or cool completely. Store at room temperature in tightly covered container up to 2 days.   *Makes 18 muffins*

*Or, prepare muffin batter in airtight container. Cover with lid and refrigerate up to one week. Bake refrigerated batter for 30 to 35 minutes.

Pesto Surprise Muffins

Pesto Surprise Muffins

2 cups all-purpose flour
2 tablespoons grated Parmesan cheese
1 tablespoon baking powder
½ teaspoon salt
1 cup milk
¼ cup vegetable oil
1 egg
¼ cup prepared pesto sauce
   Additional grated Parmesan cheese (optional)

Preheat oven to 400°F. Grease 12 (2½-inch) muffin cups.

Combine flour, 2 tablespoons Parmesan cheese, baking powder and salt in large bowl. Combine milk, oil and egg in small bowl until blended; stir into flour mixture just until moistened. Spoon into prepared muffin cups, filling ⅓ full. Stir pesto sauce to blend; spoon 1 teaspoon pesto sauce into each muffin cup. Spoon remaining batter evenly over pesto sauce. Sprinkle additional Parmesan cheese over tops of muffins, if desired.

Bake 25 to 30 minutes or until golden brown and wooden pick inserted in center comes out clean. Remove from pan. Cool on wire rack 10 minutes. Serve warm.   *Makes 12 muffins*

Tex-Mex Pumpkin Corn Muffins with Corn Stick and Corn Bread variations

Tex-Mex Pumpkin Corn Muffins

1 cup yellow cornmeal
1 cup all-purpose flour
2 tablespoons granulated sugar
4 teaspoons baking powder
½ teaspoon salt
½ teaspoon chili powder
2 eggs
1 cup LIBBY'S® Solid Pack Pumpkin
1 cup milk
2 tablespoons vegetable oil
1 can (4 ounces) chopped green chiles
¾ cup grated Cheddar cheese

In large bowl, combine cornmeal, flour, sugar, baking powder, salt, and chili powder; set aside. In small mixer bowl, beat eggs; mix in pumpkin, milk, oil, and chiles. Add liquid ingredients to dry ingredients; mix until just blended. Spoon batter into 18 greased 2½-inch muffin cups. Sprinkle with cheese.

Bake in preheated 400°F. oven for 20 to 25 minutes, or until toothpick inserted in center comes out clean. Serve warm.

Makes 18 muffins

Note: For variation, batter may be baked in any of the following well-greased pans, in preheated 425°F. oven for 20 to 25 minutes, or until toothpick comes out clean:

> One 10-inch cast iron skillet
> Two 9-inch divided metal pans
> Corn-stick pans (omit cheese on top)

Hint: Grease pans thoroughly for easy removal. To avoid sticking, be sure cheese is not too close to edges of pan.

Sun-Dried Tomato 'n' Cheese Muffins

1 jar (7½ ounces) sun-dried tomatoes in olive oil
2 tablespoons butter or margarine
¼ teaspoon dried rosemary leaves, crushed
1 clove garlic, minced
2 cups all-purpose flour
2 tablespoons sugar
2 teaspoons baking powder
½ teaspoon baking soda
½ teaspoon salt
1 cup (4 ounces) shredded provolone cheese
1 cup buttermilk
1 egg

Drain tomatoes; reserve 2 tablespoons oil. Chop enough tomatoes to measure ⅓ cup; set aside.

Heat reserved oil and butter in small saucepan over medium-low heat. Cook and stir rosemary and garlic 30 seconds until garlic is soft. Cool.

Preheat oven to 400°F. Grease or paper-line 12 (2½-inch) muffin cups.

Combine flour, sugar, baking powder, baking soda and salt in large bowl; stir in cheese. Combine buttermilk and egg in small bowl until blended; stir in tomatoes and garlic mixture. Stir tomato mixture into flour mixture just until moistened. Spoon evenly into prepared muffin cups.

Bake 20 to 25 minutes or until golden brown and toothpick inserted in center comes out clean. Remove from pan. Cool on wire rack 10 minutes. Serve warm.

Makes 12 muffins

Pizza Muffins

½ cup WISH-BONE® Italian Dressing
¾ cup chopped onions
2 cups all-purpose flour
⅔ cup grated Parmesan cheese
1 tablespoon baking powder
¼ teaspoon crushed red pepper
1 egg
1 can (6 ounces) tomato paste
½ cup water
2 tablespoons chopped fresh basil leaves*
⅔ cup shredded provolone cheese

Preheat oven to 375°F.

In medium skillet, heat ¼ cup Italian dressing and cook onions over medium heat, stirring occasionally, 2 minutes or until tender; set aside.

In medium bowl, combine flour, Parmesan cheese, baking powder and pepper; set aside. In large bowl, beat egg with tomato paste until blended. Stir in remaining ¼ cup Italian dressing, water, basil and provolone cheese. Gradually stir in flour mixture just until blended. (Batter will be thick.) Evenly spoon batter into greased and floured 3-inch muffin cups. Top, if desired, with additional Parmesan cheese.

Bake in lower third of oven 30 minutes or until slightly browned.

Makes 12 muffins

*Substitution: Use ½ teaspoon dried basil leaves.

Note: Also great with Wish-Bone® Robusto Italian or Lite Italian Dressing.

Bacon 'n' Peanut Butter Muffins

2 cups all-purpose flour
2 tablespoons sugar
1 tablespoon baking powder
¼ teaspoon salt
½ cup chunky or creamy peanut butter
3 tablespoons butter or margarine
4 slices bacon, diced, cooked and
　　drained
1 cup milk
1 egg

Preheat oven to 400°F. Grease or paper-line 12 (2½-inch) muffin cups.

Combine flour, sugar, baking powder and salt in large bowl. Cut in peanut butter and butter with pastry blender until mixture resembles fine crumbs. Stir in bacon. Combine milk and egg in small bowl until blended; stir into flour mixture just until moistened. Spoon evenly into prepared muffin cups.

Bake 25 to 30 minutes or until golden brown and wooden pick inserted in center comes out clean. Remove from pan. Cool on wire rack 10 minutes. Serve warm. *Makes 12 muffins*

Double Cheese Muffins

1½ cups all-purpose flour
½ cup cornmeal
¼ cup sugar
1 tablespoon baking powder
1 egg, beaten
1 cup milk
½ cup (2 ounces) shredded Wisconsin
　　Cheddar cheese
½ cup cream-style Cottage cheese
¼ cup butter, melted

Preheat oven to 400°F. Butter and flour 16 (2½-inch) muffin cups.

Combine flour, cornmeal, sugar and baking powder in large bowl. Combine egg, milk, Cheddar cheese, Cottage cheese and butter in medium bowl; add to flour mixture, stirring until moistened. Spoon into prepared muffin cups, filling ⅔ full.

Bake 20 minutes or until wooden pick inserted in center comes out clean. Cool in pan 5 minutes. Remove from pan. Serve warm. *Makes 16 muffins*

Favorite recipe from **Wisconsin Milk Marketing Board** *© 1993*

Zucchini Basil Muffins

1½ cups NABISCO® 100% Bran™
1¼ cups skim milk
⅓ cup FLEISCHMANN'S® Margarine,
　　melted
¼ cup EGG BEATERS® 99% Real Egg
　　Product
1¼ cups all-purpose flour
2 tablespoons sugar
2 teaspoons baking powder
1 teaspoon dried basil leaves
½ cup grated zucchini

Mix bran, milk, margarine and Egg Beaters®; let stand 5 minutes.

In bowl, blend flour, sugar, baking powder and basil; stir in bran mixture just until blended. Stir in zucchini. Spoon into 12 greased 2½-inch muffin-pan cups.

Bake at 400°F for 20 to 25 minutes or until toothpick inserted in center comes out clean. Serve warm. *Makes 12 muffins*

Feta-Dill Muffins

2 cups all-purpose flour
2 tablespoons sugar
1 tablespoon baking powder
1 cup milk
½ cup (4 ounces) crumbled feta cheese
⅓ cup vegetable oil
1 tablespoon chopped fresh dill *or*
    1 teaspoon dried dill weed
1 egg

Preheat oven to 400°F. Grease or paper-line 12 (2½-inch) muffin cups.

Combine flour, sugar and baking powder in large bowl. Combine milk, feta cheese, oil, dill and egg in small bowl until blended; stir into flour mixture just until moistened. Spoon evenly into prepared muffin cups.

Bake 25 to 30 minutes or until golden brown and wooden pick inserted in center comes out clean. Remove from pan. Cool on wire rack 10 minutes. Serve warm. *Makes 12 muffins*

Feta-Dill Muffins

Southern Biscuit Muffins

2½ cups all-purpose flour
¼ cup sugar
1½ tablespoons baking powder
¾ cup cold butter or margarine
1 cup cold milk

Preheat oven to 400°F. Grease 12 (2½-inch) muffin cups. (These muffins brown better on the sides and bottom when baked without paper liners.)

Combine flour, sugar and baking powder in large bowl. Cut in butter with pastry blender until mixture resembles coarse crumbs. Stir in milk just until flour mixture is moistened. Spoon evenly into prepared muffin cups.

Bake 20 minutes or until golden. Remove from pan. Cool on wire rack.

Makes 12 muffins

Tip: These muffins taste like baking powder biscuits and are very quick and easy to make. Serve them with jelly, jam or honey.

Smoky Beef, Cheddar and Onion Muffins

2 tablespoons butter or margarine
¼ cup finely chopped green onions
¼ teaspoon pepper
2 cups all-purpose flour
2 tablespoons sugar
1 tablespoon baking powder
1 package (2 ounces) smoked beef
    jerky stick, chopped
½ cup (2 ounces) shredded sharp
    Cheddar cheese
1 cup milk
1 tablespoon Dijon-style mustard
1 egg

Heat butter in small saucepan over low heat. Cook and stir green onions and pepper in hot butter until soft. Cool. Preheat oven to 400°F. Grease or paper-line 12 (2½-inch) muffin cups.

Combine flour, sugar and baking powder in large bowl. Stir in beef and cheese to coat. Combine milk, mustard and egg in small bowl until blended; stir in green onion mixture. Stir milk mixture into flour mixture just until moistened. Spoon evenly into prepared muffin cups.

Bake 20 to 25 minutes or until golden brown and wooden pick inserted in center comes out clean. Remove from pan. Cool on wire rack 10 minutes. Serve warm.

Makes 12 muffins

Tunnel of Cheese Muffins

2 cups biscuit baking mix
5 slices bacon, crisp-cooked and
    crumbled
¾ cup milk
1 egg, beaten
12 (½-inch) cubes Wisconsin Swiss
    cheese

Preheat oven to 400°F. Butter 12 (2½-inch) muffin cups.

Combine biscuit mix and bacon in medium bowl. Add milk and egg, stirring just until moistened. Spoon ½ of the batter into prepared muffin cups. Press 1 cheese cube into each muffin cup. Top with remaining batter, covering cheese completely.

Bake 25 minutes or until golden. Remove from pan. Serve hot.

Makes 12 muffins

*Favorite recipe from **Wisconsin Milk Marketing Board** © 1993*

Southern Biscuit Muffin

Buttermilk Spice Muffins

1 cup all-purpose flour
1 cup whole wheat flour
3 tablespoons packed light brown
    sugar
2 teaspoons baking powder
1 teaspoon ground cinnamon
½ teaspoon baking soda
½ teaspoon ground nutmeg
¼ teaspoon salt
1 cup buttermilk
⅓ cup vegetable oil
1 egg

Preheat oven to 400°F. Grease or paper-line 12 (2½-inch) muffin cups.

Combine flours, brown sugar, baking powder, cinnamon, baking soda, nutmeg and salt in large bowl. Combine buttermilk, oil and egg in small bowl until blended; stir into flour mixture just until moistened. Spoon evenly into prepared muffin cups.

Bake 25 to 30 minutes or until golden brown and wooden pick inserted in center comes out clean. Remove from pan. Cool on wire rack. Serve warm or cool completely. Store at room temperature in tightly covered container up to 2 days. *Makes 12 muffins*

Corn Muffins

1 cup all-purpose flour
1 cup yellow cornmeal
¼ cup sugar
4 teaspoons baking powder
¾ teaspoon salt
2 eggs
1 cup milk
¼ cup vegetable oil or shortening,
    melted

Preheat oven to 400°F.

Combine flour, cornmeal, sugar, baking powder and salt in mixing bowl. Add eggs, milk and oil. Beat just until combined; do not overbeat. Grease 2½-inch muffin cups or line with paper baking cups; fill ⅔ full.

Bake 15 to 20 minutes or until wooden pick inserted in center comes out clean. Let stand 3 minutes in pan. Loosen muffins; remove from pan. Serve warm.
Makes about 14 muffins

Favorite recipe from **The Kingsford Products Company**

Mincemeat Muffins

2 cups all-purpose flour
2 tablespoons sugar
1 tablespoon baking powder
1 teaspoon ground cinnamon
¼ teaspoon salt
½ cup butter or margarine
¾ cup milk
½ cup prepared mincemeat
1 egg

Preheat oven to 400°F. Grease or paper-line 12 (2½-inch) muffin cups.

Combine flour, sugar, baking powder, cinnamon and salt in large bowl. Cut in butter with pastry blender until mixture resembles fine crumbs. Combine milk, mincemeat and egg in small bowl until blended; stir into flour mixture just until moistened. Spoon evenly into prepared muffin cups.

Bake 25 to 30 minutes or until golden brown and wooden pick inserted in center comes out clean. Remove from pan. Cool on wire rack. Serve warm or cool completely. Store at room temperature in tightly covered container up to 2 days. *Makes 12 muffins*

Cheesy Green Onion Muffins

1 package (3 ounces) cream cheese
1¾ cups all-purpose flour
4 teaspoons baking powder
1 tablespoon sugar
1 teaspoon salt
3 cups RICE CHEX® Brand Cereal,
    crushed to 1 cup
2 eggs, beaten
1¼ cups milk
⅓ cup vegetable oil
½ cup chopped green onions with tops

Preheat oven to 400°F. Grease 18 (2½-inch) muffin cups. Cut and separate cream cheese into ¼-inch cubes; set aside.

Combine flour, baking powder, sugar and salt in large bowl. Combine cereal, eggs, milk, oil and onions in medium bowl; add all at once to flour mixture, stirring just until moistened. Fold in cheese. Spoon evenly into prepared muffin cups.

Bake 20 to 25 minutes or until wooden pick inserted in center comes out clean. Remove from pan. Serve warm.

Makes 18 muffins

Cheesy Green Onion Muffins

Bacon Cheese Muffins

Bacon Cheese Muffins

½ **pound bacon (10 to 12 slices)**
  Vegetable oil
 1 **egg, beaten**
¾ **cup milk**
1¾ **cups all-purpose flour**
¼ **cup sugar**
 1 **tablespoon baking powder**
 1 **cup (4 ounces) shredded Wisconsin
    Cheddar cheese**
½ **cup crunchy nugget-like cereal**

Preheat oven to 400°F. Butter or paper-line 12 (2½-inch) muffin cups.

Cook bacon over medium-high heat in large skillet until crisp. Drain, reserving drippings. Crumble bacon; set aside. If necessary, add oil to drippings to measure ⅓ cup. Combine drippings, egg and milk in small bowl; set aside.

Combine flour, sugar and baking powder in large bowl. Make well in center. Add egg mixture, stirring just until moistened. (Batter will be lumpy.) Fold in bacon, cheese and cereal. Spoon into prepared muffin cups, filling about ¾ full.

Bake 15 to 20 minutes or until golden brown. Remove from pan. Cool on wire rack.   *Makes 12 muffins*

Favorite recipe from **Wisconsin Milk Marketing Board** © *1993*

Sun-Dried Tomato Olive Muffins

 1 **jar (7½ ounces) sun-dried tomatoes
    in olive oil**
½ **teaspoon dried basil leaves, crushed**
¼ **teaspoon freshly ground pepper**
 1 **clove garlic, minced**
 2 **cups all-purpose flour**
 2 **tablespoons sugar**
1½ **teaspoons baking powder**
½ **teaspoon baking soda**
½ **teaspoon salt**
⅓ **cup chopped pitted ripe olives**
 2 **tablespoons chopped fresh parsley**
 1 **cup milk**
 3 **tablespoons vegetable oil**
 1 **egg**
  Grated Parmesan cheese (optional)

Drain tomatoes; reserve 1 tablespoon olive oil. Chop enough tomatoes to measure ⅓ cup; set aside.

Heat reserved oil in small saucepan over low heat. Cook and stir basil, pepper and garlic in hot oil 30 seconds or until garlic is soft. Cool.

Preheat oven to 400°F. Grease or paper-line 12 (2½-inch) muffin cups.

Combine flour, sugar, baking powder, baking soda and salt in large bowl. Stir in tomatoes, olives and parsley. Combine milk, oil and egg in small bowl until blended; stir in garlic mixture. Stir milk mixture into flour mixture just until moistened. Spoon evenly into prepared muffin cups. Sprinkle Parmesan cheese over tops of muffins, if desired.

Bake 20 to 25 minutes or until golden brown and wooden pick inserted in center comes out clean. Remove from pan. Cool on wire rack. Serve warm or cool completely.   *Makes 12 muffins*

Sausage Corn Muffins

½ pound ECKRICH® Smoked Sausage
1 cup unsifted all-purpose flour
¾ cup yellow cornmeal
¼ cup sugar
1 tablespoon baking powder
1 cup buttermilk
¼ cup vegetable oil
2 eggs, beaten
    Honey Butter (recipe follows)

Preheat oven to 375°F. Cut sausage into quarters lengthwise, then cut crosswise into ¼-inch pieces. Lightly brown sausage in medium skillet over medium heat. Drain on paper towels.

Combine flour, cornmeal, sugar and baking powder in medium bowl. Add buttermilk, oil, eggs and sausage. Stir only until blended. Spoon into paper-lined 2½-inch muffin cups, filling ⅔ full.

Bake 12 to 15 minutes or until wooden pick inserted near center comes out clean. Remove from pans. Serve warm with Honey Butter.   *Makes 15 muffins*

Honey Butter: Blend ½ cup softened butter or margarine and ¼ cup honey in small bowl.

Sausage Corn Muffins

Herbed Parmesan Muffins

2 cups all-purpose flour
¾ cup grated Parmesan cheese
2 teaspoons sugar
2 teaspoons baking powder
2 teaspoons Italian-style herb
    seasoning*
½ teaspoon baking soda
½ teaspoon salt
½ cup chopped fresh basil, parsley or
    cilantro leaves
1¼ cups buttermilk
¼ cup olive or vegetable oil
1 egg

Preheat oven to 400°F. Grease bottoms only of 12 (2½-inch) or 36 (1¾-inch) mini-muffin cups.

Combine flour, Parmesan cheese, sugar, baking powder, herb seasoning, baking soda, salt and basil in large bowl. Combine buttermilk, oil and egg in small bowl until blended; stir into flour mixture just until moistened. Spoon evenly into prepared muffin cups.

Bake 15 to 20 minutes for regular-size muffins, 12 to 15 minutes for mini muffins, or until golden brown and wooden pick inserted in center comes out clean. Remove from pan. Serve warm.
    Makes 12 regular-size or 36 mini muffins

*Italian-style herb seasoning is a blend of dried marjoram, thyme, rosemary, savory, sage, oregano and basil.

Tip: Serve these muffins with an Italian-style meal or minestrone soup.

Whole Wheat Herb Muffins

1 cup all-purpose flour
1 cup whole wheat flour
⅓ cup sugar
2 teaspoons baking powder
½ teaspoon baking soda
½ teaspoon salt
½ teaspoon dried basil leaves, crushed
¼ teaspoon dried marjoram leaves, crushed
¼ teaspoon dried oregano leaves, crushed
⅛ teaspoon dried thyme leaves, crushed
¾ cup raisins
1 cup buttermilk
2 tablespoons butter or margarine, melted
1 egg, beaten
2 tablespoons wheat germ

Preheat oven to 400°F. Grease 12 (2½-inch) muffin cups.

Combine flours, sugar, baking powder, baking soda, salt, basil, marjoram, oregano, thyme and raisins in large bowl. Combine buttermilk, butter and egg in small bowl; stir into flour mixture just until moistened. Spoon evenly into prepared muffin cups. Sprinkle wheat germ over tops of muffins.

Bake 15 to 20 minutes or until lightly browned and wooden pick inserted in center comes out clean. Remove from pan. Serve warm.   *Makes 12 muffins*

Wisconsin Blue Cheese Muffins

2 cups all-purpose flour
3 tablespoons sugar
1 tablespoon baking powder
¼ teaspoon salt
1 cup Wisconsin Blue cheese, crumbled
1 egg, beaten
1 cup milk
¼ cup butter, melted

Preheat oven to 400°F. Butter 10 (2½-inch) muffin cups.

Combine flour, sugar, baking powder, salt and cheese in large bowl. Combine egg, milk and butter in small bowl until blended; stir into flour mixture just until moistened. Spoon into prepared muffin cups, filling ¾ full.

Bake 20 to 25 minutes or until golden brown. Remove from pan. Serve warm.
Makes 10 muffins

*Favorite recipe from **Wisconsin Milk Marketing Board © 1993***

***Whole Wheat Herb Muffins
and Wisconsin Blue Cheese Muffins***

Four-Grain Savory Muffins

1 cup buttermilk
½ cup high-fiber bran cereal
½ cup all-purpose flour
½ cup whole wheat flour
½ cup wheat germ
3 tablespoons sugar
1 teaspoon baking powder
1 teaspoon baking soda
½ teaspoon salt
¼ cup butter or margarine, melted
1 egg

Preheat oven to 400°F. Grease or paper-line 12 (2½-inch) muffin cups.

Pour buttermilk over bran cereal in large bowl. Let stand 5 minutes to soften. Combine flours, wheat germ, sugar, baking powder, baking soda and salt in medium bowl. Add melted butter and egg to cereal mixture; stir until blended. Stir in flour mixture just until moistened. Spoon evenly into prepared muffin cups.

Bake 20 to 25 minutes or until browned and wooden pick inserted in center comes out clean. Remove from pan. Cool on wire rack about 10 minutes. Serve warm or cool completely. Store at room temperature in tightly covered container up to 2 days. *Makes 12 muffins*

Wheat Germ Ginger Muffins

1 cup wheat germ, divided
1½ cups all-purpose flour
3 tablespoons sugar
1 tablespoon baking powder
¼ teaspoon salt
¼ teaspoon ground nutmeg
1 cup milk
⅓ cup vegetable oil
1 teaspoon grated fresh ginger
1 egg

Preheat oven to 400°F. Grease or paper-line 12 (2½-inch) muffin cups. Reserve 2 tablespoons wheat germ; set aside.

Combine remaining wheat germ, flour, sugar, baking powder, salt and nutmeg in large bowl. Combine milk, oil, ginger and egg in small bowl until blended; stir into wheat germ mixture just until moistened. Spoon evenly into prepared muffin cups. Sprinkle reserved wheat germ over tops of muffins.

Bake 25 to 30 minutes or until golden brown and wooden pick inserted in center comes out clean. Remove from pan. Cool on wire rack. Serve warm or cool completely. Store at room temperature in tightly covered container up to 2 days. *Makes 12 muffins*

Muffin Magic

Muffin recipe for 12 muffins
12 heaping teaspoons Wisconsin Jalapeño, Cheddar, Swiss or Bacon Cold Pack cheese

Paper-line 12 (2½-inch) muffin cups.

Prepare muffin recipe for 12 muffins according to package or recipe directions. Spoon into prepared muffin cups, filling ⅓ full. Drop 1 heaping teaspoon Jalapeño, Cheddar, Swiss or Bacon Cold Pack cheese on each muffin. Spoon remaining batter evenly over cheese. Bake according to recipe directions.
Makes 12 muffins

*Favorite recipe from **Wisconsin Milk Marketing Board** © 1993*

Spanish Olive Cheddar Muffins

2 cups all-purpose flour
1 tablespoon sugar
2 teaspoons baking powder
1 teaspoon dry mustard
½ teaspoon baking soda
½ teaspoon salt
⅛ teaspoon ground red pepper
¼ cup butter or margarine, softened
1 cup (4 ounces) shredded sharp
    Cheddar cheese
½ cup chopped pimiento-stuffed olives
1 cup buttermilk
1 egg

Preheat oven to 375°F. Grease or paper-line 12 (2½-inch) muffin cups.

Combine flour, sugar, baking powder, mustard, baking soda, salt and red pepper in large bowl. Cut in butter with pastry blender until mixture resembles fine crumbs. Stir in cheese and olives. Combine buttermilk and egg in small bowl until blended; stir into flour mixture just until moistened. Spoon evenly into prepared muffin cups.

Bake 25 to 30 minutes or until golden brown and wooden pick inserted in center comes out clean. Remove from pan. Cool on wire rack. Serve warm or cool completely. *Makes 12 muffins*

Fruited Corn Muffins

2 (8½-ounce) packages *or* 1 (18-ounce)
    package corn muffin mix
1 (9-ounce) package NONE SUCH®
    Condensed Mincemeat, finely
    crumbled

Preheat oven to 400°F.

Prepare muffin mix according to package directions, stirring in mincemeat. Fill greased or paper-lined 2½-inch muffin cups ½ full.

Bake 15 to 18 minutes or until golden brown. Remove from pan. Serve warm. *Makes about 18 muffins*

Anadama Muffins

2 cups all-purpose flour, divided
3 tablespoons sugar
½ teaspoon salt
1 package active dry rapid-rise yeast
¾ cup water
⅓ cup yellow cornmeal
3 tablespoons molasses
3 tablespoons butter or margarine
1 egg

Grease or paper-line 12 (2½-inch) muffin cups.

Combine 1 cup flour, sugar, salt and yeast in large bowl; set aside. Combine water, cornmeal, molasses and butter in 1-quart saucepan. Heat over low heat until very warm (120°F to 130°F). Gradually beat water mixture into flour mixture with electric mixer at low speed until well blended. Increase speed to medium; beat 2 minutes. Add ½ cup flour and egg; beat 2 minutes more. Stir in remaining ½ cup flour with wooden spoon until mixture is well blended and forms a thick batter. Spoon evenly into prepared muffin cups. Let rise, uncovered, 30 minutes.

Preheat oven to 400°F. Bake 20 to 25 minutes or until browned and sound hollow when tapped. Remove from pans. Cool on wire rack 10 minutes. Serve warm. *Makes 12 muffins*

Spanish Olive Cheddar Muffins

Garden Vegetable Muffins

Garden Vegetable Muffins

2 cups all-purpose flour
2 tablespoons sugar
1 tablespoon baking powder
¼ teaspoon salt
1 package (3 ounces) cream cheese
¾ cup milk
½ cup finely shredded or grated carrots
¼ cup chopped green onions
¼ cup vegetable oil
1 egg

Preheat oven to 400°F. Grease or paper-line 12 (2½-inch) muffin cups.

Combine flour, sugar, baking powder and salt in large bowl. Cut in cream cheese with pastry blender until mixture resembles fine crumbs. Combine milk, carrots, green onions, oil and egg in small bowl until blended; stir into flour mixture just until moistened. Spoon evenly into prepared muffin cups.

Bake 25 to 30 minutes or until golden brown and wooden pick inserted in center comes out clean. Remove from pan. Cool on wire rack 10 minutes. Serve warm. *Makes 12 muffins*

Chili-Cheese Corn Muffins

MAZOLA® No Stick cooking spray
1 cup yellow corn meal
¾ cup flour
2 tablespoons sugar
1 tablespoon baking powder
¼ teaspoon salt
1 egg, lightly beaten
⅔ cup milk
⅓ cup HELLMANN'S® or BEST FOODS® Real Mayonnaise or Light Reduced Calorie Mayonnaise Dressing
1 can (7 ounces) corn or corn with green and red sweet peppers, drained
½ cup (2 ounces) shredded Cheddar cheese
3 to 6 tablespoons chopped green chilies, undrained

Preheat oven to 400°F. Spray 12 (2½-inch) muffin pan cups with cooking spray.

In large bowl combine corn meal, flour, sugar, baking powder and salt. In small bowl combine egg, milk and mayonnaise; stir in corn, cheese and chilies until well mixed. Stir corn mixture into flour mixture just until moistened. Spoon into prepared muffin pan cups.

Bake 20 to 25 minutes or until golden. Immediately remove from pan. Serve warm. *Makes 12 muffins*

Bayou Yam Muffins

1 cup all-purpose flour
1 cup yellow cornmeal
¼ cup sugar
1 tablespoon baking powder
1¼ teaspoons ground cinnamon
1 teaspoon salt
2 eggs
½ cup cold strong coffee
¼ cup butter or margarine, melted
1 cup mashed yams
½ teaspoon TABASCO® Brand Pepper
    Sauce

Preheat oven to 425°F. Grease 12 (3-inch) muffin-pan cups.

Combine flour, cornmeal, sugar, baking powder, cinnamon and salt in large bowl. Beat eggs in small bowl; stir in coffee, butter, yams and Tabasco® sauce. Make a well in center of flour mixture; add yam mixture and stir just to combine. Spoon batter into prepared muffin-pan cups.

Bake 20 to 25 minutes or until wooden pick inserted in center comes out clean. Cool 5 minutes on wire rack. Remove from pan. Serve warm or at room temperature. *Makes 12 muffins*

Boursin Muffins

2¼ cups all-purpose flour
1 tablespoon baking powder
¼ teaspoon salt
1 package (4 ounces) garlic-herb
    flavored soft spreadable cheese
¾ cup milk
¼ cup vegetable oil
1 egg

Preheat oven to 400°F. Grease or paper-line 12 (2½-inch) muffin cups.

Combine flour, baking powder and salt in large bowl. Cut in cheese with pastry blender until mixture resembles fine crumbs. Combine milk, oil and egg in small bowl until blended; stir into flour mixture just until moistened. Spoon evenly into prepared muffin cups.

Bake 25 to 30 minutes or until golden brown and wooden pick inserted in center comes out clean. Remove from pan. Cool on wire rack. Serve warm or cool completely. *Makes 12 muffins*

Dilly Cheese Muffins

2 cups all-purpose flour
1 tablespoon sugar
1 tablespoon baking powder
2 teaspoons dried dill weed
1 teaspoon onion powder
½ teaspoon salt
¼ teaspoon freshly ground black
    pepper
1 cup small curd creamed cottage
    cheese
¾ cup milk
¼ cup butter or margarine, melted
1 egg, beaten

Preheat oven to 400°F. Grease or paper-line 12 (2½-inch) muffin cups.

Combine flour, sugar, baking powder, dill weed, onion powder, salt and pepper in large bowl. Combine cottage cheese, milk, butter and egg in small bowl until blended; stir into flour mixture just until moistened. Spoon evenly into prepared muffin cups.

Bake 20 to 25 minutes or until golden and wooden pick inserted in center comes out clean. Remove from pan. Serve warm.
Makes 12 muffins

Tomato 'n' Fennel Muffins

2 tablespoons butter or margarine
½ cup finely chopped green onions
½ teaspoon fennel seed
2¼ cups all-purpose flour
2 tablespoons sugar
2 teaspoons baking powder
½ teaspoon salt
¼ teaspoon freshly ground pepper
1 cup milk
2 tablespoons vegetable oil
1 egg
½ cup seeded, chopped canned
tomatoes, well drained

Heat butter in small saucepan over medium-low heat. Cook and stir green onions and fennel seed in hot butter until onions are soft. Cool.

Preheat oven to 400°F. Grease or paper-line 12 (2½-inch) muffin cups.

Combine flour, sugar, baking powder, salt and pepper in large bowl. Combine milk, oil and egg in small bowl until blended; stir in green onion mixture and tomato. Stir tomato mixture into flour mixture just until moistened. Spoon evenly into prepared muffin cups.

Bake 25 to 30 minutes or until golden brown and wooden pick inserted in center comes out clean. Remove from pan. Cool on wire rack. Serve warm or cool completely.   *Makes 12 muffins*

Country Corn Muffins

2 (8½-ounce) packages corn
    muffin mix
10 slices bacon, cooked and crumbled
¾ cup BAMA® Strawberry or
    Blackberry Preserves

Preheat oven to 400°F.

Prepare muffin mix according to package directions; stir in bacon. Fill paper-lined 2½-inch muffin cups ⅓ full. Drop 2 level teaspoons preserves in center of each. Add remaining batter to fill cups ¾ full.

Bake 15 to 20 minutes or until golden brown. Remove from pans. Serve warm.
Makes 12 to 18 muffins

Anjou Pear Cheese Muffins

2 cups all-purpose flour
¼ cup packed brown sugar
3 teaspoons baking powder
½ teaspoon salt
¾ cup (3 ounces) shredded Swiss
    cheese
⅔ cup milk
1 egg, slightly beaten
2 tablespoons vegetable oil
1 USA Anjou pear, finely chopped
½ cup chopped nuts

Preheat oven to 400°F. Grease 12 (2½-inch) muffin cups.

Combine flour, brown sugar, baking powder, salt and cheese in large bowl. Combine milk, egg and oil in small bowl; add to flour mixture with pear and nuts. Mix only until moistened. Spoon evenly into prepared muffin cups.

Bake 20 to 25 minutes or until wooden pick inserted near center comes out clean.
Makes 12 muffins

Note: Anjou Pear-Cheese Muffins may be frozen in aluminum foil or freezer-proof bags then reheated, unthawed, at 350°F 20 to 25 minutes or until thoroughly heated.

*Favorite recipe from **Oregon-Washington-California Pear Bureau***

Oat Bread Muffins

2 cups all-purpose flour, divided
½ cup oat bran cereal
2 tablespoons sugar
½ teaspoon salt
1 package active dry rapid-rise yeast
½ cup milk
½ cup cottage cheese
2 tablespoons butter or margarine
1 egg
¼ cup chopped fresh parsley
1 tablespoon chopped fresh dill *or*
  1 teaspoon dried dill weed
2 tablespoons quick-cooking or old-
  fashioned oats (optional)

Grease or paper-line 12 (2½-inch) muffin cups.

Combine 1 cup flour, bran cereal, sugar, salt and yeast in large bowl; set aside. Place milk, cottage cheese and butter in 1-quart saucepan. Heat over low heat until very warm (120°F to 130°F). Gradually beat milk mixture into flour mixture with electric mixer at low speed until well blended. Increase speed to medium; beat 2 minutes. Add ½ cup flour, egg, parsley and dill; beat 2 minutes more. Stir in remaining ½ cup flour with wooden spoon until mixture is well blended and forms a thick batter. Spoon evenly into prepared muffin cups. Sprinkle oats over tops of muffins, if desired. Let rise, uncovered, 30 minutes.

Preheat oven to 400°F. Bake 20 to 25 minutes or until browned and sound hollow when tapped. Remove from pans. Cool on wire rack 10 minutes. Serve warm. *Makes 12 muffins*

Calico Bell Pepper Muffins

¼ cup *each* finely chopped red, yellow
  and green bell pepper
¼ cup butter or margarine
2 cups all-purpose flour
2 tablespoons sugar
1 tablespoon baking powder
¾ teaspoon salt
½ teaspoon dried basil leaves, crushed
1 cup milk
2 eggs

Preheat oven to 400°F. Grease or paper-line 12 (2½-inch) muffin cups. Cook peppers in butter over medium-high heat in small skillet until color is bright and peppers are tender crisp, about 3 minutes; set aside.

Combine flour, sugar, baking powder, salt and basil in large bowl. Combine milk and eggs in small bowl until blended. Add milk mixture and peppers with drippings to flour mixture, stirring just until moistened. Spoon evenly into prepared muffin cups.

Bake 15 minutes or until golden brown and wooden pick inserted in center comes out clean. Remove from pan. Serve warm. *Makes 12 muffins*

Calico Bell Pepper Muffins

Sesame-Mushroom Muffins

6 tablespoons vegetable oil, divided
1½ cups chopped fresh mushrooms
⅓ cup chopped green onions
1 clove garlic, minced
2 cups all-purpose flour
2 tablespoons sugar
1½ teaspoons baking powder
½ teaspoon salt
½ teaspoon baking soda
½ cup milk
½ cup sour cream
1 egg
2 tablespoons sesame seed

Heat 2 tablespoons oil in 10-inch skillet over medium heat. Cook and stir mushrooms, onions and garlic in hot oil 5 minutes or until mushrooms are brown and liquid is evaporated. Remove from heat; set aside.

Preheat oven to 400°F. Grease or paper-line 10 (2½-inch) muffin cups.

Combine flour, sugar, baking powder, salt and baking soda in large bowl. Combine remaining 4 tablespoons oil, milk, sour cream and egg in small bowl until blended; stir in cooked vegetables. Stir vegetable mixture into flour mixture just until moistened. Spoon evenly into prepared muffin cups. Sprinkle sesame seed over tops of muffins.

Bake 25 to 30 minutes or until golden brown and wooden pick inserted in center comes out clean. Remove from pan. Cool on wire rack 10 minutes. Serve warm. *Makes 10 muffins*

Jalapeño Corn Muffins

MAZOLA® No Stick cooking spray
1 cup flour
1 cup yellow corn meal
2 teaspoons baking powder
¼ teaspoon salt
2 eggs
½ cup KARO® Light Corn Syrup
¼ cup MAZOLA® Corn Oil
1 cup cream-style corn
1 cup (4 ounces) shredded Monterey Jack cheese
2 tablespoons seeded chopped jalapeño peppers, fresh or pickled*

Preheat oven to 400°F. Spray 12 (2½-inch) muffin pan cups with cooking spray.

In medium bowl combine flour, corn meal, baking powder and salt. In large bowl combine eggs, corn syrup and corn oil. Stir in flour mixture until well blended. Stir in corn, cheese and peppers. Spoon into prepared muffin pan cups.

Bake 15 to 20 minutes or until lightly browned and firm to touch. Cool in pan on wire rack 5 minutes; remove from pan. *Makes 12 muffins*

*Wear rubber gloves when working with hot peppers or wash hands in warm soapy water after handling. Avoid touching face or eyes.

Sesame-Mushroom Muffins

Green Chili Cheese Muffins

2 cups all-purpose flour
2 tablespoons sugar
2 teaspoons baking powder
½ teaspoon baking soda
½ teaspoon salt
½ cup (2 ounces) shredded Monterey Jack cheese
½ cup milk
¼ cup vegetable oil
¼ teaspoon hot pepper sauce
1 egg
1 can (4 ounces) chopped green chilies

Preheat oven to 400°F. Grease or paper-line 10 (2½-inch) muffin cups.

Combine flour, sugar, baking powder, baking soda and salt in large bowl. Stir in cheese. Combine milk, oil, hot pepper sauce and egg in small bowl until blended; stir in chilies. Stir milk mixture into flour mixture just until moistened. Spoon evenly into prepared muffin cups.

Bake 20 to 25 minutes or until golden brown and wooden pick inserted in center comes out clean. Remove from pan. Cool on wire rack 10 minutes. Serve warm. *Makes 10 muffins*

Red Wine Muffins

2 cups all-purpose flour
¼ cup sugar
2 teaspoons baking powder
½ teaspoon salt
¼ cup butter or margarine, softened
½ cup dry red wine
½ cup milk
1 egg
   Slivered almonds or pine nuts (optional)

Preheat oven to 400°F. Grease or paper-line 12 (2½-inch) muffin cups.

Combine flour, sugar, baking powder and salt in large bowl. Cut in butter with pastry blender until mixture resembles fine crumbs. Combine wine, milk and egg in small bowl until blended; stir into flour mixture just until moistened. Spoon evenly into prepared muffin cups. Sprinkle almonds over tops of muffins, if desired.

Bake 20 to 25 minutes or until golden brown and wooden pick inserted in center comes out clean. Remove from pan. Cool on wire rack. Serve warm or cool completely. *Makes 12 muffins*

Herb Cheese Muffins

1½ cups all-purpose flour
2 teaspoons baking powder
½ teaspoon salt
¼ teaspoon freshly ground black pepper
⅔ cup milk
1 package (4 ounces) soft spreadable herbed cream cheese
1 egg, beaten
2 teaspoons minced fresh chives

Preheat oven to 375°F. Grease or paper-line 12 (2½-inch) muffin cups.

Combine flour, baking powder, salt and pepper in large bowl. Combine milk, cream cheese, egg and chives in small bowl until blended; stir into flour mixture just until moistened. Spoon evenly into prepared muffin cups.

Bake 15 to 20 minutes or until wooden pick inserted in center comes out clean. Remove from pan. Serve warm.
Makes 12 muffins

Tip: These muffins are great served with any chicken or fish dish.

Indian Corn Muffins

Indian Corn Muffins

　1 cup all-purpose flour
　1 cup cornmeal
　⅓ cup granulated sugar
　1 tablespoon baking powder
　½ teaspoon salt
　2 eggs, lightly beaten
　1 cup LIBBY'S® Solid Pack Pumpkin
　¼ cup vegetable oil
　¼ cup water

In large bowl, combine flour, cornmeal, sugar, baking powder, and salt. Mix well; set aside. In small mixer bowl, combine eggs, pumpkin, oil, and water; beat well. Add wet ingredients to dry ingredients; mix thoroughly. Spoon batter into 10 greased or paper-lined muffin cups.

Bake in preheated 375°F. oven for 25 to 30 minutes, or until toothpick comes out clean. Serve warm.　　*Makes 10 muffins*

Squash Muffins

　1 cup all-purpose flour
　1 cup whole wheat flour
　⅓ cup packed light brown sugar
　2 teaspoons baking powder
1½ teaspoons ground cinnamon
　½ teaspoon baking soda
　½ teaspoon salt
　½ teaspoon ground cloves
　¼ teaspoon ground nutmeg
　6 tablespoons butter or margarine
　½ cup golden raisins
　¾ cup milk
　½ of a 12-ounce package frozen cooked
　　　squash, thawed and well drained
　　　(½ cup)
　1 egg

Preheat oven to 400°F. Grease or paper-line 12 (2½-inch) muffin cups.

Combine flours, brown sugar, baking powder, cinnamon, baking soda, salt, cloves and nutmeg in large bowl. Cut in butter with pastry blender until mixture resembles fine crumbs. Stir in raisins. Combine milk, squash and egg in small bowl until blended; stir into flour mixture just until moistened. Spoon evenly into prepared muffin cups.

Bake 25 to 30 minutes or until golden brown and wooden pick inserted in center comes out clean. Remove from pan. Cool on wire rack 10 minutes. Serve warm.　　*Makes 12 muffins*

Cheddar Pepper Muffins

2 cups all-purpose flour
1 tablespoon sugar
1 tablespoon baking powder
1 teaspoon coarsely ground black
    pepper
½ teaspoon salt
1¼ cups milk
¼ cup vegetable oil
1 egg
1 cup (4 ounces) shredded sharp
    Cheddar cheese, divided

Preheat oven to 400°F. Generously grease 12 (2½-inch) muffin cups.

Combine flour, sugar, baking powder, pepper and salt in large bowl. Combine milk, oil and egg in small bowl until blended; stir into flour mixture just until moistened. Fold in ¾ cup cheese. Spoon evenly into prepared muffin cups. Sprinkle remaining ¼ cup cheese over tops of muffins.

Bake 15 to 20 minutes or until light golden brown. Let cool in pan on wire rack 5 minutes. Remove from pan. Serve warm. *Makes 12 muffins*

Cheddar Pepper Muffins

Pumpkin-Chutney Muffins

1½ cups all-purpose flour
1½ teaspoons ground cinnamon
1 teaspoon baking soda
½ teaspoon baking powder
½ teaspoon salt
¼ teaspoon ground allspice
½ cup chopped walnuts
¾ cup mashed cooked pumpkin
½ cup mango chutney
⅓ cup buttermilk
¼ cup packed dark brown sugar
¼ cup vegetable oil
1 egg

Preheat oven to 375°F. Grease or paper-line 12 (2½-inch) muffin cups.

Combine flour, cinnamon, baking soda, baking powder, salt and allspice in large bowl. Stir in walnuts. Combine pumpkin, chutney, buttermilk, brown sugar, oil and egg in medium bowl until blended; stir into flour mixture just until moistened. Spoon evenly into prepared muffin cups.

Bake 25 to 30 minutes or until wooden pick inserted in center comes out clean. Remove from pan. Cool on wire rack. Serve warm or cool completely. Store at room temperature in tightly covered container up to 2 days.

Makes 12 muffins

Whole Wheat Muffins

¾ cup all-purpose flour
¾ cup whole wheat flour
2 teaspoons baking powder
½ teaspoon salt
1 egg
½ cup packed brown sugar
½ cup milk
¼ cup vegetable oil

Preheat oven to 375°F. Grease 12 (2½-inch) muffin cups.

Combine flours, baking powder and salt in large bowl. Make well in center. Combine egg, brown sugar, milk and oil in medium bowl until well blended; stir into flour mixture just until moistened. Spoon into prepared muffin cups, filling ⅔ full.

Bake 20 to 25 minutes or until wooden pick inserted in center comes out clean. Remove from pan. Serve warm.

Makes 12 muffins

Turkey Ham, Cheese & Pepper Muffins

¼ cup butter or margarine
½ cup minced sweet onion
¼ cup minced green bell pepper
1 clove garlic, minced
2 cups all-purpose flour
1 tablespoon baking powder
1 teaspoon salt
½ teaspoon coarsely ground black pepper
1 cup milk
2 eggs
1 cup (4 ounces) finely diced turkey ham
½ cup (2 ounces) diced Cheddar cheese
¼ cup roasted shelled sunflower seeds

Preheat oven to 375°F. Generously grease or paper-line 12 (2½-inch) or 36 (1¾-inch) mini-muffin cups.

Melt butter in small skillet over medium-high heat. Add onion, green pepper and garlic; cook and stir 5 to 7 minutes or until onion is translucent. Combine flour, baking powder, salt and black pepper in large bowl. Combine milk and eggs in small bowl until blended. Add milk mixture, vegetables with drippings, turkey and cheese to flour mixture. Stir mixture just until moistened. Spoon evenly into prepared muffin cups. Sprinkle sunflower seeds over tops of muffins.

Bake 25 to 30 minutes for regular-size muffins, 15 to 20 minutes for mini muffins, or until wooden pick inserted in center comes out clean. Remove from pan.

Makes 12 regular-size or 36 mini muffins

Tip: Serve these savory muffins baked in mini-muffin cups as an appetizer. Larger muffins are a perfect accompaniment to a salad or soup.

Favorite Corn Muffins

1 cup all-purpose flour
¾ cup cornmeal
¼ cup wheat bran cereal
2 teaspoons baking powder
1½ teaspoons salt
½ teaspoon baking soda
1 cup dairy sour cream
2 eggs
¼ cup honey
¼ cup butter, melted

Preheat oven to 425°F. Generously butter 12 (2½-inch) muffin cups.

Combine flour, cornmeal, cereal, baking powder, salt and baking soda in large bowl. Beat sour cream, eggs, honey and butter in medium bowl until blended; add to flour mixture, stirring just until moistened. Spoon evenly into prepared muffin cups.

Bake 15 to 20 minutes or until wooden pick inserted in center comes out clean. Cool in pan on wire rack 5 minutes. Remove from pan. Serve warm.

Makes 12 muffins

*Favorite recipe from **Wisconsin Milk Marketing Board** © 1993*

Old World Pumpernickel Muffins

1 cup all-purpose flour
½ cup rye flour
½ cup whole wheat flour
2 teaspoons caraway seed
1 teaspoon baking soda
½ teaspoon salt
1 cup buttermilk
¼ cup vegetable oil
¼ cup light molasses
1 egg
½ square (½ ounce) unsweetened
    chocolate, melted and cooled

Preheat oven to 400°F. Grease or paper-line 12 (2½-inch) muffin cups.

Combine flours, caraway seed, baking soda and salt in large bowl. Combine buttermilk, oil, molasses and egg in small bowl until blended; stir in melted chocolate. Stir into flour mixture just until moistened. Spoon evenly into prepared muffin cups.

Bake 20 to 25 minutes or until wooden pick inserted in center comes out clean. Remove from pan. Cool on wire rack 10 minutes. Serve warm or cool completely. Store at room temperature in tightly covered container up to 2 days.

Makes 12 muffins

Cheesy Red Pepper Corn Muffins

1 package (8½ ounces) corn muffin mix
½ cup (2 ounces) shredded sharp
    Cheddar cheese
¼ cup drained, chopped roasted red
    peppers
2 tablespoons grated Parmesan cheese
    Generous dash ground red pepper

Preheat oven to 400°F. Grease or paper-line 10 (2½-inch) muffin cups.

Prepare corn muffins according to package directions in large bowl. Stir in Cheddar cheese, chopped red peppers, Parmesan cheese and ground red pepper. Let batter stand for 2 minutes. Spoon evenly into prepared muffin cups.

Bake 15 to 20 minutes or until golden brown and wooden pick inserted in center comes out clean. Remove from pan. Cool on wire rack 10 minutes. Serve warm.

Makes 10 muffins

Pear-Cheese Muffins

2 cups all-purpose flour
⅓ cup sugar
1 tablespoon baking powder
½ teaspoon salt
¼ teaspoon pumpkin pie spice
1 cup (4 ounces) shredded Colby
    cheese
2 medium pears, peeled, cored, cut
    into large pieces
1 cup milk
2 large eggs
¼ cup butter, melted

In large bowl, combine flour, sugar, baking powder, salt and spice; stir in cheese. In blender or food processor, process pears, milk, eggs and butter until pears are finely chopped. Pour pear mixture into flour mixture, stirring just until moistened. Spoon into paper-lined 2½-inch muffin cups, filling ⅔ full.

Bake in preheated 425°F oven 20 to 25 minutes or until wooden pick inserted in center comes out clean. Serve warm.

Makes about 15 muffins

*Favorite recipe from **American Dairy Association***

Old World Pumpernickel Muffins

Chili Corn Muffins

½ cup all-purpose flour
½ cup stone ground cornmeal
1 tablespoon sugar
1 teaspoon baking powder
½ teaspoon baking soda
½ teaspoon salt
½ teaspoon chili powder
½ cup frozen or fresh whole kernel corn
¼ cup chopped green bell pepper
⅓ cup buttermilk
¼ cup vegetable oil
1 egg, beaten

Microwave Directions: Line 6 microwavable muffin cups with double paper liners.

Combine flour, cornmeal, sugar, baking powder, baking soda, salt and chili powder in large bowl. Stir in corn and pepper. Combine buttermilk, oil and egg until blended in small bowl; stir into flour mixture just until moistened. Spoon into prepared muffin cups, filling ½ full.

Microwave at HIGH 2½ to 4½ minutes or until tops appear dry. Rotate dish ½ turn halfway through cooking. Let stand 5 minutes. Remove from pan. Repeat procedure with remaining batter.

Makes about 12 muffins

Chili Corn Muffins

Zucchini Cheese Muffins

1 cup all-purpose flour
¾ cup PROGRESSO® Italian Style or Plain Bread Crumbs
¾ cup sugar
1½ teaspoons baking powder
1 teaspoon salt
1 cup (4 ounces) shredded Cheddar cheese
2 eggs, beaten
1 can (5 fluid ounces) PET® Evaporated Milk
¼ cup butter, melted
1½ cups shredded zucchini

Preheat oven to 400°F. Grease 18 (2½-inch) muffin cups.

Combine flour, bread crumbs, sugar, baking powder and salt in large bowl; stir in cheese. Combine eggs, evaporated milk and butter in medium bowl; stir in zucchini. Add zucchini mixture to flour mixture; stir until moistened. Spoon evenly into prepared muffin cups.

Bake 20 to 22 minutes or until lightly browned. Remove from pan. Serve warm.

Makes 18 muffins

Estimated preparation time: 10 minutes
Baking time: 22 minutes

Blueberry Orange Corn Muffins

⅓ cup margarine or butter, softened
½ cup sugar
2 to 3 teaspoons grated orange peel
¾ cup MOTT'S® Regular Apple Sauce
1 egg
1 cup all-purpose flour
½ cup cornmeal
½ teaspoon baking powder
½ teaspoon baking soda
¼ teaspoon salt
1 cup fresh blueberries

Preheat oven to 375°F. Grease bottoms only of 12 (2½-inch) muffin cups or line with paper baking cups.

Beat margarine and sugar in large bowl until fluffy. Add orange peel, apple sauce and egg; blend well. Stir in flour, cornmeal, baking powder, baking soda and salt. Blend just until dry ingredients are moistened. Gently fold in blueberries. Spoon into prepared muffin cups, filling ⅔ full.

Bake 20 to 25 minutes or until wooden pick inserted in center comes out clean. Cool 5 minutes; remove from pan. Serve warm.   *Makes 12 muffins*

Spicy Garden Vegetable Muffins

½ cup shredded carrots
½ cup shredded zucchini
3 cups wheat bran cereal
1¼ cups whole milk
1 egg
2 tablespoons butter, melted
½ teaspoon vanilla extract
1½ cups all-purpose flour
½ cup sugar
1 tablespoon baking powder
1½ teaspoons ground cinnamon
¼ teaspoon ground cloves

Preheat oven to 400°F. Spray 12 (2½-inch) muffin cups with nonstick cooking spray or paper-line.

Combine carrots, zucchini, cereal, milk, egg, butter and vanilla in medium bowl. Let stand 5 minutes to soften. Combine flour, sugar, baking powder, cinnamon and cloves in large bowl. Add cereal mixture to flour mixture all at once, stirring just until moistened. Spoon evenly into prepared muffin cups.

Bake 20 to 25 minutes or until wooden pick inserted in center comes out clean. Remove from pan.   *Makes 12 muffins*

Buttermilk Herb Muffins

2 cups NABISCO® 100% Bran™
1¼ cups buttermilk
¼ cup FLEISCHMANN'S® Margarine, melted
¼ cup EGG BEATERS® 99% Real Egg Product
1 cup all-purpose flour
2 tablespoons sugar
1 tablespoon DAVIS® Baking Powder
1 teaspoon dried dill weed

Mix bran, buttermilk, margarine and Egg Beaters®; let stand 5 minutes.

In bowl, blend flour, sugar, baking powder and dill; stir in bran mixture just until blended. (Batter will be lumpy.) Spoon batter into 12 greased 2½-inch muffin-pan cups. Bake at 400°F for 18 to 20 minutes or until toothpick inserted in center comes out clean. Serve warm.
Makes 1 dozen muffins

Microwave Directions: Prepare batter as above. In each of 6 microwavable muffin-pan cups, place 2 paper liners. Spoon batter into cups, filling ⅔ full. Microwave on HIGH (100% power) for 1 minute; rotate pan ½ turn. Microwave on HIGH for 1 minute more or until toothpick inserted in center comes out clean. Let stand in pan 1 minute; remove from pan. Repeat 2 more times to make a total of 18 muffins. Serve warm.

Oatmeal Green Onion Muffins

1¾ cups all-purpose flour
¾ cup old-fashioned oats
2 tablespoons sugar
1 tablespoon baking powder
½ teaspoon salt
¾ cup milk
½ cup cottage cheese
⅓ cup vegetable oil
¼ cup chopped green onions
1 egg

Preheat oven to 400°F. Grease or paper-line 12 (2½-inch) muffin cups.

Combine flour, oats, sugar, baking powder and salt in large bowl. Combine milk, cottage cheese, oil, green onions and egg in small bowl until blended; stir into flour mixture just until moistened. Spoon evenly into prepared muffin cups.

Bake 25 to 30 minutes or until golden brown and wooden pick inserted in center comes out clean. Remove from pan. Cool on wire rack 10 minutes. Serve warm.   *Makes 12 muffins*

Sunflower Muffins

1½ cups all-purpose flour
¾ cup whole wheat flour
⅓ cup packed light brown sugar
1 tablespoon baking powder
1 teaspoon ground cinnamon
¼ teaspoon salt
½ cup unsalted sunflower seeds
1 cup milk
⅓ cup vegetable oil
1 egg

Preheat oven to 400°F. Grease or paper-line 12 (2½-inch) muffin cups.

Combine flours, brown sugar, baking powder, cinnamon and salt in large bowl; stir in sunflower seeds. Combine milk, oil and egg in small bowl until blended; stir into flour mixture just until moistened. Spoon evenly into prepared muffin cups.

Bake 25 to 30 minutes or until golden brown and wooden pick inserted in center comes out clean. Remove from pan. Cool on wire rack. Serve warm or cool completely. Store at room temperature in tightly covered container up to 2 days.   *Makes 12 muffins*

Tomato-Basil Muffins

2 cups all-purpose flour
2 tablespoons sugar
2 teaspoons baking powder
½ teaspoon salt
½ teaspoon baking soda
½ teaspoon dried basil leaves, crushed
¼ teaspoon garlic powder
¼ cup butter or margarine, softened
¾ cup milk
1 egg
½ cup seeded, chopped canned tomatoes, well drained

Preheat oven to 400°F. Grease or paper-line 12 (2½-inch) muffin cups.

Combine flour, sugar, baking powder, salt, baking soda, basil and garlic powder in large bowl. Cut in butter with pastry blender until mixture resembles fine crumbs. Combine milk and egg in small bowl until blended; stir in tomatoes. Stir tomato mixture into flour mixture just until moistened. Spoon evenly into prepared muffin cups.

Bake 20 to 25 minutes or until golden brown and wooden pick inserted in center comes out clean. Remove from pan. Cool on wire rack. Serve warm or cool completely.   *Makes 12 muffins*

Louisiana Corn Muffins

1 cup all-purpose flour
1 cup yellow cornmeal
2 tablespoons sugar
2½ teaspoons baking powder
½ teaspoon salt
1 cup milk
½ cup vegetable oil
2 eggs, slightly beaten
½ teaspoon TABASCO® Brand Pepper
   Sauce
1 can (8¾ ounces) whole kernel corn,
   drained *or* 1 cup fresh or thawed
   frozen corn kernels

Microwave Directions: Line 6
microwavable muffin-pan cups or 6-
ounce microwavable custard cups with
double paper liners.

Combine flour, cornmeal, sugar, baking
powder and salt in large bowl. Make well
in center. Combine milk, oil, eggs and
Tabasco® sauce in medium bowl. Add
milk mixture to flour mixture, stirring
just until moistened. Fold in corn. Spoon
about ⅓ cup batter into each cup.

Microwave at HIGH (100%) 4 to 5½
minutes or until wooden pick inserted in
center comes out clean. Rotate muffin pan
½ turn or rearrange custard cups halfway
through cooking. Let stand 5 minutes;
remove from pan. Repeat procedure with
remaining batter. Serve warm.

Makes about 12 muffins

Conventional Directions: Preheat oven
to 400°F. Grease 12 (3-inch) muffin-pan
cups. Prepare batter as directed. Spoon
evenly into prepared muffin cups. Bake
15 to 20 minutes or until wooden pick
inserted in center comes out clean. Cool
in pan on wire rack 5 minutes. Remove
from pan. Serve warm.

Makes 12 muffins

Salsa Muffins

Salsa Muffins

1 cup all-purpose flour
1 cup yellow cornmeal
3 tablespoons sugar
1 tablespoon baking powder
½ teaspoon salt
6 tablespoons butter or margarine,
   softened
¾ cup bottled chunky salsa
½ cup milk
1 egg

Preheat oven to 400°F. Grease or paper-
line 12 (2½-inch) muffin cups.

Combine flour, cornmeal, sugar, baking
powder and salt in large bowl. Cut in
butter with pastry blender until mixture
resembles fine crumbs. Combine salsa,
milk and egg in small bowl until blended;
stir into flour mixture just until
moistened. Spoon evenly into prepared
muffin cups.

Bake 25 to 30 minutes or until golden
brown and wooden pick inserted in
center comes out clean. Remove from
pan. Cool on wire rack 10 minutes. Serve
warm. *Makes 12 muffins*

SWEET-SNACKIN' MUFFINS

Sparkling Cranberry Muffins

1 cup chopped fresh cranberries
2 tablespoons sugar
2 cups all-purpose flour
⅓ cup sugar
2 teaspoons baking powder
½ teaspoon salt
½ cup LAND O LAKES® Butter
¾ cup orange juice
1 egg, slightly beaten
¼ cup LAND O LAKES® Butter, melted
¼ cup sugar

Heat oven to 400°F.

In small bowl combine cranberries and 2 tablespoons sugar; set aside. In large bowl stir together flour, ⅓ cup sugar, baking powder and salt. Cut in ½ cup butter until mixture is crumbly. Stir in orange juice and egg just until moistened. Fold in cranberry-sugar mixture. Spoon batter into greased 12-cup muffin pan.

Bake for 20 to 25 minutes or until golden brown. Cool 5 minutes; remove from pan. Dip top of each muffin in ¼ cup melted butter, then in ¼ cup sugar. Serve warm.

Makes 1 dozen muffins

Orange Glazed Muffins

1½ cups all-purpose flour
½ cup KRETSCHMER® Original or Honey Crunch Wheat Germ
¼ cup granulated sugar
1 tablespoon baking powder
1 tablespoon grated orange peel
½ teaspoon salt (optional)
⅔ cup milk
⅓ cup margarine, melted
2 eggs, slightly beaten
½ cup powdered sugar
1 tablespoon orange juice

Heat oven to 400°F. Line 12 (2½-inch) muffin cups with paper baking cups or grease lightly.

In large bowl, combine flour, wheat germ, granulated sugar, baking powder, orange peel and salt. In small bowl, combine milk, margarine and eggs. Add to flour mixture, stirring just until moistened. Fill muffin cups ⅔ full.

Bake 20 to 25 minutes or until light golden brown and wooden pick inserted in center comes out clean. Remove to wire rack. In small bowl, combine powdered sugar and orange juice. Drizzle over slightly cooled muffins.

Makes 12 muffins

Sparkling Cranberry Muffins

Chocolate Pumpkin Muffins

1½ cups all-purpose flour
½ cup sugar
2 teaspoons baking powder
½ teaspoon cinnamon
½ teaspoon salt
1 cup milk
½ cup solid pack canned pumpkin
¼ cup butter, melted
1 egg
One 6-oz. pkg. (1 cup) NESTLÉ® Toll House® Semi-Sweet Chocolate Morsels
¼ cup finely chopped nuts

Preheat oven to 400°F. Grease 12 (2½-inch) muffin cups.

In large bowl, combine flour, sugar, baking powder, cinnamon and salt; make well in center. In small bowl, combine milk, pumpkin, butter and egg; add to well in flour mixture. Add semi-sweet chocolate morsels; stir until dry ingredients are just moistened. Spoon into prepared muffin cups, filling each ¾ full. Sprinkle 1 teaspoon nuts over each muffin.

Bake 18 to 20 minutes or until wooden toothpick inserted into center comes out clean. Cool 5 minutes; remove from pans. Cool completely on wire racks.

Makes 12 muffins

Chocolate Pumpkin Muffins

Walnut Streusel Muffins

3 cups all-purpose flour, divided
1½ cups packed brown sugar
¾ cup butter or margarine
1 cup chopped DIAMOND® Walnuts, divided
2 teaspoons baking powder
1 teaspoon ground nutmeg
1 teaspoon ground ginger
½ teaspoon baking soda
½ teaspoon salt
1 cup buttermilk or sour milk*
2 eggs, beaten

Combine 2 cups flour and brown sugar in medium bowl; cut in butter to form fine crumbs. Combine ¾ cup of the crumbs and ¼ cup walnuts in small bowl; set aside. Into remaining crumb mixture, stir in remaining 1 cup flour, baking powder, nutmeg, ginger, baking soda, salt and remaining ¾ cup walnuts. Combine buttermilk and eggs in another small bowl; stir into dry ingredients just to moisten. Spoon into 18 greased or paper-lined 2¾-inch muffin cups, filling about ⅔ full. Top each with a generous spoonful of reserved crumb-nut mixture.

Bake in preheated 350°F oven 20 to 25 minutes or until wooden pick inserted in center comes out clean. Cool in pans on wire rack 10 minutes. Loosen and remove from pans. Serve warm.

Makes 18 muffins

To make sour milk: Use 1 tablespoon vinegar plus milk to equal 1 cup. Stir; let stand 5 minutes.

Apple-Cranberry Muffins

Apple-Cranberry Muffins

1¾ cups plus 2 tablespoons all-purpose
    flour, divided
½ cup sugar, divided
1½ teaspoons baking powder
½ teaspoon baking soda
½ teaspoon salt
1 egg
¾ cup milk
¾ cup sweetened applesauce
¼ cup butter or margarine, melted
1 cup fresh cranberries, coarsely
    chopped
½ teaspoon ground cinnamon

Preheat oven to 400°F. Grease 12
(2¾-inch) muffin cups.

Combine 1¾ cups flour, ¼ cup sugar,
baking powder, baking soda and salt in
medium bowl. Combine egg, milk,
applesauce and butter in small bowl; mix
well. Add egg mixture to flour mixture;
stir just until moistened. (Batter will be
lumpy; do not overmix.) Toss cranberries
with remaining 2 tablespoons flour in
small bowl; fold into batter. Spoon evenly
into prepared muffin cups. Combine
remaining ¼ cup sugar and cinnamon in
another small bowl. Sprinkle evenly over
tops of muffins.

Bake 20 to 25 minutes or until golden
brown. Remove to wire rack to cool.

Makes 12 muffins

*Favorite recipe from **Western New York Apple Growers
Association, Inc.***

Cherry Peanut Butter Muffins

2 cups all-purpose flour
⅓ cup sugar
2½ teaspoons baking powder
½ teaspoon salt
½ teaspoon grated orange peel
½ cup peanut butter
2 tablespoons butter or margarine
½ cup maraschino cherries, chopped
⅔ cup milk
2 eggs, lightly beaten

Preheat oven to 400°F. Grease 12
(2½-inch) muffin cups.

Combine flour, sugar, baking powder, salt
and orange peel in medium bowl; cut in
peanut butter and butter with pastry
blender until mixture resembles coarse
crumbs. Stir in cherries. Combine milk
and eggs in small bowl; stir into dry
ingredients just until moistened. Spoon
evenly into prepared muffin cups.

Bake 15 minutes or until wooden pick
inserted near center comes out clean.
Remove from pan.   *Makes 12 muffins*

*Favorite recipe from **National Cherry Foundation***

Chocolate & Orange Muffins

One 6-oz. pkg. (1 cup) NESTLÉ® Toll
   House® Semi-Sweet Chocolate
   Morsels
1¾ cups all-purpose flour
½ cup walnuts, chopped
⅓ cup plus 1 tablespoon sugar,
   divided
1 tablespoon baking powder
½ teaspoon salt
One 8-oz. container plain yogurt
½ cup (1 stick) butter, melted
2 eggs
½ teaspoon grated orange rind

Preheat oven to 375°F. Grease or paper-line 12 to 15 muffin cups. Melt semi-sweet chocolate morsels; set aside.

In large bowl, combine flour, walnuts, ⅓ cup sugar, baking powder and salt. In small bowl, combine yogurt, butter and eggs; stir into flour mixture just until dry ingredients are moistened. Divide batter in half. Blend melted chocolate into one half of batter. Stir orange rind and remaining 1 tablespoon sugar into remaining half of batter. Spoon 1 rounded measuring tablespoonful of each batter, side by side, into each prepared muffin cup.

Bake 20 to 23 minutes until wooden toothpick inserted into center comes out clean. Cool 5 minutes; remove from cups. Serve warm or cool completely.

Makes 12 to 15 muffins

Swiss Coconut Banana Muffins

½ cup milk
2 teaspoons lemon juice
3 cups all-purpose flour
4 teaspoons baking powder
1 teaspoon baking soda
½ teaspoon salt
⅔ cup butter, softened
⅔ cup sugar
3 eggs
3 ripe bananas, mashed (1 cup)
½ cup cream of coconut
1 teaspoon vanilla extract
2 cups (8 ounces) finely shredded
   Wisconsin Swiss cheese, divided

Preheat oven to 375°F. Butter or paper-line 24 (2½-inch) muffin cups.

Combine milk and lemon juice in small bowl; set aside. Combine flour, baking powder, baking soda and salt in medium bowl. Cream butter and sugar with electric mixer in large bowl. Add eggs, one at a time, beating well after each addition. Add bananas, cream of coconut, vanilla and milk mixture. Add flour mixture; blend just until moistened. Stir in 1¾ cups cheese. Spoon into prepared muffin cups, filling about ⅔ full. Sprinkle with remaining ¼ cup cheese.

Bake for 30 to 35 minutes or until wooden pick inserted in center comes out clean. Remove from pan.   *Makes 24 muffins*

Favorite recipe from **Wisconsin Milk Marketing Board** *© 1993*

Deluxe Blueberry Muffins

Deluxe Blueberry Muffins

1⅔ cups all-purpose flour
  1 teaspoon baking soda
½ teaspoon baking powder
½ teaspoon salt
  1 teaspoon ground cinnamon
½ teaspoon ground allspice
  1 cup LIBBY'S® Solid Pack Pumpkin
¼ cup *undiluted* CARNATION®
     Evaporated Milk
⅓ cup shortening
  1 cup packed light brown sugar
  1 egg
  1 cup blueberries
  1 tablespoon all-purpose flour
     Streusel Topping (recipe follows)

In large bowl, combine *1⅔ cups* flour, baking soda, baking powder, salt, cinnamon, and allspice; set aside. In small bowl, blend pumpkin and evaporated milk. In large mixer bowl, cream shortening and sugar. Add egg; beat until fluffy. Alternately add flour and pumpkin mixtures to shortening mixture; beat well after each addition. Combine blueberries and *1 tablespoon* flour. Gently stir into batter. Fill greased or paper-lined muffin cups ¾ full. Sprinkle Streusel Topping over muffins.

Bake in preheated 350°F. oven for 35 to 40 minutes, or until toothpick comes out clean. Cool 3 to 4 minutes. Remove from pan; cool on wire rack.

Makes 18 muffins

Streusel Topping: In small bowl, combine 2 tablespoons all-purpose flour, 2 tablespoons granulated sugar, and ¼ teaspoon ground cinnamon. Cut in 1 tablespoon butter or margarine until mixture is crumbly.

Chocolate Macadamia Muffins

1½ cups (¾ of 12-oz. pkg.) NESTLÉ® Toll House® Semi-Sweet Chocolate Morsels, divided
1½ cups all-purpose flour
2 tablespoons sugar
1 teaspoon baking soda
¼ teaspoon salt
¾ cup macadamia nuts, chopped
¾ cup sour cream
2 eggs
⅓ cup vegetable oil

Preheat oven to 375°F. Grease or paper-line 12 (2½-inch) muffin cups. Melt 1 cup semi-sweet chocolate morsels; set aside.

In large bowl, combine flour, sugar, baking soda and salt; stir in macadamia nuts and remaining ½ cup semi-sweet chocolate morsels. In small bowl, combine melted chocolate, sour cream, eggs and oil; stir into flour mixture just until dry ingredients are moistened. Spoon into prepared muffin cups, filling about ¾ full.

Bake 18 to 20 minutes until wooden toothpick inserted into center comes out clean. Cool 5 minutes; remove from cups. Serve warm or cool completely.

Makes 12 muffins

Mini Crumbcakes

Topping:
½ cup walnuts, chopped
⅓ cup firmly packed brown sugar
2 tablespoons (¼ stick) butter, melted
1 tablespoon all-purpose flour
One 12-oz. pkg. (2 cups) NESTLÉ® Toll House® Semi-Sweet Chocolate Mini Morsels, divided

Cake:
2 cups all-purpose flour
1½ cups NESTLÉ® Toll House® Semi-Sweet Chocolate Mini Morsels, reserved from 12-oz. pkg.
3 tablespoons granulated sugar
1 tablespoon baking powder
¼ teaspoon salt
⅔ cup milk
½ cup (1 stick) butter, melted
2 eggs
1 teaspoon vanilla extract

Topping: In small bowl, combine walnuts, brown sugar, butter and flour; stir in ½ cup mini morsels; set aside.

Cake: Preheat oven to 400°F. Grease or paper-line 18 (2½-inch) muffin cups. In large bowl, combine flour, remaining 1½ cups mini morsels, granulated sugar, baking powder and salt. In small bowl, combine milk, butter, eggs and vanilla extract. Add to flour mixture, stirring just until dry ingredients are moistened. Spoon into prepared muffin cups, filling each about ¾ full. Sprinkle each with Topping.

Bake 18 to 20 minutes until wooden toothpick inserted into center comes out clean. Cool 5 minutes; remove from cups. Serve warm or cool completely.

Makes 18 crumbcakes

Clockwise from top left: Chocolate Macadamia Muffins, Chocolate Streusel Pecan Muffins (page 120) and Mini Crumbcakes

Chocolate Streusel Pecan Muffins

Topping:
- ¼ cup all-purpose flour
- ¼ cup firmly packed brown sugar
- 2 tablespoons (¼ stick) butter, melted
- ¼ teaspoon cinnamon
- ¼ cup pecans, chopped

Muffins:
- One 11½-oz pkg. (2 cups) NESTLÉ® Toll House® Milk Chocolate Morsels, divided
- 3 tablespoons butter
- 1 cup all-purpose flour
- 2 tablespoons granulated sugar
- 2 teaspoons baking powder
- ¾ cup pecans, chopped
- 1 egg
- ⅓ cup milk
- ½ teaspoon vanilla extract

Topping: In small bowl, combine flour, brown sugar, melted butter and cinnamon; stir with fork until mixture resembles coarse crumbs. Stir in pecans.

Muffins: Preheat oven to 375°F. Grease or paper-line 12 (2½-inch) muffin cups. Melt 1 cup milk chocolate morsels and butter, stirring until smooth; set aside.

In large bowl, combine flour, granulated sugar and baking powder; stir in pecans and remaining 1 cup milk chocolate morsels. In small bowl, combine egg, milk, vanilla extract and melted chocolate; stir into flour mixture just until dry ingredients are moistened. Spoon into prepared muffin cups, filling each ⅔ full. Sprinkle each with Topping.

Bake 20 to 25 minutes until wooden toothpick inserted into center comes out clean. Cool 5 minutes; remove from cups. Serve warm or cool completely.

Makes 12 muffins

Popover-Pan Muffins

- 2 cups all-purpose flour
- ¾ cup sugar
- 2 teaspoons pumpkin pie spice
- ¾ teaspoon baking powder
- ¾ teaspoon baking soda
- ¾ teaspoon salt
- 3 eggs
- ¾ cup almond oil
- 2 teaspoons vanilla extract
- 1 cup grated zucchini
- ½ cup chopped toasted almonds
- ½ cup seedless raisins

Preheat oven to 375°F. Grease 6 popover pans.*

Combine flour, sugar, spice, baking powder, baking soda and salt in large bowl. Beat eggs with oil and vanilla in small bowl; stir into flour mixture with zucchini, almonds and raisins just until moistened. Spoon into popover pans.

Bake in center of oven 25 minutes or until browned. Remove from pans; serve warm. *Makes 6 popover-pan muffins*

*To make standard-size muffins, divide batter among 18 greased (2½-inch) muffin cups. Bake in preheated 375°F oven 20 minutes or until browned.

Makes 18 muffins

*Favorite recipe from **Almond Board of California***

Apricot-Pecan Muffins

2 cups all-purpose flour
2½ teaspoons baking powder
1 teaspoon ground cinnamon
½ teaspoon salt
⅓ to ½ cup packed brown sugar
¾ cup chopped California dried
    apricots*
½ cup chopped pecans
1 egg, slightly beaten
½ cup milk
½ cup apricot nectar
¼ cup vegetable oil

Preheat oven to 400°F. Grease or paper-line 12 (2½-inch) muffin cups.

Sift together flour, baking powder, cinnamon and salt in large bowl. Stir in brown sugar, apricots and nuts. Mix together egg, milk, apricot nectar and oil; add to apricot-flour mixture, stirring with spoon just until combined. (Batter will be lumpy; do not overmix.) Spoon into prepared muffin cups, filling about ⅔ full.

Bake 20 minutes or until golden brown. Serve warm. *Makes 12 muffins*

*California apricots are halved and dried. Lower quality imports are dried whole.

Favorite recipe from **California Apricot Advisory Board**

Apricot-Pecan Muffins

Top to bottom: Chocolate Chip Fruit Muffins and Mini Chips Surprise Muffins

Chocolate Chip Fruit Muffins

  1 package (about 15 oz.) banana quick bread mix
  2 eggs
  1 cup milk
  ¼ cup vegetable oil
  1 cup HERSHEY'S Semi-Sweet Chocolate Chips, MINI CHIPS Semi-Sweet Chocolate or Milk Chocolate Chips
  ½ cup dried fruit bits

Heat oven to 400°F. Grease or paper-line 18 muffin cups (2½ inches in diameter).

In bowl, stir together quick bread mix, eggs, milk and oil; beat with spoon 30 seconds. Stir in chocolate chips and fruit bits. Fill muffin cups ¾ full with batter.

Bake 18 to 20 minutes or until lightly browned. Serve warm.

Makes about 1½ dozen muffins

Mini Chips Surprise Muffins

  1 package (about 16 oz.) nut quick bread mix
  1 egg
  1 cup milk
  ¼ cup vegetable oil
  1 cup HERSHEY'S MINI CHIPS Semi-Sweet Chocolate
  ⅓ cup fruit preserves, any flavor

Heat oven to 400°F. Grease or paper-line 18 muffin cups (2½ inches in diameter).

In bowl, combine bread mix, egg, milk and oil; beat with spoon 1 minute. Stir in small chocolate chips. Fill muffin cups ¼ full with batter. Spoon ½ teaspoon preserves onto center of batter. Fill muffin cups ¾ full with batter.

Bake 20 to 22 minutes or until lightly browned. Serve warm.

Makes about 1½ dozen muffins

Almond Date Muffins

  1 cup DOLE® Sliced Almonds
  3 to 4 extra-ripe, medium DOLE® Bananas, peeled
  1 cup cooked, mashed pumpkin
  3 eggs
1½ cups sugar
  1 cup vegetable oil
  5 cups all-purpose flour
  1 tablespoon baking soda
  2 teaspoons ground cinnamon
  ½ teaspoon ground cloves
  2 cups DOLE® Chopped Dates
  Topping (recipe follows)

Preheat oven to 350°F. Generously grease 12 (2½-inch) muffin cups *and* 2 (8½×4½-inch) loaf pans. Sprinkle bottoms of pans equally with almonds.

Purée bananas in blender (2 cups). Combine puréed bananas, pumpkin, eggs and sugar in mixer bowl. Beat in oil. Combine flour, baking soda, cinnamon and cloves; stir in dates. Beat flour mixture into banana mixture until just blended. Spoon ¼ cup batter into each muffin cup. Pour remaining batter evenly into loaf pans. Prepare Topping. Sprinkle 1 to 2 teaspoons Topping on top of each muffin. Sprinkle remaining Topping evenly on loaves.

Bake muffins 25 minutes or until wooden pick inserted in center comes out clean. Bake loaves 60 minutes or until wooden pick inserted in center comes out clean. Cool in pans on wire racks 5 minutes. Remove from pans. Cool completely on wire racks.

Makes 12 muffins and 2 loaves of bread

Topping: Combine 1 cup Dole® Sliced Almonds, ½ cup melted margarine and ¼ cup packed brown sugar in medium bowl.

Streusel Raspberry Muffins

Pecan Streusel Topping
(recipe follows)
1½ cups all-purpose flour
½ cup sugar
2 teaspoons baking powder
½ cup milk
½ cup butter or margarine, melted
1 egg, beaten
1 cup fresh or individually frozen whole unsweetened raspberries

Preheat oven to 375°F. Grease or paper-line 12 (2½-inch) muffin cups. Prepare Pecan Streusel Topping; set aside.

Combine flour, sugar and baking powder in large bowl. Combine milk, butter and egg in small bowl until blended; stir into flour mixture just until moistened. Spoon ½ of batter into muffin cups. Divide raspberries among cups, then top with remaining batter. Sprinkle Pecan Streusel Topping over tops of muffins.

Bake 25 to 30 minutes or until golden and wooden pick inserted in center comes out clean. Remove from pan.

Makes 12 muffins

Pecan Streusel Topping: Combine ¼ cup *each* chopped pecans, packed brown sugar and all-purpose flour in small bowl. Stir in 2 tablespoons melted butter or margarine until mixture resembles moist crumbs.

Oreo Muffins

1¾ cups all-purpose flour
½ cup sugar
1 tablespoon DAVIS® Baking Powder
½ teaspoon salt
¾ cup milk
⅓ cup sour cream
1 egg
¼ cup BLUE BONNET® Margarine, melted
20 OREO® Chocolate Sandwich Cookies, coarsely chopped

In medium bowl, combine flour, sugar, baking powder and salt; set aside.

In small bowl, combine milk, sour cream and egg; stir into flour mixture with margarine until just blended. Gently stir in cookies. Spoon batter into 12 greased 2½-inch muffin-pan cups.

Bake at 400°F for 20 to 25 minutes or until toothpick inserted in center comes out clean. Remove from pan; cool on wire rack. Serve warm or cold.

Makes 1 dozen muffins

Pecan Peach Muffins

Topping (recipe follows)
1½ cups all-purpose flour
½ cup granulated sugar
2 teaspoons baking powder
1 teaspoon ground cinnamon
¼ teaspoon salt
½ cup butter or margarine, melted
¼ cup milk
1 egg
2 medium peaches, peeled and diced
(about 1 cup)

Preheat oven to 400°F. Grease* or paper-line 12 (2½-inch) muffin cups. Prepare Topping; set aside.

Combine flour, granulated sugar, baking powder, cinnamon and salt in large bowl. Combine butter, milk and egg in small bowl until blended; stir into flour mixture just until moistened. Fold in peaches. Spoon evenly into prepared muffin cups. Sprinkle Topping over tops of muffins.

Bake 20 to 25 minutes or until wooden pick inserted in center comes out clean. Remove from pan.   *Makes 12 muffins*

Topping: Combine ½ cup chopped pecans, ⅓ cup packed brown sugar, ¼ cup all-purpose flour and 1 teaspoon ground cinnamon in small bowl. Add 2 tablespoons melted butter or margarine, stirring until mixture is crumbly.

*Muffins can be difficult to remove from pan. For best results, use paper liners.

Lemony Apple Oat Muffins

1¼ cups unsifted flour
½ cup packed light brown sugar
1½ teaspoons baking powder
1 teaspoon baking soda
1 teaspoon ground cinnamon
½ teaspoon salt
¼ teaspoon ground nutmeg
1 egg
½ cup BORDEN® or MEADOW
GOLD® Milk
¼ cup vegetable oil
2 tablespoons REALEMON® Lemon
Juice from Concentrate
¾ cup quick-cooking oats
1 cup finely chopped all-purpose
apples
½ cup chopped nuts
Lemon Glaze (recipe follows)

Preheat oven to 400°F.

In small bowl, combine flour, sugar, baking powder, baking soda, cinnamon, salt and nutmeg. In medium bowl, beat egg; stir in milk, oil, then ReaLemon® brand. Add oats; mix well. Add flour mixture, apples and nuts; stir only until moistened (batter will be thick). Spoon into greased or paper-lined 2½-inch muffin cups.

Bake 20 minutes or until golden. Spoon Lemon Glaze over muffins. Remove from pans; serve warm.

Makes about 12 muffins

Lemon Glaze: In small bowl, combine ½ cup confectioners' sugar, 1 tablespoon ReaLemon® brand and 1 tablespoon melted margarine or butter.

Makes about ¼ cup glaze

Pecan Peach Muffins

Mandarin Muffins

1 can (8¼ ounces) DOLE® Crushed
    Pineapple in Syrup or Juice
  Milk
2 cups all-purpose flour
⅓ cup packed brown sugar
2 tablespoons toasted wheat germ
1 tablespoon baking powder
½ teaspoon salt
1 egg, beaten
¾ cup finely shredded carrots
⅓ cup vegetable oil
½ teaspoon vanilla extract
2 tablespoons granulated sugar
½ teaspoon ground cinnamon

Preheat oven to 400°F. Paper-line 15
(2½-inch) muffin cups.

Drain pineapple, reserving syrup. (Press
pineapple with back of spoon to remove
as much syrup as possible.) Add enough
milk to syrup to measure ¾ cup liquid.

Combine flour, brown sugar, wheat germ,
baking powder and salt in large bowl.
Make well in center. Combine egg,
carrots, oil, vanilla, milk-syrup mixture
and pineapple in medium bowl. Add
pineapple mixture all at once to dry
ingredients, stirring just until moistened.
(Batter will be lumpy.) Spoon into
prepared muffin cups, filling ⅔ full.
Combine granulated sugar and cinnamon
in small bowl; sprinkle over tops of
muffins.

Bake 20 to 25 minutes or until wooden
pick inserted in center comes out clean.
Remove from pans.   *Makes 15 muffins*

Strawberry Muffins

Strawberry Muffins

1¼ cups all-purpose flour
2½ teaspoons baking powder
½ teaspoon salt
1 cup uncooked rolled oats
½ cup sugar
1 cup milk
½ cup butter or margarine, melted
1 egg, beaten
1 teaspoon vanilla extract
1 cup chopped strawberries

Preheat oven to 425°F. Grease 12
(2½-inch) muffin cups.

Combine flour, baking powder and salt in
large bowl; stir in oats and sugar.
Combine milk, butter, egg and vanilla in
small bowl; stir into flour mixture just
until moistened. Fold in strawberries.
Spoon into prepared muffin cups, filling
about ⅔ full.

Bake 15 to 18 minutes or until lightly
browned and wooden pick inserted in
center comes out clean. Remove
from pan.   *Makes 12 muffins*

Cranberry Muffins and Creamy Orange Spread

2 cups all-purpose flour
7 tablespoons sugar
2 teaspoons baking powder
½ teaspoon salt
¾ cup milk
½ cup PARKAY® Margarine, melted
1 egg, beaten
¾ cup coarsely chopped cranberries
1 (8-ounce) package PHILADELPHIA BRAND® Cream Cheese,* softened
1 tablespoon orange juice
1 teaspoon grated orange peel

In large bowl, combine flour, 4 tablespoons sugar, baking powder and salt; mix well. In medium bowl, combine milk, margarine and egg. Pour into flour mixture, mixing just until moistened. In small bowl, combine 2 tablespoons sugar and cranberries; fold into batter. Spoon into greased 2½-inch muffin cups, filling each ⅔ full.

Bake at 400°F 20 to 25 minutes or until golden brown. Remove from pan.

In small bowl, combine cream cheese, remaining 1 tablespoon sugar, orange juice and peel until well blended. Cover and chill. Serve with muffins.

Makes 12 muffins

*Light Philadelphia Brand® Neufchatel Cheese may be substituted.

Lemon Glazed Zucchini Muffins

2 cups all-purpose flour
⅔ cup granulated sugar
1 tablespoon baking powder
1 teaspoon salt
½ teaspoon ground nutmeg
2 teaspoons grated lemon peel
¾ cup chopped walnuts, pecans or hazelnuts
½ cup dried fruit bits or golden raisins
½ cup milk
⅓ cup vegetable oil
2 eggs
1 cup packed shredded zucchini, undrained
½ cup powdered sugar
2 to 3 teaspoons fresh lemon juice

Preheat oven to 400°F. Grease well or paper-line 12 (2½-inch) muffin cups.

Combine flour, granulated sugar, baking powder, salt, nutmeg and lemon peel in large bowl; stir in nuts and fruit. Combine milk, oil and eggs in small bowl until blended. Pour into flour mixture; add zucchini, stirring just until moistened. Spoon evenly into prepared muffin cups.

Bake 20 to 25 minutes or until wooden pick inserted in center comes out clean. Remove from pan. Meanwhile, combine powdered sugar and lemon juice in small bowl until smooth. Drizzle over warm muffins.

Makes 12 muffins

Sweet Surprise Muffins

1¾ cups unsifted flour
¼ cup sugar
2 teaspoons baking powder
1 teaspoon ground cinnamon
¾ teaspoon salt
2 eggs
¾ cup BORDEN® or MEADOW GOLD® Milk
¼ cup margarine or butter, melted
½ cup chopped nuts
¾ cup BAMA® Blackberry or Strawberry Preserves

Preheat oven to 400°F.

In small bowl, combine flour, sugar, baking powder, cinnamon and salt. In medium bowl, beat eggs; stir in milk and margarine. Add dry ingredients; stir only until moistened (batter will be slightly lumpy). Stir in nuts. Fill paper-lined 2½-inch muffin cups ⅓ full; drop 2 level teaspoons preserves into center of each. Add remaining batter to fill cups ⅔ full.

Bake 20 minutes or until golden brown. Remove from pans; serve warm.

Makes about 12 muffins

Banana Scotch Muffins

1 ripe, large DOLE® Banana, peeled
1 egg, beaten
½ cup sugar
¼ cup milk
¼ cup vegetable oil
1 teaspoon vanilla extract
1 cup all-purpose flour
1 cup quick-cooking rolled oats
1 teaspoon baking powder
½ teaspoon baking soda
½ teaspoon salt
½ cup butterscotch chips

Preheat oven to 400°F. Grease 12 (2½-inch) muffin cups.

Purée banana in blender (⅔ cup). Combine puréed banana, egg, sugar, milk, oil and vanilla in medium bowl. Combine flour, oats, baking powder, baking soda and salt in large bowl. Stir banana mixture into dry ingredients with butterscotch chips until just blended. Spoon evenly into prepared muffin cups.

Bake 12 to 15 minutes or until wooden pick inserted in center comes out clean. Remove from pan. *Makes 12 muffins*

Gingered Muffins

Vegetable cooking spray
2 fresh California nectarines, chopped (about 1⅓ cups)
1 cup sugar
½ cup vegetable oil or margarine
1 egg
1½ cups all-purpose flour
½ cup oat bran
2 teaspoons baking soda
¼ to ½ teaspoon ground ginger

Preheat oven to 375°F. Coat muffin pan cups with vegetable cooking spray.

Beat nectarines, sugar, oil and egg in large bowl until sugar is dissolved. Combine remaining ingredients and stir into nectarine mixture until just combined. Spoon evenly into prepared muffin cups.

Bake 20 to 25 minutes or until wooden pick inserted in center comes out clean. Remove from oven and let cool 5 minutes. Turn out onto wire rack to cool completely. *Makes 12 muffins*

*Favorite recipe from **California Tree Fruit Agreement***

Blueberry Poppy Seed Muffins

1 cup all-purpose flour
½ cup whole wheat flour
⅓ cup packed brown sugar
2 tablespoons poppy seeds
2 teaspoons baking powder
½ teaspoon salt
1 egg
1 cup milk
¼ cup vegetable oil
1 cup fresh blueberries
2 tablespoons granulated sugar

Preheat oven to 425°F. Grease 12 (2½-inch) muffin cups.

Combine flours, brown sugar, poppy seeds, baking powder and salt in large bowl. Combine egg, milk and oil in small bowl until blended; stir into flour mixture just until moistened. Fold in blueberries. Spoon evenly into prepared muffin cups. Sprinkle granulated sugar over tops of muffins.

Bake 15 to 20 minutes or until wooden pick inserted in center comes out clean. Remove from pan; serve warm.

Makes 12 muffins

Apple Streusel Muffins

2½ cups all-purpose flour
2 cups granulated sugar
1 tablespoon pumpkin pie spice
1 teaspoon baking soda
½ teaspoon salt
2 eggs, lightly beaten
1 cup LIBBY'S® Solid Pack Pumpkin
½ cup vegetable oil
2 cups peeled, finely chopped apples
Streusel Topping (recipe follows)

In large bowl, combine flour, sugar, pumpkin pie spice, baking soda, and salt; set aside. In medium bowl, combine eggs, pumpkin, and oil. Add liquid ingredients to dry ingredients; stir just until moistened. Stir in apples. Spoon batter into greased or paper-lined muffin cups, filling ⅔ full. Sprinkle Streusel Topping over batter.

Bake in preheated 350°F oven for 35 to 40 minutes, or until toothpick comes out clean. *Makes 18 muffins*

Streusel Topping: In small bowl, combine 2 tablespoons all-purpose flour, ¼ cup sugar, and ½ teaspoon ground cinnamon. Cut in 4 teaspoons butter until mixture is crumbly.

Variation: For 6 giant muffins, follow directions above increasing baking time to 40 to 45 minutes.

Apple Streusel Muffins

Glazed Strawberry Lemon Streusel Muffins

Lemon Streusel Topping
(recipe follows)
1½ cups all-purpose flour
½ cup granulated sugar
2 teaspoons baking powder
1 teaspoon ground cinnamon
¼ teaspoon salt
½ cup milk
½ cup butter or margarine, melted
1 egg
1½ cups fresh strawberries, chopped
1 teaspoon grated lemon peel
Lemony Glaze (recipe follows)

Preheat oven to 375°F. Paper-line 12 (2½-inch) muffin cups. Prepare Lemon Streusel Topping; set aside.

Combine flour, sugar, baking powder, cinnamon and salt in large bowl. Combine milk, butter and egg in small bowl; stir into flour mixture just until moistened. Fold in strawberries and lemon peel. Spoon evenly into prepared muffin cups. Sprinkle Lemon Streusel Topping evenly over tops of muffins.

Bake 20 to 25 minutes or until wooden pick inserted in center comes out clean. Remove from pan. Prepare Lemony Glaze; drizzle over warm muffins.

Makes 12 muffins

Lemon Streusel Topping: Combine ¼ cup chopped pecans, ¼ cup packed light brown sugar, 2 tablespoons all-purpose flour, ½ teaspoon ground cinnamon and ½ teaspoon grated lemon peel in medium bowl. Add 1 tablespoon melted butter or margarine, stirring until crumbly.

Lemony Glaze: Combine ½ cup powdered sugar and 1 tablespoon fresh lemon juice in small bowl, stirring until smooth.

Glazed Strawberry Lemon Streusel Muffins

Cocoa Applesauce Muffins

Cocoa Crunch Topping
(recipe follows)
¼ cup HERSHEY'S Cocoa
¼ cup vegetable oil
¾ cup chunky applesauce
1 egg, beaten
1¼ cups all-purpose flour
¾ cup sugar
¾ teaspoon baking soda
¼ teaspoon salt
¼ teaspoon ground cinnamon
½ cup chopped nuts

Microwave Directions: Prepare Cocoa Crunch Topping; set aside. Paper-line six microwave-safe 6-ounce custard cups or microwave-safe cupcake or muffin pan.

In small bowl, stir together cocoa and oil until smooth. Add applesauce and egg; blend well. Stir together flour, sugar, baking soda, salt and cinnamon; add applesauce mixture and nuts, stirring just until dry ingredients are moistened. Fill cups half full with batter. Sprinkle heaping teaspoonful Cocoa Crunch Topping on top of each muffin.

Microwave at HIGH (100%) 2½ to 3½ minutes, turning ¼ turn after each minute, or until wooden pick inserted in center comes out clean. (Tops may still appear moist.) Let stand several minutes. (Moist spots will disappear upon standing.) Remove from cups to wire rack. Repeat cooking procedure with remaining batter. Serve warm.

Makes about 1 dozen muffins

Cocoa Crunch Topping: In bowl, stir together ¼ cup packed light brown sugar, ¼ cup chopped nuts, if desired, 2 tablespoons butter or margarine, 2 tablespoons HERSHEY'S Cocoa and 2 tablespoons all-purpose flour until crumbly. (Leftover topping can be stored in covered container in refrigerator.)

Orange Coconut Muffins

¾ cup all-purpose flour
¾ cup whole wheat flour
⅔ cup toasted wheat germ
½ cup sugar
½ cup coconut
1½ teaspoons baking soda
½ teaspoon salt
1 cup dairy sour cream
2 eggs
1 can (11 ounces) mandarin oranges,
    drained
½ cup chopped nuts

Preheat oven to 400°F. Butter 12 (2½-inch) muffin cups.

Combine flours, wheat germ, sugar, coconut, baking soda and salt in large bowl. Blend sour cream, eggs and oranges in small bowl; stir into flour mixture just until moistened. Fold in nuts. Spoon into prepared muffin cups, filling ¾ full.

Bake 18 to 20 minutes or until wooden pick inserted in center comes out clean. Remove from pan. Cool on wire rack.

Makes 12 muffins

Favorite recipe from **Wisconsin Milk Marketing Board** © 1993

Orange Coconut Muffins

Cinnamon Apple Nut Muffins

¾ cup peeled, finely chopped apple
½ cup sugar, divided
1 teaspoon ground cinnamon
1 cup all-purpose flour
¾ cup whole wheat flour
2 teaspoons baking powder
¼ teaspoon salt
1 cup low-fat (1%) milk
2 tablespoons margarine, melted
2 egg whites, lightly beaten
¼ cup chopped walnuts
    Sugar, for topping (optional)

Preheat oven to 400°F. Lightly grease 12 (2½-inch) muffin cups.

Toss apple with ¼ cup sugar and cinnamon in small bowl. Combine remaining ¼ cup sugar, flours, baking powder and salt in large bowl. Mix together milk, melted margarine and egg whites; stir into dry ingredients just until moistened. Add apple and walnuts. Spoon into prepared muffin cups, filling ¾ full. Sprinkle each lightly with sugar, if desired.

Bake 20 to 25 minutes or until wooden pick inserted in center comes out clean.

Makes 1 dozen muffins

Favorite recipe from **The Sugar Association**

Apple Butter Pumpkin Muffins

½ cup pecans, toasted and chopped
½ cup whole wheat flour
½ cup all-purpose flour
½ cup rolled oats
2 teaspoons ground allspice
1 teaspoon ground cinnamon
1 teaspoon baking soda
¼ teaspoon baking powder
1 cup LIBBY'S® Solid Pack Pumpkin
¾ cup packed dark brown sugar
½ cup vegetable oil
2 eggs
¼ cup apple butter
1 tablespoon granulated sugar
   (optional)

In large bowl, combine pecans, flours, oats, allspice, cinnamon, baking soda, and baking powder. Mix well; set aside. In small bowl, combine pumpkin, brown sugar, oil, eggs, and apple butter; blend thoroughly. Add liquid ingredients to dry ingredients; stir just until ingredients are moistened. Spoon batter into 8 greased or paper-lined muffin cups. Sprinkle with granulated sugar, if desired.

Bake in preheated 375°F oven for 25 to 30 minutes, or until toothpick comes out clean. Immediately remove from pan; cool on rack.   *Makes 8 muffins*

Berry Filled Muffins

Berry Filled Muffins

1 package DUNCAN HINES®
   Blueberry Muffin Mix
1 egg
½ cup water
¼ cup strawberry jam
2 tablespoons sliced natural almonds

1. Preheat oven to 400°F. Place 8 (2½-inch) paper or foil liners in muffin cups.

2. Rinse blueberries from Mix with cold water and drain.

3. Empty muffin mix into bowl. Break up any lumps. Add egg and water. Stir until moistened, about 50 strokes. Fill cups half full with batter.

4. Fold blueberries into jam. Spoon on top of batter in each cup. Spread gently. Cover with remaining batter. Sprinkle with almonds. Bake at 400°F for 17 to 20 minutes or until set and golden brown. Cool in pan 5 to 10 minutes. Loosen carefully before removing from pan.
                Makes 8 muffins

Tip: For a delicious flavor variation, try using blackberry or red raspberry jam for the strawberry jam.

Cream Cheese Pumpkin Muffins

Batter:

2¼ cups all-purpose flour
1½ teaspoons ground cinnamon
1 teaspoon baking soda
½ teaspoon ground coriander
½ teaspoon salt
2 eggs, lightly beaten
2 cups granulated sugar
1 cup LIBBY'S® Solid Pack Pumpkin
½ cup vegetable oil
½ teaspoon vanilla extract

Filling:

6 ounces cream cheese, softened
1 egg
1 tablespoon granulated sugar

Topping:

¾ cup flaked coconut
½ cup pecans, chopped
¼ cup granulated sugar
½ teaspoon ground cinnamon

Cream Cheese Pumpkin Muffins

For Batter: In large bowl, combine flour, cinnamon, baking soda, coriander, and salt; set aside. In small bowl, combine eggs, sugar, pumpkin, oil, and vanilla; mix well. Add liquid ingredients to dry ingredients; stir just until moistened.

For Filling: In small bowl, combine cream cheese, egg, and sugar; mix well.

For Topping: In small bowl, combine coconut, pecans, sugar, and cinnamon.

To Assemble: Spoon *half* of batter into 24 paper-lined muffin cups, filling ½ full. Spoon cream cheese filling evenly over partially filled muffin cups. Spoon remaining batter over cream cheese filling, carefully spreading to edges. Sprinkle topping over muffins.

Bake in preheated 350°F. oven for 20 to 25 minutes, or until toothpick comes out clean. Cool in pans 3 to 4 minutes. Remove from pans; cool on wire rack.

Makes 24 muffins

Lemon Glazed Peach Muffins

1 cup all-purpose flour
3 tablespoons sugar
2 teaspoons baking powder
½ teaspoon salt
½ teaspoon pumpkin pie spice
1 can (16 ounces) sliced cling peaches in light syrup
1 cup KELLOGG'S® ALL-BRAN® cereal
½ cup skim milk
1 egg white
2 tablespoons vegetable oil
Lemon Sauce (recipe follows)

Stir together flour, sugar, baking powder, salt and pumpkin pie spice. Set aside.

Drain peaches, reserving ⅓ cup syrup. Set aside 8 peach slices; chop remaining peach slices.

Measure Kellogg's® All-Bran® cereal, milk and the ⅓ cup syrup into large mixing bowl. Stir to combine. Let stand 2 minutes or until cereal is softened. Add egg white and oil. Beat well. Stir in chopped peaches. Add flour mixture, stirring only until combined. Portion batter evenly into 8 lightly greased 2½-inch muffin-pan cups. Place 1 peach slice over top of each muffin.

Bake at 400°F about 25 minutes or until golden brown. Serve warm with Lemon Sauce. *Makes 8 muffins*

Lemon Sauce

⅓ cup sugar
2 tablespoons cornstarch
1½ cups cold water
1 tablespoon lemon juice
1 teaspoon grated lemon peel

Combine sugar and cornstarch in 2-quart saucepan. Add water, stirring until smooth. Cook over medium heat, stirring constantly, until mixture boils. Continue cooking and stirring 3 minutes longer. Remove from heat; stir in lemon juice and peel. Serve hot over warm peach muffins.

Cinnamon Chip Muffins

2 cups all-purpose biscuit baking mix
¼ cup sugar
1 egg
⅔ cup milk
1 cup HERSHEY®'S MINI CHIPS Semi-Sweet Chocolate
¼ cup finely chopped nuts (optional)
Sugar-Cinnamon Topping (recipe follows)

Heat oven to 400°F. Grease or paper-line 12 muffin cups (2½ inches in diameter).

In bowl, stir together baking mix, sugar, egg and milk; beat with spoon 30 seconds. Stir in small chocolate chips and nuts, if desired. Fill muffin cups ¾ full with batter. Sprinkle each with about ½ teaspoon Sugar-Cinnamon Topping.

Bake 15 to 17 minutes or until very lightly browned. Serve warm.
Makes about 1 dozen muffins

Sugar-Cinnamon Topping: In small bowl, stir together 2 tablespoons sugar and 2 teaspoons ground cinnamon.

Cottage Cakes

2¼ cups all-purpose flour
2 teaspoons baking powder
½ teaspoon baking soda
1 teaspoon ground cinnamon
¼ teaspoon ground nutmeg
¼ teaspoon salt
½ cup butter, softened
½ cup packed light brown sugar
½ cup granulated sugar
3 eggs
1¾ cups (16-ounce can) LIBBY'S® Solid Pack Pumpkin
¼ cup milk
2 teaspoons orange zest
1 cup chopped assorted dried fruits or raisins
Quick Drizzle Frosting (recipe follows)

In medium bowl, combine flour, baking powder, baking soda, cinnamon, nutmeg, and salt; set aside. In large mixer bowl, cream butter and sugars. Add eggs; beat until light and fluffy. Blend in pumpkin, milk, and orange zest. Add dry ingredients; mix well. Stir in chopped fruits. Spoon mixture into greased 2½-inch muffin cups, filling ¾ full.

Bake in preheated 350°F. oven for 25 to 30 minutes, or until toothpick comes out clean. Immediately remove from pans; cool on wire racks. Drizzle with frosting.

Makes 20 small cakes

Quick Drizzle Frosting: In small bowl, combine 1 cup sifted powdered sugar and 2 to 3 tablespoons cream or fresh lemon juice.

Banana Pumpkin Muffins

1 ripe, medium DOLE® Banana, peeled
½ cup canned pumpkin
½ cup sugar
¼ cup milk
¼ cup vegetable oil
1 egg
1¾ cups all-purpose flour
2 teaspoons baking powder
1 teaspoon pumpkin pie spice
½ teaspoon salt
Sugar 'n' Spice Mix (recipe follows)

Preheat oven to 375°F. Grease 12 (2½-inch) muffin cups.

Purée banana in blender (½ cup). Mix puréed banana, pumpkin, sugar, milk, oil and egg in medium bowl until well blended. Combine flour, baking powder, spice and salt in large bowl. Stir banana mixture into flour mixture just until moistened. Spoon evenly into prepared muffin cups. Sprinkle 1 tablespoon Sugar 'n' Spice Mix on top of each muffin.

Bake 20 minutes or until wooden pick inserted in center comes out clean. Cool on wire rack. *Makes 12 muffins*

Sugar 'n' Spice Mix: Combine ½ cup packed brown sugar, ½ cup chopped nuts or oats and ½ teaspoon pumpkin pie spice in small bowl until blended.

Cottage Cakes

Black Cherry Muffins

Black Cherry Muffins

2 cups all-purpose flour
1 tablespoon baking powder
¼ teaspoon salt
1 cup pitted fresh or frozen dark sweet
    cherries, coarsely chopped and
    well drained
6 tablespoons butter or margarine,
    softened
⅔ cup sugar
2 eggs
1 teaspoon vanilla extract
½ cup milk

Preheat oven to 400°F. Grease or paper-line 12 (2½-inch) muffin cups.

Combine flour, baking powder and salt in small bowl. Toss 1 tablespoon flour mixture with cherries in small bowl. Beat butter and sugar with electric mixer in large bowl until light and fluffy. Add eggs and vanilla; beat 3 minutes. Alternately beat in flour mixture and milk. Fold in cherries. Spoon batter evenly into prepared muffin cups.

Bake 18 to 20 minutes or until golden and wooden pick inserted in center comes out clean. Remove from pan. Cool on wire rack. *Makes 12 muffins*

Quick Apple Muffins

2 cups buttermilk baking mix
½ cup sugar
1 teaspoon ground cinnamon
½ teaspoon ground nutmeg
2 eggs
5 tablespoons vegetable or corn oil
⅔ cup buttermilk
1 can SOLO® *or* 1 jar BAKER® Apple
   Filling
   Fruit Butter (recipe follows)
   (optional)

Preheat oven to 400°F. Line one 12-cup
and one 6-cup muffin pan with cupcake
liners or spray pans with nonstick
cooking spray; set aside.

Stir baking mix, sugar, cinnamon and
nutmeg in large bowl until blended. Beat
eggs, oil and buttermilk in medium bowl
with electric mixer until blended. Add to
dry ingredients, stirring until just
moistened. (Batter will be lumpy.) Stir in
filling. Spoon batter into prepared muffin
cups, filling about ⅔ full.

Bake 15 to 18 minutes or until wooden
pick inserted in center comes out clean.
Cool in pans on wire racks 1 minute.
Remove from pans; serve warm or cool
completely on racks. Serve with Fruit
Butter, if desired.   *Makes 18 muffins*

Fruit Butter

½ cup unsalted butter, softened*
1 can SOLO® *or* 1 jar BAKER®
   Strawberry, Raspberry, Cherry,
   Apricot, Pineapple or Prune
   Filling

*Do not substitute salted butter or
margarine for unsalted butter in Fruit
Butter recipe. Fruit Butter may be served
with waffles, pancakes, muffins or on
toast.

Beat butter in medium bowl with electric
mixer until creamy and fluffy. Add
strawberry filling, ⅓ at a time, beating
constantly until thoroughly blended.

Spoon into serving dish; cover with
plastic wrap. Refrigerate or freeze until
ready to use.   *Makes about 1½ cups*

Peanut Butter Banana Muffins

1½ cups unsifted flour
1 teaspoon baking powder
1 teaspoon baking soda
½ cup BORDEN® or MEADOW
   GOLD® Whipping Cream
6 tablespoons margarine or butter,
   softened
⅓ cup LAURA SCUDDER'S® All
   Natural or BAMA® Peanut Butter
¼ cup packed light brown sugar
2 large, ripe bananas, mashed
½ cup CARY'S®, MAPLE ORCHARD®
   or MACDONALD'S™ Pure
   Maple Syrup
1 egg
1 teaspoon vanilla
¼ cup chopped peanuts

Preheat oven to 350°F.

In small bowl, combine flour, baking
powder and baking soda. In large mixer
bowl, beat cream, margarine, peanut
butter and sugar until smooth. Add
bananas, maple syrup, egg and vanilla;
mix well. Add flour mixture; stir until
moistened. Fill paper-lined 2½-inch
muffin cups ¾ full; sprinkle with nuts.

Bake 25 to 30 minutes or until golden
brown. Remove from pans; serve warm.
Makes about 12 muffins

Chocolate Chunk Sour Cream Muffins

1½ cups all-purpose flour
½ cup sugar
1½ teaspoons CALUMET® Baking
    Powder
½ teaspoon cinnamon
¼ teaspoon salt
2 eggs, lightly beaten
½ cup milk
½ cup sour cream or plain yogurt
¼ cup (½ stick) margarine, melted
1 teaspoon vanilla
1 package (4 ounces) BAKER'S®
    GERMAN'S® Sweet Chocolate,
    chopped

HEAT oven to 375°F.

MIX flour, sugar, baking powder, cinnamon and salt; set aside. Stir eggs, milk, sour cream, margarine and vanilla in large bowl until well blended. Add flour mixture; stir just until moistened. Stir in chocolate.

FILL 12 paper- or foil-lined muffin cups ⅔ full with batter.

BAKE for 30 minutes or until toothpick inserted in center comes out clean. Remove from pan to cool on wire rack.
Makes 12 muffins

Prep time: 15 minutes
Baking time: 30 minutes

Blueberry Orange Muffins

Blueberry Orange Muffins

1 package DUNCAN HINES®
    Blueberry Muffin Mix
2 egg whites
½ cup orange juice
1 teaspoon grated orange peel

1. Preheat oven to 400°F. Grease 2½-inch muffin cups (or use paper liners).

2. Rinse blueberries from Mix with cold water and drain.

3. Empty muffin mix into large bowl. Break up any lumps. Add egg whites, orange juice and orange peel. Stir until moistened, about 50 strokes. Fold blueberries *gently* into batter.

4. For large muffins, fill cups two-thirds full. Bake at 400°F for 18 to 21 minutes or until toothpick inserted in center comes out clean. (For medium muffins, fill cups half full. Bake at 400°F for 16 to 19 minutes or until toothpick inserted in center comes out clean.) Cool in pan 5 to 10 minutes. Loosen carefully before removing from pan. Serve warm or cool completely.
Makes 8 large or 12 medium muffins

Tip: Freeze extra grated orange peel for future use.

Raspberry Apple Streusel Muffins

Batter:

  2 cups all-purpose flour
½ cup sugar
  2 teaspoons baking powder
½ teaspoon baking soda
½ teaspoon salt
  1 cup MOTT'S® Regular or Natural
    Apple Sauce
½ cup vegetable oil
  1 teaspoon grated lemon peel
  2 eggs
  1 cup fresh or frozen raspberries

Topping:

⅓ cup sugar
¼ cup flour
  2 tablespoons margarine or butter,
    softened

Preheat oven to 400°F. Grease bottoms only of 12 (2½-inch) muffin cups or line with paper baking cups.

For batter, combine flour, sugar, baking powder, baking soda and salt in large bowl; mix well. Combine apple sauce, oil, lemon peel and eggs in small bowl; blend well. Add to dry ingredients; stir just until moistened. Carefully fold in raspberries. Spoon into prepared muffin cups, filling ¾ full. Combine all topping ingredients in small bowl. Sprinkle over tops of muffins.

Bake 18 to 20 minutes or until light brown and wooden pick inserted in center comes out clean. Cool 5 minutes; remove from pan. Serve warm.

Makes 12 muffins

Apple Nugget Muffins

½ cup margarine or butter, softened
½ cup firmly packed brown sugar
1½ cups MOTT'S® Natural Apple Sauce
¼ cup milk
  1 teaspoon vanilla extract
  2 eggs
1½ cups all-purpose flour
½ cup whole wheat flour
  1 teaspoon baking powder
  1 teaspoon baking soda
¼ teaspoon salt
  1 cup chopped walnuts
  1 cup grated apple
½ cup raisins

Preheat oven to 375°F. Grease bottoms only of 12 (2½-inch) muffin cups or line with paper baking cups.

Beat margarine and brown sugar in large bowl until fluffy. Add apple sauce, milk, vanilla and eggs; blend well. Stir in flours, baking powder, baking soda and salt. Blend just until dry ingredients are moistened; stir in walnuts, apple and raisins. Spoon evenly into prepared muffin cups. Bake 20 to 25 minutes or until wooden pick inserted in center comes out clean. Cool 5 minutes; remove from pan. *Makes 12 muffins*

Clockwise from top: Apple Nugget Muffins, Blueberry Orange Corn Muffins (page 108) and Raspberry Apple Streusel Muffins

Chocolate Cherry Cordial Muffins

2 cups all-purpose flour
¼ cup granulated sugar
¼ cup firmly packed brown sugar
2 teaspoons baking powder
½ teaspoon baking soda
½ teaspoon salt
One 11½-oz. pkg. (2 cups) NESTLÉ® Toll
    House® Milk Chocolate Morsels,
    divided
½ cup candied cherries, chopped, or
    raisins
¾ cup milk
⅓ cup vegetable oil
1 egg

Preheat oven to 400°F. Grease or paper-line 12 (2½-inch) muffin cups.

In large bowl, combine flour, granulated sugar, brown sugar, baking powder, baking soda and salt. Stir in 1¾ cups milk chocolate morsels and cherries; set aside. In small bowl, combine milk, oil and egg. Stir into flour mixture just until moistened. Spoon into prepared muffin cups (muffin cups will be full). Sprinkle with remaining ¼ cup milk chocolate morsels.

Bake 18 to 21 minutes until golden brown. Cool 5 minutes; remove from pan.
Makes 1 dozen muffins

Banana Blueberry Muffins

1 package DUNCAN HINES® Bakery
    Style Blueberry Muffin Mix
2 egg whites
½ cup water
1 medium-size ripe banana, mashed
    (about ½ cup)

1. Preheat oven to 400°F. Place 12 (2½-inch) paper liners in muffin cups.

2. Rinse blueberries from Mix with cold water and drain.

3. Empty muffin mix into bowl. Break up any lumps. Add egg whites, water and mashed banana. Stir until moistened, about 50 strokes. Fold in blueberries. Fill muffin cups two-thirds full. Sprinkle with contents of topping packet from Mix. Bake at 400°F for 18 to 22 minutes or until toothpick inserted in center comes out clean. Cool in pan 5 to 10 minutes. Serve warm or cool completely.
Makes 12 muffins

Tip: To reheat leftover muffins, wrap muffins tightly in foil. Place in 400°F oven for 10 to 15 minutes.

Apple-Walnut Muffins

2 cups all-purpose flour
⅔ cup sugar
2¼ teaspoons baking powder
¾ teaspoon salt
¼ teaspoon ground cinnamon
1 egg
⅔ cup milk
3 tablespoons vegetable oil
1 teaspoon grated lemon peel
¾ teaspoon vanilla extract
1 cup chopped DIAMOND® Walnuts
¾ cup coarsely grated peeled apple

Sift together flour, sugar, baking powder, salt and cinnamon in medium bowl. Beat egg in small bowl; add milk, oil, lemon peel and vanilla. Stir into dry ingredients, mixing just until flour is moistened. Fold in walnuts and apple. Spoon evenly into 12 greased 2½-inch muffin cups.

Bake in preheated 400°F oven 20 to 25 minutes or until golden brown and wooden pick inserted in center comes out clean.
Makes 12 muffins

Chocolate Cherry Cordial Muffins

Orange Pineapple Muffins

1 can (8 ounces) DOLE® Crushed
    Pineapple in Juice
1¾ cups all-purpose flour
¼ cup packed brown sugar
2 teaspoons baking powder
½ teaspoon salt
2 eggs, slightly beaten
¾ cup milk
3 tablespoons margarine, melted
½ cup chopped walnuts
2 teaspoons grated orange peel

Preheat oven to 400°F. Grease 16 (2½-inch) muffin cups.

Drain pineapple. Combine flour, brown sugar, baking powder and salt in large bowl. Combine eggs, milk and margarine in small bowl; stir in pineapple, walnuts and orange peel. Make well in center of dry ingredients; pour in milk mixture. Stir just until moistened. Spoon evenly into prepared muffin cups.

Bake 20 to 25 minutes or until wooden pick inserted in center comes out clean. Remove from pans; serve warm.

Makes 16 muffins

Quick Poppy Muffins

2 cups buttermilk baking mix
½ cup sugar
½ cup chopped nuts
½ teaspoon grated lemon peel
2 eggs
5 tablespoons vegetable or corn oil
⅔ cup buttermilk
1 can SOLO® *or* 1 jar BAKER® Poppy
    Filling
Fruit Butter (page 139) (optional)

Preheat oven to 400°F. Line one 12-cup and one 6-cup muffin pan with cupcake liners or spray pans with nonstick cooking spray; set aside.

Stir baking mix, sugar, nuts and peel in large bowl until blended. Beat eggs, oil and buttermilk in medium bowl with electric mixer until blended. Add to dry ingredients, stirring until just moistened. (Batter will be lumpy.) Stir in filling. Spoon batter into prepared muffin cups, filling about ⅔ full.

Bake 15 to 18 minutes or until wooden pick inserted in center comes out clean. Cool in pans on wire racks 1 minute. Remove from pans; serve warm or cool completely on racks. Serve with Fruit Butter, if desired.

Makes 18 muffins

Easy Mix Pumpkin Muffins

1 egg
⅔ cup LIBBY'S® Pumpkin Pie Mix
1 package (13.5 ounces) muffin mix
    with cinnamon streusel topping

In medium bowl, combine egg and pumpkin pie mix; mix with fork. Add muffin mix; blend just until moistened (batter will be slightly lumpy). Spoon batter into greased or paper-lined muffin cups, filling ¼ *full* (reserve remaining batter). Sprinkle *2 level teaspoons* streusel over top of batter in each muffin cup (reserve remaining streusel for topping). Add *remaining* batter, filling each cup ⅔ full. Sprinkle with *remaining* streusel.

Bake in preheated 400°F. oven for 15 to 20 minutes, or until toothpick comes out clean. Cool 3 to 4 minutes. Remove from pan; cool on wire rack.

Makes 8 to 10 muffins

Streusel-Topped Blueberry Muffins

1½ cups plus ⅓ cup all-purpose flour,
    divided
½ cup plus ⅓ cup sugar, divided
1 teaspoon ground cinnamon
3 tablespoons butter or margarine, cut
    into small pieces
2 teaspoons baking powder
½ teaspoon salt
1 egg, beaten
1 cup milk
¼ cup butter or margarine, melted and
    slightly cooled
1 teaspoon vanilla extract
1 cup fresh blueberries

Preheat oven to 375°F. Paper-line 12 (2½-inch) muffin cups.

Combine ⅓ cup flour, ⅓ cup sugar and cinnamon in small bowl; mix well. Cut in 3 tablespoons butter with pastry blender until mixture resembles coarse crumbs; set aside for topping.

Combine remaining 1½ cups flour, ½ cup sugar, baking powder and salt in large bowl. Combine egg, milk, ¼ cup melted butter and vanilla in small bowl; stir into flour mixture until just moistened. (Do not overmix.) Fold in blueberries. Spoon evenly into prepared muffin cups. Sprinkle reserved topping over tops of muffins.

Bake 20 to 25 minutes or until wooden pick inserted in center comes out clean. Remove from pan; cool on wire rack.

Makes 12 muffins

Streusel-Topped Blueberry Muffins

Banana Poppy Seed Muffins

2 ripe, medium DOLE® Bananas, peeled
1 egg
¾ cup sugar
¼ cup vegetable oil
2 teaspoons grated orange peel
2 cups all-purpose flour
1½ tablespoons poppy seeds
2 teaspoons baking powder
½ teaspoon salt
   Citrus Glaze (recipe follows)

Preheat oven to 375°F. Grease 12 (2½-inch) muffin cups.

Purée bananas in blender (1 cup). Mix puréed bananas, egg, sugar, oil and orange peel in medium bowl until well blended. Combine flour, poppy seeds, baking powder and salt in large bowl. Stir banana mixture into flour mixture until just moistened. Spoon evenly into prepared muffin cups.

Bake 20 minutes or until wooden pick inserted in center comes out clean. Remove from pan; cool on wire rack. Top with Citrus Glaze while warm.

Makes 12 muffins

Citrus Glaze: Combine 1¼ cups powdered sugar, ¼ cup orange juice, 1 teaspoon grated orange peel and 1 teaspoon vanilla extract in medium bowl until smooth.

Banana Poppy Seed Muffins

Fresh Peach Muffins

   Vegetable cooking spray
3 fresh California peaches, chopped (about 1⅔ cups)
⅔ cup sugar
¼ cup extra-light olive or vegetable oil
¼ cup low-fat milk
1 egg
2⅓ cups all-purpose flour
⅓ cup flaked coconut
⅓ cup chopped walnuts
1 teaspoon baking soda
1 teaspoon finely grated lemon peel
½ teaspoon salt

Preheat oven to 375°F. Coat muffin pan cups with vegetable cooking spray.

Beat peaches, sugar, oil, milk and egg in large bowl until sugar is dissolved. Combine remaining ingredients and stir into peach mixture until just combined. Spoon evenly into prepared muffin cups.

Bake 25 minutes or until wooden pick inserted in center comes out clean. Remove from oven and let cool 5 minutes. Turn out onto wire rack to cool completely. *Makes 12 muffins*

Favorite recipe from California Tree Fruit Agreement

Cherry Blossom Muffins

1 egg
⅔ cup BAMA® Cherry or Strawberry Preserves
¼ cup BORDEN® or MEADOW GOLD® Milk
½ cup sugar
2 cups biscuit baking mix
⅔ cup chopped pecans
1 tablespoon flour
¾ teaspoon ground cinnamon
2 tablespoons cold margarine or butter
   Additional chopped pecans

Preheat oven to 400°F.

In medium bowl, beat egg; stir in preserves, milk and ¼ cup sugar. Add biscuit mix; stir only until moistened (batter will be slightly lumpy). Stir in ⅔ cup nuts. Fill greased or paper-lined 2½-inch muffin cups ¾ full. In small bowl, combine remaining ¼ cup sugar, flour and cinnamon. Cut in margarine until crumbly; sprinkle over batter. Top with additional nuts.

Bake 15 to 20 minutes or until golden brown. Remove from pans; serve warm.

Makes about 12 muffins

Premier White Spice Muffins

Topping:
   ½ **cup all-purpose flour**
   ¼ **cup firmly packed brown sugar**
   ½ **teaspoon cinnamon**
   ⅛ **teaspoon nutmeg**
   3 **tablespoons butter**

Muffins:
 1¾ **cups all-purpose flour**
   1 **teaspoon baking powder**
   1 **teaspoon baking soda**
   ½ **teaspoon salt**
   ½ **teaspoon cinnamon**
   ¼ **teaspoon nutmeg**
One 10-oz. pkg. (1½ cups) NESTLÉ® Toll House® Treasures Premier White Deluxe Baking Pieces
   ½ **cup raisins**
   1 **cup applesauce**
   ½ **cup vegetable oil**
   ⅓ **cup firmly packed brown sugar**
   2 **eggs**

Premier White Spice Muffins

Topping: In small bowl, combine flour, brown sugar, cinnamon and nutmeg. With pastry blender or 2 knives, cut in butter until mixture resembles fine crumbs; set aside.

Muffins: Preheat oven to 400°F. Grease or paper-line 16 muffin cups. In large bowl, combine flour, baking powder, baking soda, salt, cinnamon and nutmeg. Stir in Treasures Premier White deluxe baking pieces and raisins.

In small bowl, combine applesauce, oil, brown sugar and eggs; stir into flour mixture just until dry ingredients are moistened. Spoon into prepared muffin cups, filling each about ¾ full. Sprinkle each with 1 measuring tablespoonful Topping.

Bake 20 to 25 minutes until wooden toothpick inserted into center comes out clean. Cool 5 minutes; remove from cups. Serve warm or cool completely.

Makes 16 muffins

Newton Muffins

1¾ cups all-purpose flour
¼ cup sugar
 1 tablespoon DAVIS® Baking Powder
⅓ cup FLEISCHMANN'S® Margarine, melted
 1 egg, slightly beaten
¾ cup apple juice
10 Fat Free FIG or APPLE NEWTONS® Fruit Chewy Cookies, coarsely chopped

In medium bowl, combine flour, sugar and baking powder. Stir in margarine, egg and apple juice just until blended. (Batter will be lumpy.) Stir in cookies. Fill 12 greased 2½-inch muffin-pan cups.

Bake at 400°F for 15 to 20 minutes or until toothpick inserted in center comes out clean. Serve warm or cold.

Makes 1 dozen muffins

Home-Style Blueberry Muffins

1 8-oz. pkg. PHILADELPHIA BRAND® Cream Cheese, softened
¼ cup sugar
1 egg yolk
1 teaspoon vanilla
1 23.5-oz. pkg. bakery style blueberry muffin mix
¾ cup water
1 egg
1 teaspoon grated lemon peel
1 teaspoon cinnamon

- Preheat oven to 400°F.
- Beat cream cheese, sugar, egg yolk and vanilla in small mixing bowl at medium speed with electric mixer until well blended.

Top to bottom: Home-Style Blueberry Muffins and Caramel-Pecan Sticky Buns (page 161)

- Rinse and drain blueberries. Stir together muffin mix, water, egg and peel in large bowl (mixture will be lumpy). Fold in blueberries. Pour into well greased medium-sized muffin pan.
- Spoon cream cheese mixture over batter; sprinkle with combined topping mix and cinnamon.
- Bake 18 to 22 minutes or until lightly browned. Cool 5 minutes. Loosen muffins from rim of pan; cool before removing from pan.

Makes 1 dozen muffins

Prep time: 20 minutes
Cooking time: 22 minutes

Peanut Butter Bran Muffins

½ cup peanut butter
 2 tablespoons butter or margarine
¼ cup packed brown sugar
 1 egg
 1 cup wheat bran cereal
 1 cup milk
¾ cup all-purpose flour
 1 tablespoon baking powder
½ teaspoon salt
½ cup raisins

Preheat oven to 400°F. Grease 12 (2½-inch) muffin cups.

Beat peanut butter, butter, brown sugar and egg in medium bowl until well blended. Stir in cereal and milk until blended. Combine flour, baking powder and salt in large bowl; make well in center. Pour cereal mixture into flour mixture, stirring just until flour mixture is moistened. (Batter will be lumpy.) Fold in raisins. Spoon into prepared muffin cups, filling about ⅔ full.

Bake 20 to 25 minutes or until golden and wooden pick inserted in center comes out clean. Remove from pan; serve warm.

Makes 12 muffins

In-the-Chips Carrot Muffins

12 CHIPS AHOY!® Chocolate Chip
   Cookies, finely rolled
   (about 1¼ cups crumbs)
1 cup all-purpose flour
1 cup grated carrots
⅓ cup walnuts, chopped
3 tablespoons firmly packed light
   brown sugar
1 tablespoon DAVIS® Baking Powder
1 egg
¾ cup milk
¼ cup BLUE BONNET® Margarine,
   melted
   Soft cream cheese, optional

In medium bowl, combine cookie crumbs, flour, carrots, walnuts, brown sugar and baking powder; set aside.

In small bowl, blend egg, milk and margarine; stir into flour mixture just until moistened. Spoon into 12 greased 2½-inch muffin-pan cups.

Bake at 400°F for 20 to 25 minutes or until toothpick inserted in center comes out clean. Cool slightly; serve topped with cream cheese, if desired.

Makes 12 muffins

Microwave Directions: Prepare batter as above. In each of 6 microwavable muffin-pan cups, place 2 paper liners. Spoon batter into cups, filling ⅔ full. Microwave on HIGH (100% power) for 2½ to 3½ minutes or until toothpick inserted in center comes out clean, rotating dish ½ turn after 1 minute. Let stand 1 minute on heat-proof surface; remove to rack. Repeat with remaining batter.

Lemon Tea Muffins

2 cups unsifted flour
2 teaspoons baking powder
½ teaspoon salt
1 cup margarine or butter, softened
1 cup granulated sugar
4 eggs, separated
½ cup REALEMON® Lemon Juice from
   Concentrate
¼ cup finely chopped nuts
2 tablespoons light brown sugar
¼ teaspoon ground nutmeg

Preheat oven to 375°F.

In medium bowl, combine flour, baking powder and salt. In large bowl, beat margarine and granulated sugar until fluffy. Add egg yolks; beat until light. Gradually stir in ReaLemon® brand alternately with dry ingredients (do not overmix). In small bowl, beat egg whites until stiff but not dry. Fold ⅓ egg whites into batter; fold in remaining egg whites. Fill paper-lined or greased 2½-inch muffin cups ¾ full. In another small bowl, combine remaining ingredients; sprinkle evenly over muffins.

Bake 15 to 20 minutes or until set. Cool in pans on wire rack 5 minutes. Remove from pans. Serve warm.

Makes about 18 muffins

Lemon Tea Muffins

Butterscotch Apple Muffins

1⅓ cups whole-wheat flour
  1 cup all-purpose flour
  1 cup (half of 12-oz. pkg.) NESTLÉ®
     Toll House® Butterscotch Flavored
     Morsels
  ½ cup sugar
  4 teaspoons baking powder
  ½ teaspoon cinnamon
  ¼ teaspoon salt
1½ cups skim milk
  6 tablespoons vegetable oil
  1 egg
  1 apple, chopped

Preheat oven to 400°F. Grease or paper-line 18 (2½-inch) muffin cups.

In large bowl, combine whole-wheat flour, all-purpose flour, butterscotch morsels, sugar, baking powder, cinnamon and salt. In small bowl, combine milk, oil, egg and apple. Stir into flour mixture just until dry ingredients are moistened. Spoon into prepared muffin cups, filling each ¾ full.

Bake 18 to 20 minutes until wooden toothpick inserted into center comes out clean. (Muffins will be light in color.) Cool 5 minutes; remove from cups. Serve warm or cool completely.

Makes 18 muffins

Zucchini Muffins

  1 package DUNCAN HINES® Bakery
     Style Cinnamon Swirl Muffin Mix
  ½ teaspoon baking powder
  2 egg whites
  ⅔ cup water
  ½ cup grated zucchini

1. Preheat oven to 400°F. Grease 12 (2½-inch) muffin cups (or use paper liners).

Zucchini Muffins

2. Combine muffin mix and baking powder in large bowl. Break up any lumps. Add egg whites, water and zucchini. Stir until well blended, about 50 strokes.

3. Knead swirl packet from Mix for 10 seconds before opening. Cut off one end of swirl packet. Squeeze contents on top of batter. Swirl into batter with knife or spatula, folding from bottom of bowl to get an even swirl. (Do not completely mix into batter.) Spoon batter into muffin cups. Sprinkle with contents of topping packet from Mix. Bake at 400°F for 20 to 25 minutes or until toothpick inserted in center comes out clean. Cool in pan 5 to 10 minutes. Serve warm or cool completely. *Makes 12 muffins*

Tip: Zucchini can be grated ahead and frozen. Thaw and drain well before using.

MASQUERADING MUFFINS

Bacon Brunch Buns

1 loaf (1 pound) frozen bread dough
2 tablespoons (½ package) HIDDEN VALLEY RANCH® Original Ranch® with Bacon salad dressing mix
¼ cup unsalted butter or margarine, melted
1 cup shredded Cheddar cheese
2 egg yolks
1½ tablespoons cold water
3 tablespoons sesame seeds

Thaw bread dough following package directions. Preheat oven to 375°F. Grease jelly-roll pan.

On floured board, roll dough into rectangle about 18×7 inches. Whisk together salad dressing mix and butter in small bowl. Spread mixture on dough; sprinkle with cheese. Roll up tightly, jelly-roll style, pinching seam to seal. Cut into 16 slices. Place slices cut-side down on prepared pan.

Cover with plastic wrap and let rise until doubled in bulk, about 1 hour. Beat egg yolks and water in small bowl; brush mixture over buns. Sprinkle with sesame seeds.

Bake 25 to 30 minutes or until golden brown. Serve warm.   *Makes 16 buns*

Raisin Scones

2 cups all-purpose flour
2 tablespoons sugar
2 teaspoons baking powder
½ teaspoon baking soda
½ teaspoon salt
½ teaspoon ground nutmeg
½ cup butter or margarine, cut into chunks
1 cup SUN-MAID® Raisins
¾ cup buttermilk
1 egg white, lightly beaten, for glaze
    Sugar, for glaze

Preheat oven to 425°F. Grease 2 baking sheets.

Combine flour, 2 tablespoons sugar, baking powder, baking soda, salt and nutmeg in large bowl. Cut in butter until mixture resembles coarse crumbs. Stir in raisins; mix in buttermilk with fork. Gather dough into ball and knead on lightly floured surface about 2 minutes. Roll or pat dough into circle, ¾ inch thick. With sharp knife, cut into 3-inch triangles. Space apart on prepared baking sheets. Brush tops with egg white; sprinkle with sugar.

Bake about 15 minutes or until nicely browned. Serve warm with butter or jam.
    Makes about 1 dozen scones

Bacon Brunch Buns

Apple & Raisin Scones

½ cup dried apples
1½ cups KRETSCHMER® Original or
    Honey Crunch Wheat Germ
½ cup whole wheat flour
¼ cup sugar
 1 tablespoon baking powder
⅓ cup (5⅓ tablespoons) margarine
½ cup raisins
⅓ cup 2% low-fat milk
 2 egg whites, slightly beaten

Heat oven to 400°F. Coarsely chop apples; set aside.

Combine dry ingredients; cut in margarine until mixture resembles coarse crumbs. Stir in raisins and reserved apples. Add combined milk and egg whites, mixing just until moistened.

Turn dough out onto ungreased cookie sheet; pat into 9-inch circle. Cut into eight wedges; do not separate.

Bake 12 to 15 minutes or until light golden brown. Break apart; serve warm with margarine, fruit spread or honey, if desired.   *Makes 8 scones*

Apple & Raisin Scones

Food Processor Directions: Insert metal blade into work bowl. Process apples, pulsing 20 seconds or until coarsely chopped; remove. Add dry ingredients and margarine to work bowl; process 20 seconds or until mixture resembles coarse crumbs. Add milk, egg whites, raisins and reserved apples; pulse 30 to 35 seconds or until mixture forms a ball. Proceed as recipe directs above.

Cheddar Cheese Biscuits

 2 cups all-purpose flour
 1 tablespoon baking powder
½ teaspoon salt
¼ cup shortening
 1 egg, beaten
¾ cup milk
½ cup (2 ounces) shredded sharp
    Wisconsin Cheddar cheese
 1 tablespoon butter, melted
  Poppy seeds

Preheat oven to 450°F.

Stir together flour, baking powder and salt in medium bowl. Cut in shortening with pastry blender until mixture resembles coarse crumbs. Make well in center. Combine egg and milk in small bowl; add all at once to dry ingredients. Add cheese. Stir just until dough clings together.

Knead gently on lightly floured surface 10 to 12 times. Roll or pat dough to ½-inch thickness. Cut with floured 2½-inch biscuit cutter; dip cutter in flour between cuts. Place biscuits on ungreased baking sheet. Brush tops with melted butter; sprinkle with poppy seeds.

Bake 10 to 12 minutes or until golden brown. Serve warm.   *Makes 10 biscuits*

Favorite recipe from Wisconsin Milk Marketing Board © 1993

Cranberry-Apricot Tea Cakes

1¼ cups boiling water
¾ cup dried apricots
½ cup butter or margarine, softened
¾ cup granulated sugar
2 eggs
1½ teaspoons vanilla extract
1¾ cups all-purpose flour
2 teaspoons baking powder
½ teaspoon baking soda
½ teaspoon salt
1 cup OCEAN SPRAY® fresh or frozen Cranberries, coarsely chopped
½ cup chopped nuts
Powdered sugar
OCEAN SPRAY® Cranberries, for garnish

Pour boiling water over apricots in medium bowl; let soak 15 minutes to soften. Drain, reserving ¾ cup of the liquid. Coarsely chop apricots; set aside.

Preheat oven to 375°F. Grease and flour or paper-line 2½-inch muffin cups.

Cream butter and granulated sugar until light and fluffy in large bowl. Beat in eggs, one at a time, until well blended; beat in vanilla. Sift together flour, baking powder, baking soda and salt in medium bowl. With mixer on low speed, alternately add flour mixture and reserved ¾ cup apricot soaking liquid to the butter mixture, beating well after each addition. Fold in chopped cranberries, apricots and nuts. Spoon into prepared muffin cups, filling ¾ full.

Bake 20 to 23 minutes or until wooden pick inserted in center comes out clean. Cool in pan on wire rack 5 minutes. Remove from pan. Dust with powdered sugar. Garnish each tea cake with a whole cranberry, if desired.

Makes about 24 tea cakes

Cheesy Corn Sticks

Cheesy Corn Sticks

½ cup all-purpose flour
½ cup cornmeal
2 teaspoons baking powder
¼ teaspoon salt
½ cup milk
1 egg, beaten
3 tablespoons vegetable oil
½ cup (2 ounces) shredded Cheddar cheese

Preheat oven to 425°F. Heat cast-iron corn stick pan in oven while preparing batter.

Combine flour, cornmeal, baking powder and salt in medium bowl. Combine milk, egg and oil in small bowl; add to flour mixture, stirring just until moistened. Carefully brush hot pan with additional oil. Spoon batter into prepared pan. Sprinkle batter with cheese.

Bake 10 minutes or until lightly browned.

Makes 7 to 9 corn sticks

Cornmeal Bacon Shortcakes

1¼ cups all-purpose flour
¾ cup cornmeal
2 tablespoons sugar
1½ tablespoons low sodium baking powder
¾ cup unsalted margarine or butter, cold
12 slices ARMOUR® Lower Salt Bacon, cooked crisp and finely crumbled
⅓ cup skim milk
1 egg

Preheat oven to 400°F. Spray 6 shortcake or muffin cups with nonstick cooking spray.

Combine flour, cornmeal, sugar and baking powder in large bowl. Cut in margarine until crumbly. Stir in bacon. Add milk and egg; stir until just moistened. (Do not overmix.) Spoon ⅓ cup of the batter into each prepared cup.

Bake 10 to 12 minutes or until golden brown. Garnish with fresh basil, if desired.   *Makes 6 shortcakes or muffins*

High Tea Oatmeal Scones

2 cups all-purpose flour
¾ cup firmly packed brown sugar
4 teaspoons baking powder
¼ teaspoon salt
10 tablespoons (1¼ sticks) butter
One 12-oz. pkg. (2 cups) NESTLÉ® Toll House® Semi-Sweet Chocolate Mini Morsels
2 cups quick oats, uncooked
4 eggs, beaten
½ cup heavy or whipping cream *or* milk
2 tablespoons granulated sugar

Preheat oven to 425°F.

In large bowl, combine flour, brown sugar, baking powder and salt. With pastry blender or 2 knives, cut in butter until mixture resembles coarse crumbs. Stir in mini morsels and oats. Reserve 2 tablespoons beaten eggs. Combine remaining beaten eggs with heavy cream. Stir into dry ingredients just until moistened.

On lightly floured board, roll dough ½ inch thick; cut into 2-inch diamonds. Place on ungreased cookie sheets. Brush with reserved beaten egg; sprinkle with granulated sugar.

Bake 10 minutes or until golden brown. Serve warm.   *Makes about 36 scones*

Sweet Potato Biscuits

2½ cups all-purpose flour
1 tablespoon DAVIS® Baking Powder
½ teaspoon salt
1 tablespoon firmly packed light brown sugar
¾ cup mashed cooked sweet potato
½ cup BLUE BONNET® Margarine
½ cup milk
1 egg

In bowl, combine flour, baking powder, salt and brown sugar; cut in potatoes and margarine until mixture resembles coarse crumbs. Lightly mix in milk and egg.

On lightly floured surface, knead dough lightly 15 times. Roll to ¾-inch thickness. Cut with a floured 3-inch biscuit cutter. Place on baking sheet.

Bake at 375°F for 20 minutes or until golden. Serve warm.

Makes 1 dozen biscuits

Country Recipe Biscuits

2 cups all-purpose flour
1 tablespoon baking powder
½ cup prepared HIDDEN VALLEY
   RANCH® Original Ranch® salad
   dressing
½ cup buttermilk

Preheat oven to 425°F.

Sift together flour and baking powder in small bowl. Make a well in flour mixture; add salad dressing and buttermilk. Stir with fork until dough forms a ball. Drop by rounded spoonfuls onto ungreased baking sheet.

Bake 12 to 15 minutes or until lightly browned. *Makes 12 biscuits*

Cinnamon Rolls

Rolls

1 package DUNCAN HINES® Moist
   Deluxe Yellow Cake Mix
5 cups all-purpose flour
2 packages (¼ ounce each) active dry
   yeast
2½ cups hot water
   Butter or margarine, softened
   Ground cinnamon
   Granulated sugar

Topping

½ cup butter or margarine, melted
¼ cup firmly packed brown sugar
¼ cup light corn syrup
1 cup chopped nuts

1. Grease two 13×9×2-inch pans.

2. **For rolls,** combine cake mix, flour and yeast in large bowl. Stir until well blended. Stir in hot water. Cover and let rise for 1 hour or until doubled.

Cinnamon Rolls

3. Divide dough in half. Roll half the dough into large rectangle on floured surface. Spread with generous amount of softened butter. Sprinkle with cinnamon and granulated sugar. Roll up jelly-roll fashion and cut into 12 slices. Place rolls in one pan. Repeat with remaining dough. Cover and let rise in pans for 30 to 40 minutes or until doubled.

4. Preheat oven to 375°F.

5. **For topping,** combine melted butter, brown sugar, corn syrup and nuts in liquid measuring cup. Pour evenly over rolls. Bake at 375°F for 25 minutes or until light golden brown. Serve warm or cool completely. *Makes 24 rolls*

Tip: For a special touch, place 1 cup confectioners sugar in small bowl. Add 1 to 2 tablespoons water, stirring until smooth and desired consistency. Drizzle glaze over baked rolls.

Pumpkin-Ginger Scones

½ cup sugar, divided
2 cups all-purpose flour
2 teaspoons baking powder
1 teaspoon ground cinnamon
½ teaspoon baking soda
½ teaspoon salt
5 tablespoons butter or margarine, divided
1 egg
½ cup canned pumpkin
¼ cup sour cream
½ teaspoon grated fresh ginger *or* 2 tablespoons finely chopped crystallized ginger

Preheat oven to 425°F.

Reserve 1 tablespoon sugar. Combine remaining sugar, flour, baking powder, cinnamon, baking soda and salt in large bowl. Cut in 4 tablespoons butter with pastry blender until mixture resembles coarse crumbs. Beat egg in small bowl. Add pumpkin, sour cream and ginger; beat until well combined. Add pumpkin mixture to flour mixture; stir until mixture forms soft dough that leaves side of bowl.

Turn out onto well-floured surface. Knead dough 10 times. Roll dough using floured rolling pin into 9×6-inch rectangle. Cut dough into 6 (3-inch) squares. Cut each square diagonally in half, making 12 triangles. Place triangles, 2 inches apart, on ungreased baking sheets. Melt remaining 1 tablespoon butter. Brush triangles with butter and sprinkle with reserved sugar.

Bake 10 to 12 minutes or until golden brown. Cool on wire racks 10 minutes. Serve warm.   *Makes 12 scones*

Fresh Sage & Pepper Popovers

Popovers

3 eggs, room temperature
1¼ cups milk, room temperature
1¼ cups all-purpose flour
1½ teaspoons fresh sage leaves,* rubbed
¼ teaspoon coarsely ground pepper
¼ teaspoon salt

Sage Butter

½ cup LAND O LAKES® Butter, softened
1½ teaspoons fresh sage leaves,* rubbed
¼ teaspoon coarsely ground pepper

Heat oven to 450°F.

For popovers, in small mixer bowl beat eggs at medium speed, scraping bowl often, until light yellow, 1 to 2 minutes. Add milk; continue beating for 1 minute to incorporate air. By hand, stir in all remaining popover ingredients. Pour batter into greased 6 cup popover pan or 6 custard cups.

Bake for 15 minutes; *reduce temperature to 350°F. Do not open oven.* Continue baking for 25 to 30 minutes or until golden brown.

For Sage Butter, in small mixer bowl beat all Sage Butter ingredients at low speed, scraping bowl often, until light and fluffy, 1 to 2 minutes; set aside.

Insert knife in popovers to allow steam to escape. Serve immediately with Sage Butter.   *Makes 6 popovers*

Tip: Eggs and milk should be at room temperature (72°F) to help ensure successful popovers.

*You may substitute ½ teaspoon dried sage leaves, crumbled, for the 1½ teaspoons fresh sage leaves, rubbed.

Pumpkin-Ginger Scones

Hot Cross Buns

Buns:

  2 pkgs. active dry yeast
  ½ cup warm water (105° to 115°F)
  1 cup warm milk (105° to 115°F)
  ½ cup (1 stick) butter, softened
  ½ cup granulated sugar
  3 eggs
  ½ teaspoon salt
  ½ teaspoon vanilla extract
  5 to 5½ cups all-purpose flour,
     divided
  1 cup raisins
  ½ teaspoon cinnamon
One 12-oz. pkg. (2 cups) NESTLÉ® Toll
     House® Semi-Sweet Chocolate
     Morsels

Glaze:

  1 cup confectioners' sugar
  2 tablespoons milk

Buns: Grease two 13×9-inch baking pans. In small bowl, dissolve yeast in warm water; let stand 10 minutes. In large bowl, combine warm milk, butter, granulated sugar, eggs, salt and vanilla extract. Add yeast mixture. Stir in 2 cups flour, raisins and cinnamon. Gradually stir in enough remaining flour to make a soft dough. Turn dough onto lightly floured surface. Knead 2 minutes. Knead in semi-sweet chocolate morsels; knead 3 minutes or until dough is smooth and elastic.

Hot Cross Buns

Place dough in lightly greased bowl; turn over to grease surface. Cover with cloth towel; let rise in warm place (70° to 75°F) until double in bulk, about 1 hour. Punch down dough; cover and let rise 30 minutes longer.

Punch down dough; divide into 24 pieces. Shape each piece into a smooth ball. Place 12 balls in each prepared pan. Cover; let rise in warm place until double in bulk, about 45 minutes.

Preheat oven to 350°F. Bake 20 to 25 minutes until golden brown. Cool 15 minutes.

Glaze: In small bowl, combine confectioners' sugar and milk, stirring until smooth. Drizzle Glaze over buns, forming a cross on each. Serve warm or cool completely. *Makes 24 buns*

Flaky Southern Biscuits

  2 cups flour
  1 tablespoon baking powder
  ½ teaspoon salt
  ½ cup chilled vegetable shortening
  ¾ cup *cold* milk

Preheat oven to 425°F.

In large bowl combine flour, baking powder and salt. With pastry blender or 2 knives, cut in shortening until mixture resembles coarse crumbs. Stir in milk just until dough holds together. On lightly floured board knead gently about 1 minute. With floured rolling pin roll dough ½ inch thick. With floured biscuit cutter cut dough into 2½- to 3-inch rounds. Place 1 inch apart on ungreased cookie sheet.

Bake 12 to 15 minutes or until lightly browned. Serve hot. *Makes 10 biscuits*

*Favorite recipe from **McIlhenny Company***

Caramel-Pecan Sticky Buns

1 8-oz. pkg. PHILADELPHIA
  BRAND® Cream Cheese, cubed
¾ cup cold water
1 16-oz. pkg. hot roll mix
1 egg
⅓ cup granulated sugar
1 teaspoon cinnamon
1 cup pecan halves
¾ cup packed brown sugar
½ cup light corn syrup
¼ cup PARKAY® Margarine, melted

- Preheat oven to 350°F.
- Stir together 6 ounces cream cheese and water in small saucepan. Cook over low heat until mixture reaches 115° to 120°, stirring occasionally.
- Stir together hot roll mix and yeast packet in large bowl. Add cream cheese mixture and egg, mixing until dough pulls away from sides of bowl.
- Knead dough on lightly floured surface 5 minutes or until smooth and elastic. Cover; let rise in warm place 20 minutes.
- Beat remaining cream cheese, granulated sugar and cinnamon in small mixing bowl at medium speed with electric mixer until well blended.
- Roll out dough to 18×12-inch rectangle; spread cream cheese mixture over dough to within 1 inch from outer edges of dough.
- Roll up from long end; sealing edges. Cut into twenty-four ¾-inch slices.
- Stir together remaining ingredients in small bowl. Spoon 2 teaspoonfuls mixture into bottoms of greased medium-sized muffin pans.
- Place dough, cut side up, in cups. Cover; let rise in warm place 30 minutes.
- Bake 20 to 25 minutes or until golden brown. Invert onto serving platter immediately.   *Makes 2 dozen*

Prep time: 30 minutes plus rising
Cooking time: 25 minutes

Five-Fruit Granola Scones

1 can (16 ounces) California fruit
  cocktail in juice or extra light
  syrup
2 cups flour
⅓ cup sugar, divided
1 tablespoon baking powder
½ teaspoon salt
¼ cup butter or margarine
1 cup granola
2 eggs, beaten

Preheat oven to 375°F. Grease baking sheet.

Drain fruit cocktail thoroughly. Combine flour, ¼ cup sugar, baking powder and salt in large bowl; blend well. Cut in butter with pastry blender until crumbly; stir in granola. Stir in eggs and drained fruit cocktail; blend until just moistened. Turn out onto lightly floured surface. Roll into 7-inch circle and place on prepared baking sheet. Sprinkle top with remaining sugar.

Bake 45 minutes or until wooden pick inserted near center comes out clean. Cut into 6 wedges. Serve warm.

Makes 6 scones

Favorite recipe from **Canned Fruit Promotion Service**

Oatmeal Drop Biscuits

Oatmeal Drop Biscuits

1½ cups all-purpose flour
 ½ cup quick-cooking oats
 1 tablespoon baking powder
 2 teaspoons sugar
 ½ teaspoon salt
 ½ teaspoon grated orange peel
 6 tablespoons butter or margarine
 ¾ cup milk

Preheat oven to 450°F.

Combine flour, oats, baking powder, sugar, salt and orange peel in large bowl. Cut in butter with pastry blender until mixture resembles coarse crumbs. Stir milk into flour mixture until well mixed. Drop by rounded tablespoonfuls, 2 inches apart, onto ungreased baking sheets.

Bake 10 to 12 minutes or until golden brown on bottoms. Serve warm.

Makes about 16 biscuits

Tabasco® Corn Bread Wedges

1 package corn bread mix
¼ cup butter or margarine
1 cup finely grated sharp Cheddar
   cheese
¼ teaspoon Worcestershire sauce
¼ teaspoon TABASCO® Brand Pepper
   Sauce
1 egg white, stiffly beaten
  Paprika

Prepare corn bread according to package directions and bake in a 9-inch pie plate.

Meanwhile, combine butter, cheese, Worcestershire sauce and Tabasco® sauce in small bowl, beating until smooth. Fold in egg white. Remove corn bread from oven when done; cut into 8 wedges. Top with cheese mixture; spread evenly over wedges. Sprinkle with paprika.

Preheat broiler to 400°F; broil corn bread about 4 minutes until cheese topping is puffy and golden brown.

Makes 8 wedges

Wheat Germ Scones

½ cup wheat germ, divided
1½ cups all-purpose flour
 2 tablespoons packed brown sugar
 1 tablespoon baking powder
½ teaspoon salt
 6 tablespoons butter or margarine
⅓ cup golden raisins, coarsely chopped
 2 eggs
¼ cup milk

Preheat oven to 425°F.

Reserve 1 tablespoon wheat germ. Combine remaining wheat germ, flour, brown sugar, baking powder and salt in large bowl. Cut in butter with pastry blender until mixture resembles coarse crumbs. Stir in raisins. Beat eggs in small bowl. Add milk; beat until well blended. Reserve 2 tablespoons milk mixture. Add remaining milk mixture to flour mixture; stir until mixture forms soft dough that leaves side of bowl.

Turn out onto well-floured surface. Knead dough 10 times.* Roll dough using floured rolling pin into 9×6-inch rectangle. Cut dough into 6 (3-inch) squares. Cut each square diagonally in half, making 12 triangles. Place triangles, 2 inches apart, on ungreased baking sheets. Brush triangles with reserved milk mixture and sprinkle with reserved wheat germ.

Bake 10 to 12 minutes until golden brown. Cool on wire racks 10 minutes. Serve warm. *Makes 12 scones*

*To knead dough, fold dough in half toward you and press dough away from you with heels of hands. Give dough a quarter turn and continue folding, pushing and turning.

Wheat Germ Scones

Mini Fruitcakes

1 can (8¼ ounces) DOLE® Crushed
   Pineapple in Syrup or Juice
1½ cups chopped figs
1 cup DOLE® Raisins
1 cup chopped walnuts
½ cup glace cherries
1½ cups all-purpose flour, divided
½ cup margarine, softened
¼ cup packed brown sugar
¼ cup honey
3 eggs
2 tablespoons bourbon whiskey
   Grated peel from 1 DOLE® Lemon
   (1 teaspoon)
1 teaspoon baking soda
1 teaspoon salt
½ teaspoon ground cinnamon
½ teaspoon ground nutmeg
½ cup whipping cream, whipped
16 maraschino cherries

Preheat oven to 300°F. Paper-line 16 (2½-inch) muffin cups. Drain pineapple well; reserve ¼ cup syrup.

Combine figs, raisins, walnuts and glace cherries in medium bowl. Toss with ½ cup flour. Beat margarine and sugar in large bowl until fluffy. Beat in honey. Beat in eggs, one at a time, until well blended. Stir in pineapple, reserved syrup, bourbon and lemon peel. Combine remaining 1 cup flour, baking soda, salt and spices in small bowl. Add to creamed mixture; beat until smooth. Stir in dried fruit mixture. Spoon into prepared muffin cups, filling to top.

Bake 55 minutes or until wooden pick inserted in center comes out clean. Remove from pans. Cool.

To serve, remove paper; dollop with whipped cream and top with maraschino cherry. *Makes 16 mini fruitcakes*

Almond Popovers

3 eggs
⅔ cup milk
⅓ cup almond-flavored liqueur
3 tablespoons butter or margarine, melted
1 cup all-purpose flour
¼ cup ground toasted almonds
¼ teaspoon salt
3 tablespoons sliced natural almonds

Position rack in lower third of oven. Preheat oven to 375°F. Grease 6 (6-ounce) custard cups. Set custard cups in jelly-roll pan for easier handling.

Beat eggs in large bowl with electric mixer at low speed 1 minute. Beat in milk, liqueur and butter until blended. Beat in flour, ground almonds and salt until batter is smooth. Pour evenly into prepared custard cups. Sprinkle with sliced almonds.

Bake 40 minutes. Quickly make small slit in top of each popover to let out steam. Bake 5 to 10 minutes longer or until browned. Remove popovers from cups. Serve warm. *Makes 6 popovers*

Easy Sticky Buns

1 cup NABISCO® 100% Bran™
⅓ cup firmly packed light brown sugar
¼ cup FLEISCHMANN'S® Margarine, melted
1 apple, cored and sliced
2 cups buttermilk baking mix
¼ cup EGG BEATERS® 99% Real Egg Product*
½ cup water

*2 egg whites may be substituted.

Mix ¼ cup bran, brown sugar and margarine; spread in 8×8×2-inch baking pan. Top with apple slices; set aside.

In bowl, blend baking mix, remaining bran, Egg Beaters® and water until soft dough forms. Drop by ¼ cupfuls into prepared pan.

Bake at 450°F for 13 to 15 minutes or until golden brown. Invert onto heat-proof plate, leaving pan over buns for 2 to 3 minutes. Remove pan; cool slightly. Serve warm. *Makes 9 servings*

Baking Powder Biscuits

2 cups all-purpose flour
1 tablespoon baking powder
½ teaspoon salt
¼ cup butter or margarine
3 tablespoons shortening
About ¾ cup milk

Preheat oven to 450°F. Grease baking sheet.

Combine flour, baking powder and salt in medium bowl. Cut in butter and shortening with pastry blender until mixture resembles coarse crumbs. Stir in enough milk to make soft dough.

Turn out onto lightly floured surface. Knead dough lightly.* Roll dough to ½-inch thickness. Cut out biscuits with 2-inch round cutter. Place on prepared baking sheet.

Bake 8 to 10 minutes or until browned. *Makes 16 biscuits*

*To knead dough, fold dough in half toward you and press dough away from you with heels of hands. Give dough a quarter turn and continue folding, pushing and turning.

Almond Popovers

Apricot Scones

Apricot Scones

1½ cups flour
1 cup oat bran
2 tablespoons sugar
1 tablespoon baking powder
½ teaspoon salt
½ cup margarine
1 egg, beaten
3 tablespoons low-fat milk
1 can (17 ounces) California apricot halves, drained and chopped

Preheat oven to 400°F.

Combine flour, oat bran, sugar, baking powder and salt in large bowl. Cut in margarine with pastry blender until mixture resembles fine crumbs. Add egg, milk and canned apricots; stir just until dough leaves side of bowl.

Divide dough in half; turn onto floured surface. Sprinkle surface of dough with additional flour. Roll or pat dough into 6-inch circle, 1 inch thick. Repeat with remaining dough. Cut each circle with floured knife into six wedges. Place on ungreased cookie sheet.

Bake 12 minutes or until golden brown.

Makes 12 scones

*Favorite recipe from **California Apricot Advisory Board***

Ham & Swiss Cheese Biscuits

2 cups all-purpose flour
2 teaspoons baking powder
½ teaspoon baking soda
½ cup butter or margarine, chilled, cut into pieces
½ cup (2 ounces) shredded Swiss cheese
2 ounces ham, minced
About ⅔ cup buttermilk

Preheat oven to 450°F. Grease baking sheet.

Combine flour, baking powder and baking soda in medium bowl. Cut in butter with pastry blender until mixture resembles coarse crumbs. Stir in cheese, ham and enough buttermilk to make soft dough.

Turn out dough onto lightly floured surface; knead lightly.* Roll out dough to ½-inch thickness. Cut out biscuits with 2-inch round cutter. Place on prepared baking sheet.

Bake about 10 minutes or until browned.

Makes about 18 biscuits

*To knead dough, fold dough in half toward you and press dough away from you with heels of hands. Give dough a quarter turn and continue folding, pushing and turning.

Tip: This classy combination is terrific as a breakfast biscuit, and any leftovers make great snacks.

Easter Buns With Vanilla Glaze

1 8-oz. container PHILADELPHIA BRAND® Soft Cream Cheese with Pineapple
1 8-oz. container pina colada flavored yogurt
2 tablespoons PARKAY® Margarine
1 16-oz. pkg. hot roll mix
⅓ cup granulated sugar
1 egg
   Vanilla Glaze

- Preheat oven to 350°F.

- Stir together cream cheese, yogurt and margarine in small saucepan until well blended. Cook over low heat until mixture reaches 115° to 120°, stirring occasionally.

- Stir together hot roll mix, yeast packet and granulated sugar in large bowl. Add cream cheese mixture and egg, mixing until dough pulls away from sides of bowl.

- Knead dough on lightly floured surface 5 minutes or until smooth and elastic. Cover; let rise in warm place 20 minutes.

- Divide dough into twenty-four balls. Place 2 inches apart on greased cookie sheet. Cut crisscross design with knife on top of balls, ½ inch deep. Cover; let rise in warm place 30 minutes.

- Bake 20 to 22 minutes or until lightly browned. Dip warm buns into Vanilla Glaze. *Makes 2 dozen buns*

Vanilla Glaze

1½ cups powdered sugar
3 tablespoons light corn syrup
3 tablespoons cold water
2 teaspoons vanilla

- Stir together ingredients in small bowl until smooth.

Prep time: 30 minutes plus rising
Cooking time: 22 minutes

French Breakfast Puffs

1½ cups all-purpose flour
½ cup confectioners sugar
1 teaspoon baking powder
1 teaspoon salt
¾ teaspoon ground nutmeg
½ cup milk
½ cup water
¼ cup CRISCO® Oil
1½ teaspoons grated lemon peel
3 eggs
   CRISCO® Oil for frying
   Confectioners sugar

1. Mix flour, ½ cup confectioners sugar, baking powder, salt and nutmeg in small mixing bowl. Set aside. Combine milk, water, Crisco® Oil and lemon peel in medium saucepan. Heat to rolling boil over medium-high heat. Add flour mixture all at once. Beat with wooden spoon until mixture pulls away from sides of pan into a ball. Remove from heat; cool slightly. Add eggs, one at a time, beating well after each addition.

2. Heat 2 to 3 inches Crisco® Oil in deep-fryer or large saucepan to 350°F.

3. Drop dough by tablespoonfuls into hot Crisco® Oil. Fry 3 or 4 puffs at a time, 4 to 6 minutes, or until golden brown, turning over several times. Drain on paper towels. Sprinkle top of each puff with confectioners sugar. *Makes 32 puffs*

Quicky Sticky Buns

3 tablespoons packed brown sugar, divided
¼ cup KARO® Light or Dark Corn Syrup
¼ cup coarsely chopped pecans
2 tablespoons softened MAZOLA® Margarine, divided
1 can (8 ounces) refrigerated crescent dinner rolls
1 teaspoon cinnamon

Preheat oven to 350°F.

In small bowl combine 2 tablespoons of the brown sugar, the corn syrup, pecans and 1 tablespoon of the margarine. Spoon about 2 teaspoons mixture into each of 9 (2½-inch) muffin pan cups. Unroll entire crescent roll dough; pinch seams together to form 1 rectangle. Combine remaining 1 tablespoon brown sugar and the cinnamon. Spread dough with remaining 1 tablespoon margarine; sprinkle with cinnamon mixture. Roll up from short end. Cut into 9 slices. Place one slice in each prepared muffin pan cup.

Bake 25 minutes or until golden brown. Immediately invert pan onto cookie sheet or tray; cool 10 minutes.

Makes 9 buns

Quicky Sticky Buns

Orange-Dijon Muffin Sticks

1¾ cups all-purpose flour
¼ cup firmly packed brown sugar
1 tablespoon DAVIS® Baking Powder
¾ cup milk
½ cup orange juice
¼ cup FLEISCHMANN'S® Margarine, melted
1 egg, sightly beaten
2 tablespoons GREY POUPON® Dijon Mustard
1 teaspoon grated orange peel

In medium bowl, combine flour, brown sugar and baking powder; set aside.

In small bowl, combine milk, orange juice, margarine, egg, mustard and orange peel; stir into dry ingredients just until moistened. Fill 12 greased corn stick pans or 2½-inch muffin-pan cups ¾ full.

Bake at 400°F for 20 to 25 minutes or until browned. Serve warm or cool.

Makes 12 sticks or muffins

Cheddar Cheese Popovers

4 tablespoons butter
1⅓ cups all-purpose flour
¼ teaspoon dry mustard
⅔ cup water
⅔ cup milk
4 eggs
½ cup (2 ounces) shredded Wisconsin Mild Cheddar cheese

Preheat oven to 375°F. Place eight 6-ounce custard cups on baking sheet. Measure 1½ teaspoons butter into each cup.

Combine flour and dry mustard in large bowl. Gradually stir in water and milk until blended. Beat in eggs, one at a time, until mixture is smooth. Fold in cheese.

Place baking sheet with custard cups in oven 3 to 5 minutes until butter melts and custard cups are hot. Fill cups ½ to ⅔ full with batter.

Bake 45 minutes. Do not open oven until end of baking time. Remove popovers from custard cups; serve warm.

Makes 8 popovers

Favorite recipe from **Wisconsin Milk Marketing Board** © *1993*

Jamaican Sweet Buns

  2 cups all-purpose flour
¼ cup sugar
  4 teaspoons baking powder
  2 teaspoons grated lemon peel
¼ teaspoon salt
½ cup butter or margarine
½ cup milk
  2 egg yolks, lightly beaten
¾ cup SUN-MAID® Raisins
¾ cup shredded coconut
  1 egg white, beaten, for glaze
     Sugar, for glaze

Preheat oven to 450°F. Grease 6 (4-inch) tart pans.

Combine flour, ¼ cup sugar, baking powder, peel and salt in medium bowl. Cut in butter until mixture resembles coarse crumbs. Combine milk and egg yolks in small bowl; mix into flour mixture to form soft dough. Stir in raisins and coconut just to blend. Evenly divide dough into prepared tart pans; flatten tops. Brush generously with egg white; sprinkle heavily with sugar (about 2 teaspoons on each). Space apart on baking sheet.

Bake 15 minutes or until springy to the touch and well browned. Cool in pans. Serve with whipped sweet butter.

Makes 6 buns

Apple Cheddar Nut Scones

Apple Cheddar Nut Scones

1½ cups all-purpose flour
½ teaspoon baking powder
½ teaspoon baking soda
¼ teaspoon salt
¼ cup margarine or butter
  2 cups (8 ounces) shredded Cheddar cheese
¼ cup unsalted sunflower nuts
½ cup MOTT'S® Regular Apple Sauce

Preheat oven to 400°F.

Combine flour, baking powder, baking soda and salt in medium bowl. Cut in margarine with pastry blender or fork until mixture is crumbly. Stir in cheese and nuts. Add apple sauce; stir until moistened.

On floured surface, knead dough gently 5 or 6 times. Place on ungreased cookie sheet; press into 8-inch circle, about ½ inch thick. Cut into wedges; separate slightly.

Bake 12 to 16 minutes or until lightly browned. Serve warm.

Makes 8 to 12 servings

Roasted Red Pepper Biscuits

2 cups buttermilk biscuit mix
½ cup PROGRESSO® Grated Parmesan Cheese
1 teaspoon dried oregano leaves, crushed
⅛ teaspoon cayenne pepper
1 jar (7 ounces) PROGRESSO® Roasted Peppers (red), drained, patted dry with paper towel and chopped
⅔ cup milk

Preheat oven to 425°F. Grease baking sheet.

Stir together biscuit mix, Parmesan cheese, oregano and cayenne pepper in medium bowl. Add roasted peppers and milk; stir just until moistened. Drop dough by heaping tablespoonfuls, 2 inches apart, onto prepared baking sheet.

Bake 12 to 14 minutes or until browned.

Makes 1 dozen

Estimated preparation time: 10 minutes
Baking time: 14 minutes

Chocolate Chip Scones

1¾ cups all-purpose flour
3 tablespoons sugar
2½ teaspoons baking powder
½ teaspoon salt
⅓ cup LAND O LAKES® Butter
1 egg, slightly beaten
½ cup semi-sweet chocolate chips
4 to 6 tablespoons half-and-half
1 egg, slightly beaten

Heat oven to 400°F.

In medium bowl combine flour, sugar, baking powder and salt. Cut butter into flour mixture until it resembles fine crumbs. Stir in 1 egg, chocolate chips and just enough half-and-half so dough leaves side of bowl. Turn dough onto lightly floured surface; knead lightly 10 times. Roll into ½-inch-thick circle; cut into 12 wedges. Place on ungreased cookie sheet. Brush with remaining egg.

Bake for 10 to 12 minutes or until golden brown. Immediately remove from cookie sheet. Serve warm.

Makes 1 dozen scones

Mini Chips-Cinnamon Crescents

1 can (8 oz.) refrigerated quick crescent dinner rolls
Ground cinnamon
½ cup HERSHEY®'S MINI CHIPS Semi-Sweet Chocolate
Powdered sugar

Heat oven to 375°F.

On ungreased cookie sheet, unroll dough to form 8 triangles. Lightly sprinkle cinnamon and 1 tablespoon small chocolate chips on top of each. Gently press into dough to adhere. Starting at shortest side of triangle, roll dough to opposite point.

Bake 10 to 12 minutes or until golden brown. Sprinkle with powdered sugar. Serve warm.

Makes 8 crescents

Roasted Red Pepper Biscuits

Paul Bunyan Sticky Buns

1 package (16 ounces) hot roll mix
½ cup butter or margarine, melted and divided
2 tablespoons water
1 cup packed brown sugar
1 cup chopped DIAMOND® Walnuts, divided
¾ cup granulated sugar
1 tablespoon ground cinnamon

Prepare dough as package directs for rolls. Knead gently on lightly floured surface 1 minute. Place dough in lightly greased bowl; turn once to grease surface. Cover; let rise in warm place (85°F) until doubled, about 1 hour.

To prepare syrup, combine ¼ cup butter, water and brown sugar in small saucepan. Stir over medium heat until sugar dissolves. Bring to a boil; reduce heat to low and simmer gently 1 minute. Pour at once into 11×7-inch baking pan, tilting to spread evenly. Sprinkle ½ cup walnuts over syrup layer; set aside.

Turn out dough onto lightly floured surface. Let rest 5 minutes, then stretch and roll into 30×5-inch rectangle. Brush with remaining ¼ cup butter. Combine granulated sugar and cinnamon in small bowl; sprinkle over butter. Arrange remaining ½ cup walnuts on top. Starting from 5-inch side, roll up loosely, jelly-roll fashion, pinching edges to seal. Cut roll into 6 equal pieces. Place cut sides up in prepared pan, spreading pinwheels open slightly. Cover; let rise in warm place 35 to 45 minutes or until almost doubled.

Cover lower shelf of oven with foil. Bake buns on center shelf in preheated 375°F oven 25 to 35 minutes or until golden. Immediately invert onto tray. Cool 5 minutes. Serve warm.

Makes 6 large buns

Country Biscuits

Country Biscuits

2 cups all-purpose flour
1 tablespoon baking powder
1 teaspoon salt
⅓ cup CRISCO® Shortening
¾ cup milk

1. Preheat oven to 425°F. Combine flour, baking powder and salt in medium bowl. Cut in Crisco® using pastry blender or two knives to form coarse crumbs. Add milk. Mix with fork until particles are moistened and cling together. Form dough into ball.

2. Transfer dough to lightly floured surface. Knead gently 8 to 10 times. Roll dough ½ inch thick. Cut with floured 2-inch round cutter. Place on ungreased baking sheet.

3. Bake 12 to 14 minutes or until golden.
Makes 12 to 16 biscuits

Sour Cream Biscuits

1¼ cups flour
1½ teaspoons baking powder
½ teaspoon salt
¼ teaspoon baking soda
½ cup sour cream
¼ cup light cream or milk

Preheat oven to 375°F. Lightly grease baking sheet.

Stir together flour, baking powder, salt and baking soda in bowl. Combine sour cream and light cream in small bowl. Make a well in center of dry ingredients; add sour cream mixture. Stir just until dough clings together and forms a ball.

Knead dough gently on lightly floured surface 10 to 12 times. Roll or pat to ½-inch thickness. Cut dough into 2¼-inch rounds. Carefully transfer cut biscuits to prepared baking sheet. Bake 15 minutes or until golden. Serve warm.

Makes 8 biscuits

Favorite recipe from **The Kingsford Products Company**

Dill Sour Cream Scones

2 cups all-purpose flour
2 teaspoons baking powder
½ teaspoon baking soda
½ teaspoon salt
4 tablespoons butter or margarine
2 eggs
½ cup sour cream
1 tablespoon chopped fresh dill *or*
    1 teaspoon dried dill weed

Preheat oven to 425°F.

Combine flour, baking powder, baking soda and salt. Cut in butter with pastry blender until mixture resembles coarse crumbs. Beat eggs with fork in small bowl. Add sour cream and dill; beat until well combined. Stir into flour mixture until mixture forms soft dough that leaves side of bowl.

Turn out onto well-floured surface. Knead dough 10 times.* Roll dough using floured rolling pin into 9×6-inch rectangle. Cut dough into 6 (3-inch) squares. Cut each square diagonally in half, making 12 triangles. Place triangles, 2 inches apart, on ungreased baking sheets.

Bake 10 to 12 minutes or until golden brown. Cool on wire racks 10 minutes. Serve warm.   *Makes 12 scones*

*To knead dough, fold dough in half toward you and press dough away from you with heels of hands. Give dough a quarter turn and continue folding, pushing and turning.

Dill Sour Cream Scones

Freezer Buttermilk Biscuits

3 cups all-purpose flour
1 tablespoon baking powder
1 tablespoon sugar
1 teaspoon baking soda
½ teaspoon salt
⅔ cup shortening
1 cup buttermilk

Combine flour, baking powder, sugar, baking soda and salt in large bowl. Cut in shortening with pastry blender until mixture resembles coarse crumbs. Stir buttermilk into flour mixture until mixture forms soft dough that leaves side of bowl.

Turn out onto well-floured surface. Knead dough 10 times. (To knead dough, fold dough in half toward you and press dough away from you with heels of hands. Give dough a quarter turn and continue folding, pushing and turning.) Roll dough into 8-inch square. Cut dough into 16 (2-inch) squares.*

Line baking sheet with plastic wrap. Place squares on lined sheet. Freeze about 3 hours or until firm. Remove frozen squares from sheet and place in freezer container. Freeze up to 1 month.

Preheat oven to 400°F. Place frozen squares, 1½ inches apart, on ungreased baking sheets.

Bake 20 to 25 minutes until golden brown. Serve warm.

Makes 16 biscuits

*To bake biscuits immediately, preheat oven to 450°F. Prepare dough as directed, but do not freeze. Place squares, 1½ inches apart, on ungreased baking sheets. Bake 10 to 12 minutes until golden brown. Serve warm.

Dilled Popovers

1 cup skim milk
¾ cup EGG BEATERS® 99% Real Egg Product
3 tablespoons FLEISCHMANN'S® Sweet Unsalted Margarine, melted
¾ cup all-purpose flour
¼ cup CREAM OF RICE® Hot Cereal
1 teaspoon dried dill weed
½ teaspoon onion powder

In medium bowl, beat milk, Egg Beaters® and margarine until blended.

In small bowl, combine flour, cereal, dill and onion powder; beat into egg mixture until well blended. Pour into 8 well-greased 6-ounce custard cups.

Bake at 450°F for 15 minutes; *reduce heat to 350°F.* Bake for 5 to 10 minutes or until puffed and lightly browned. Carefully slit tops of popovers; bake 5 minutes more. Serve immediately.   *Makes 8 popovers*

Cinnamon-Toast Croissants

¼ cup sugar
1 teaspoon ground cinnamon
2 croissants, halved lengthwise
   Butter or margarine, softened

Position oven rack about 4 inches from heat source. Preheat broiler.

Combine sugar and cinnamon. Lightly spread cut sides of croissants with butter; sprinkle with sugar mixture. Place on baking sheet. Broil until lightly browned.

Makes 2 servings

Freezer Buttermilk Biscuits

Mini Morsel Tea Biscuits

Mini Morsel Tea Biscuits

  4 cups all-purpose flour
⅓ cup sugar
  2 tablespoons baking powder
½ teaspoon salt
½ cup (1 stick) butter or margarine
  1 cup (half of 12-oz. pkg.) NESTLÉ®
    Toll House® Semi-Sweet Chocolate
    Mini Morsels
  4 eggs, divided
  1 cup CARNATION® Evaporated Milk
1½ teaspoons vanilla extract
  2 tablespoons milk

Preheat oven to 400°F. Grease two large cookie sheets.

In large bowl, combine flour, sugar, baking powder and salt. With pastry blender or 2 knives, cut in butter until mixture resembles coarse crumbs. Stir in mini morsels; set aside. In small bowl, beat three eggs with evaporated milk and vanilla extract. Stir into dry ingredients just until a soft dough forms.

Turn dough onto well-floured surface. Knead briefly. Pat dough to ¾-inch thickness. Cut with 2-inch fluted round biscuit cutter. Place on prepared cookie sheets. Beat remaining egg with milk; brush over dough.

Bake 15 to 17 minutes until golden. Serve warm.   *Makes about 1½ dozen biscuits*

Angel Biscuits

⅓ cup warm water (110°F)
  1 package (¼ ounce) active dry yeast
  5 cups all-purpose flour
  3 tablespoons sugar
  1 tablespoon baking powder
  1 teaspoon baking soda
  1 teaspoon salt
  1 cup shortening
  2 cups buttermilk

Preheat oven to 450°F. Pour warm water into small bowl. Sprinkle yeast over water and stir until dissolved. Let stand 10 minutes or until small bubbles form.

Combine flour, sugar, baking powder, baking soda and salt in large bowl. Cut in shortening with pastry blender until mixture resembles coarse crumbs. Make a well in center. Pour in yeast mixture and buttermilk; stir with fork until mixture forms dough.

Turn out onto lightly floured board. Knead 30 seconds or until dough feels light and soft but not sticky. Roll out desired amount of dough to ½-inch thickness. Cut out biscuits with 2-inch round cutter. Place desired number of biscuits close together (for soft sides) or ½ inch apart (for crispy sides) on ungreased baking sheet.

Bake 15 to 18 minutes or until tops are lightly browned.

Place remaining cut-out biscuits in airtight bag; refrigerate up to 3 days. Or place on baking sheet and freeze until frozen. Transfer frozen rounds to airtight bags; return to freezer. At baking time, place frozen rounds on ungreased baking sheet. Let stand 20 minutes or until thawed before baking. Bake as directed.

Makes about 5 dozen biscuits

Red Devil Biscuits: Prepare Angel Biscuits but add 2 tablespoons mild red chili powder to flour mixture. Cut biscuits regular size to serve as a hot bread. To serve as an appetizer, cut biscuits miniature size. Serve with your favorite cheese spread or with softened butter and thinly sliced roast beef or turkey.

Tip: In Southwestern ranch kitchens, cooks whip up a large batch of this biscuit dough, which can be stored in the refrigerator or freezer. The result is a ready-to-bake biscuit that is feather light.

Honey-Mustard Scones

3½ to 3¾ cups all-purpose flour
  5 teaspoons DAVIS® Baking Powder
  1 teaspoon salt
  ¾ cup BLUE BONNET® Margarine
  3 eggs
  ½ cup milk
  ⅓ cup GREY POUPON® Country Dijon
      Mustard
  ¼ cup honey
  ½ teaspoon A.1.® Steak Sauce
  ¾ cup finely chopped ham

In large bowl, mix 3½ cups flour, baking powder and salt. With pastry blender, cut in margarine until mixture resembles coarse crumbs; set aside.

In small bowl, with wire whisk, beat 2 eggs, milk, mustard, honey and steak sauce; add ham. Stir into flour mixture just until blended, adding extra flour if necessary to make soft dough.

On lightly floured surface, roll dough into 12×8-inch rectangle. Cut dough into eight 4×3-inch rectangles; cut each rectangle into 2 triangles. Place on greased baking sheets, about 2 inches apart. Beat remaining egg; brush tops of scones with egg.

Bake at 425°F for 10 minutes or until golden brown.   *Makes 16 scones*

Spicy Gingerbread

1½ cups all-purpose flour
  ½ cup Regular, Instant or Quick
      CREAM OF WHEAT® Cereal
  2 teaspoons ground ginger
  1 teaspoon baking soda
  1 cup buttermilk
  1 cup light molasses
  ¼ cup BLUE BONNET® Margarine,
      melted
  1 egg, beaten

In 8×8×2-inch baking pan, combine flour, cereal, ginger and baking soda. Make a well in center of flour mixture; add buttermilk, molasses, margarine and egg. Whisk mixture until well combined. Run rubber spatula around edges of pan to clean sides.

Bake at 350°F for 45 to 50 minutes or until toothpick inserted in center comes out clean. Cut into squares and serve warm.

Makes 9 servings

Cinnamon-Vanilla Popovers

2 eggs
1 cup milk
2 tablespoons butter or margarine, melted
1 teaspoon vanilla extract
1 cup all-purpose flour
2 tablespoons granulated sugar
¾ teaspoon ground cinnamon
¼ teaspoon salt
Confectioner's sugar (optional)

Position rack in lower third of oven. Preheat oven to 375°F. Grease 6 (6-ounce) custard cups. Set custard cups in jelly-roll pan for easier handling.

Beat eggs in large bowl with electric mixer at low speed 1 minute. Beat in milk, butter and vanilla until blended. Beat in flour, granulated sugar, cinnamon and salt until batter is smooth. Pour evenly into prepared custard cups.

Bake 40 minutes. Quickly make small slit in top of each popover to let out steam. Bake 5 to 10 minutes longer or until browned. Remove popovers from cups. Sprinkle with confectioner's sugar, if desired. Serve warm.

Makes 6 popovers

Puff Pastry Cheese Twists

1 envelope LIPTON® Recipe Secrets Golden Onion Recipe Soup Mix
¼ cup grated Parmesan cheese
2 teaspoons chili powder
1 teaspoon ground cumin (optional)
1 package (17¼ ounces) frozen puff pastry sheets, thawed

Preheat oven to 425°F.

In medium bowl, combine all ingredients except pastry sheets; set aside. Unfold 1 pastry sheet and sprinkle with ½ soup mixture; top with remaining pastry sheet. With rolling pin, lightly roll layered sheets into a 15×11-inch rectangle. Sprinkle top pastry sheet with remaining soup mixture, then lightly roll mixture into pastry. Cut pastry into 30 (½×11-inch) strips; twist strips. Arrange on two ungreased baking sheets.

Reduce oven temperature to 350°F. Bake 12 minutes or until golden brown.

Makes about 30 twists

Lemon Pecan Sticky Rolls

½ cup granulated sugar
½ cup firmly packed light brown sugar
¼ cup margarine or butter
¼ cup REALEMON® Lemon Juice from Concentrate
½ teaspoon ground cinnamon
½ cup chopped pecans
2 (8-ounce) packages refrigerated crescent rolls

Preheat oven to 375°F. In small saucepan, combine sugars, margarine, ReaLemon® brand and cinnamon. Bring to a boil; boil 1 minute. Reserving *¼ cup*, pour remaining lemon mixture into 9-inch round layer cake pan. Sprinkle with nuts. Separate rolls into 8 rectangles; spread with reserved lemon mixture. Roll up jellyroll-fashion, beginning with short side; seal edges. Cut in half. Place rolls, cut-side down, in prepared pan.

Bake 30 to 35 minutes or until dark golden brown. Loosen sides. Immediately invert onto serving plate; do not remove pan. Let stand 5 minutes; remove pan. Serve warm.
Makes 16 rolls

Southwestern Snack Squares

1¼ cups all-purpose flour
1 cup thinly sliced green onions
¾ cup QUAKER® Enriched Corn Meal
1 tablespoon brown sugar
2 teaspoons baking powder
1 teaspoon dried oregano
½ teaspoon ground cumin
¼ teaspoon salt (optional)
1 cup milk
¼ cup vegetable oil
1 egg
1 cup (4 ounces) shredded Cheddar
    cheese
1 can (4 ounces) chopped green chilies
¼ cup finely chopped red bell pepper
2 sliced crisp-cooked bacon, crumbled

Preheat oven to 400°F. Grease 11×7-inch baking dish.

Combine flour, green onions, corn meal, brown sugar, baking powder, oregano, cumin and salt in large bowl; mix well. Combine milk, oil and egg in small bowl. Add to corn meal mixture; mix just until moistened. Spread evenly into prepared dish. Combine cheese, chilies, pepper and bacon in medium-size bowl. Sprinkle evenly over corn meal mixture.

Southwestern Snack Squares

Bake 25 to 30 minutes or until wooden toothpick inserted into center comes out clean. Let stand 10 minutes before cutting.   *Makes about 15 appetizers*

Note: Also great as a side dish to fish, chicken or pork. Just cut into 8 squares.

Currant Biscuits

2 cups all-purpose flour
2 tablespoons sugar
2 teaspoons baking powder
½ teaspoon ground ginger
¼ teaspoon ground nutmeg
¼ teaspoon salt
1 teaspoon grated orange peel
½ cup LAND O LAKES® Butter
¼ cup shortening
½ cup half-and-half
½ cup currants *or* raisins
2 tablespoons LAND O LAKES®
    Butter, melted

Heat oven to 400°F.

In large bowl combine flour, sugar, baking powder, ginger, nutmeg, salt and orange peel. Cut in ½ cup butter and shortening until crumbly. Stir in half-and-half and currants just until moistened.

Turn out dough onto lightly floured surface; knead until smooth, 1 minute. Roll out dough to ¾-inch thickness. With 3-inch star or favorite cutter, cut out 8 to 10 biscuits. Place 1 inch apart on ungreased cookie sheet. Brush tops with some of the melted butter.

Bake for 10 to 12 minutes or until lightly browned. Brush tops with remaining melted butter.   *Makes 8 to 10 biscuits*

Tip: Serve these cutout biscuits warm, with slivered ham and honey mustard, for a festive breakfast or brunch.

Peanut Butter Chocolate Chip Scones

2 cups all-purpose flour
¼ cup packed light brown sugar
1 tablespoon baking powder
⅓ cup peanut butter
4 tablespoons butter or margarine
½ cup miniature semisweet chocolate chips
2 eggs
¼ cup milk
2 tablespoons granulated sugar

Preheat oven to 425°F.

Combine flour, brown sugar and baking powder. Cut in peanut butter and butter with pastry blender until mixture resembles coarse crumbs. Stir in chocolate chips. Beat eggs with fork in small bowl. Add milk; beat until well blended. Reserve 2 tablespoons. Add remaining milk mixture to flour mixture; stir until mixture forms soft dough that leaves side of bowl.

Turn out onto well-floured surface. Knead dough 10 times.* Roll dough using floured rolling pin into 9×6-inch rectangle. Cut dough into 6 (3-inch) squares. Cut each square diagonally in half, making 12 triangles. Place triangles, 2 inches apart, on ungreased baking sheets. Brush triangles with reserved milk mixture and sprinkle with granulated sugar.

Bake 10 to 12 minutes or until golden brown. Cool on wire racks for 10 minutes. Serve warm.   *Makes 12 scones*

*To knead dough, fold dough in half toward you and press dough away from you with heels of hands. Give dough a quarter turn and continue folding, pushing and turning.

Oatmeal Butterscotch Tea Biscuits

Oatmeal Butterscotch Tea Biscuits

1 cup all-purpose flour
1 tablespoon baking powder
¾ teaspoon salt
¼ cup vegetable shortening
1 cup quick oats, uncooked
¾ cup NESTLÉ® Toll House® Butterscotch Flavored Morsels
⅓ cup raisins
½ cup milk
1 egg
1 tablespoon honey
1 tablespoon sugar
¼ teaspoon cinnamon

Preheat oven to 425°F.

In large bowl, combine flour, baking powder and salt. Using pastry blender or 2 knives, cut in shortening until mixture resembles coarse crumbs. Stir in oats, butterscotch morsels and raisins; set aside. In small bowl, combine milk, egg and honey; mix well. Add to flour mixture, stirring until dry ingredients are just moistened. Drop by rounded tablespoonfuls onto ungreased cookie sheets. In cup, combine sugar and cinnamon; sprinkle scant ¼ teaspoon over each biscuit.

Bake 8 to 10 minutes. Cool on wire racks.
            Makes about 1½ dozen biscuits

MUFFIN IN A LOAF

◆

Apricot Date Mini-Loaves

**1 package DUNCAN HINES® Bakery
   Style Cinnamon Swirl Muffin Mix**
½ teaspoon baking powder
2 egg whites
⅔ cup water
½ cup chopped dried apricots
½ cup chopped dates

1. Preheat oven to 350°F. Grease four
5⅜×2⅝×1⅞-inch mini-loaf pans.

2. Combine muffin mix and baking
powder in large bowl. Break up any
lumps. Add egg whites, water, apricots
and dates. Stir until well blended, about
50 strokes.

3. Knead swirl packet from Mix for 10
seconds before opening. Cut off one end
of swirl packet. Squeeze contents onto
batter. Swirl into batter with knife or
spatula, folding from bottom of bowl to
get an even swirl. Do not completely mix
into batter. Divide batter evenly into
pans. Sprinkle with contents of topping
packet from Mix.

4. Bake at 350°F for 30 to 35 minutes or
until toothpick inserted in center comes
out clean. Cool 15 minutes. Loosen loaves
from pans. Lift out with knife. Cool
completely. Garnish as desired.

Makes 4 mini-loaves

Tip: This recipe may also be baked in
greased 8½×4½×2½-inch loaf pan at
350°F for 55 to 60 minutes or until
toothpick inserted in center comes out
clean. Cool 10 minutes before removing
loaf from pan.

Orange Chocolate Chip Bread

1 cup skim milk
¼ cup orange juice
⅓ cup sugar
1 egg, slightly beaten
1 tablespoon grated fresh orange peel
3 cups all-purpose biscuit baking mix
**½ cup HERSHEY'S MINI CHIPS
   Semi-Sweet Chocolate**

Heat oven to 350°F. Grease 9×5×3-inch
loaf pan. In bowl, combine milk, orange
juice, sugar, egg and orange peel; stir in
baking mix. Beat until well blended,
about 1 minute. Stir in small chocolate
chips. Pour into prepared pan.

Bake 45 to 50 minutes or until wooden
pick inserted in center comes out clean.
Cool 10 minutes; remove from pan to
wire rack. Cool completely. Slice and
serve. To store leftovers, wrap in foil or
plastic wrap. *Makes 1 loaf (16 servings)*

Apricot Date Mini-Loaves

Pear Nut Bread with Citrus Cream Cheese

Pear Nut Bread with Citrus Cream Cheese

Pear Nut Bread

1 package (14 ounces) nut bread mix
⅛ teaspoon ground nutmeg
1 fresh California Bartlett pear, cored and finely chopped (about 1¼ cups)

Citrus Cream Cheese

1 package (8 ounces) light cream cheese (Neufchatel), softened
1 tablespoon finely grated orange peel

Grease and flour 8×4×3-inch loaf pan.

Prepare bread mix according to package directions, adding nutmeg and *substituting pear for ½ the liquid required.*

Bake according to package directions. In small bowl, combine cream cheese and orange peel. Serve with bread.

Makes 1 loaf

Favorite recipe from **California Tree Fruit Agreement**

California Walnut Bread

2 cups all-purpose flour
⅔ cup sugar
2¼ teaspoons baking powder
¾ teaspoon salt
1 egg
1 cup milk
3 tablespoons vegetable oil
¾ teaspoon vanilla extract
1 cup chopped DIAMOND® Walnuts
    Additional chopped DIAMOND® Walnuts (optional)

Preheat oven to 350°F. Grease well 8×4-inch loaf pan.

Combine flour, sugar, baking powder and salt in medium bowl. Beat egg in small bowl; stir in milk, oil and vanilla until well blended. Stir into dry mixture, mixing just until flour is moistened. Stir in 1 cup chopped walnuts. Pour into prepared pan. If desired, sprinkle with additional chopped walnuts.

Bake 1 hour or until wooden pick inserted in center comes out clean. Cool in pan 10 minutes. Remove from pan; cool on wire rack. *Makes 1 loaf*

Walnut Cranberry Bread: Prepare batter as directed above, adding 1 cup whole or halved fresh cranberries and 1 tablespoon grated orange peel. Bake as directed.

Makes 1 loaf

Walnut Banana Bread: Prepare batter as directed above, omitting milk and vanilla and adding 1 additional beaten egg and 1 cup mashed ripe banana. Bake as directed. *Makes 1 loaf*

Apple Muffins: Prepare batter as directed above, reducing milk to ⅔ cup and adding ¾ cup coarsely grated peeled apple, 1 teaspoon grated lemon peel and ¼ teaspoon ground cinnamon. Spoon into 12 greased 2½-inch muffin cups. Bake in preheated 400°F oven 20 to 25 minutes or until lightly browned.

Makes 12 muffins

Chocolate Date Nut Loaf

¾ cup boiling water
1 cup cut-up pitted dates
2¼ cups all-purpose flour
⅔ cup sugar
½ cup NESTLÉ® Cocoa
1 teaspoon baking powder
1 teaspoon baking soda
½ teaspoon salt
6 tablespoons (¾ stick) butter or
    margarine
¾ cup milk
1 egg, beaten
One 6-oz. pkg. (1 cup) NESTLÉ® Toll
    House® Semi-Sweet Chocolate
    Morsels
½ cup walnuts, chopped

Topping:
1 tablespoon finely chopped walnuts
1 teaspoon sugar

Preheat oven to 350°F. Grease 9×5×3-inch loaf pan. Pour boiling water over dates; set aside.

In large bowl, combine flour, ⅔ cup sugar, cocoa, baking powder, baking soda and salt. Melt butter; stir in milk and egg. Add milk mixture and date mixture to flour mixture; stir just until moistened. Stir in semi-sweet chocolate morsels and ½ cup nuts. Pour into prepared pan.

Topping: Combine 1 tablespoon nuts and 1 teaspoon sugar. Sprinkle topping over batter.

Bake 55 to 60 minutes until skewer inserted into center comes out clean. Cool 5 minutes; remove from pan. Cool completely. To store, wrap in plastic wrap.

Makes 1 loaf

Banana Bran Loaf

1 cup mashed ripe bananas
    (about 2 large)
½ cup granulated sugar
⅓ cup liquid vegetable oil margarine
2 egg whites, slightly beaten
⅓ cup skim milk
1¼ cups all-purpose flour
1 cup QUAKER® OAT BRAN™ Hot
    Cereal, uncooked
2 teaspoons baking powder
½ teaspoon baking soda

Heat oven to 350°F. Lightly spray 8×4-inch or 9×5-inch loaf pan with no-stick cooking spray or oil lightly.

Combine bananas, sugar, margarine, egg whites and milk; mix well. Add combined flour, oat bran, baking powder and baking soda, mixing just until moistened. Pour into prepared pan.

Bake 55 to 60 minutes or until wooden pick inserted in center comes out clean. Cool 10 minutes in pan; remove to wire rack. Cool completely.

Makes 16 servings

Banana Bran Loaf

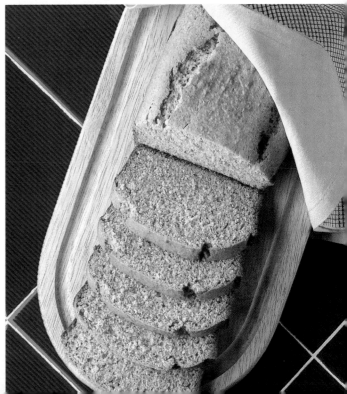

Oat Raisin Bread

1½ cups all-purpose flour
1 cup whole wheat flour
1 cup uncooked quick or old-fashioned oats
2 teaspoons baking soda
½ teaspoon salt
2 eggs
1½ cups buttermilk
½ cup KARO® Light or Dark Corn Syrup
½ cup packed brown sugar
¼ cup MAZOLA® Corn Oil
1 cup raisins

Preheat oven to 350°F. Grease and flour 2 (9×5×3-inch) loaf pans.

In large bowl combine flours, oats, baking soda and salt. In small bowl combine eggs, buttermilk, corn syrup, brown sugar and corn oil until blended. Stir into flour mixture just until moistened. Stir in raisins. Pour batter into prepared pans.

Bake 45 to 50 minutes or until toothpick inserted into center comes out clean. Cool in pans 10 minutes. Remove from pans; cool on wire rack.

Makes 2 loaves, 12 servings each

Orange Pecan Loaves

Loaves
1 package DUNCAN HINES® Moist Deluxe White Cake Mix
3 eggs
1¼ cups orange juice
⅓ cup CRISCO® Oil or CRISCO® PURITAN® Oil
½ cup finely chopped pecans

Glaze
½ cup confectioners sugar
1 tablespoon orange juice
Pecan halves, for garnish
Orange slices, for garnish

1. Preheat oven to 350°F. Grease and flour two 8½×4½×2½-inch loaf pans.

2. **For loaves,** combine cake mix, eggs, 1¼ cups orange juice and oil in large bowl. Beat at medium speed with electric mixer for 2 minutes. Stir in chopped pecans. Pour into pans. Bake at 350°F for 40 to 45 minutes or until toothpick inserted in center comes out clean. Cool in pans 15 minutes. Loosen loaves from pans. Invert onto cooling racks. Turn right-side up. Cool completely.

3. **For glaze,** combine confectioners sugar and 1 tablespoon orange juice in small bowl. Stir until smooth. Drizzle over cooled loaves. Garnish with pecan halves and orange slices.

Makes 2 loaves (24 slices)

Tip: Freeze one loaf to be served at a later time. Wrap loaf tightly in plastic wrap. Frozen loaf will keep up to 6 weeks.

Chocolate-Peanut Butter Bread

1 teaspoon baking soda
1 cup buttermilk
2 cups all-purpose flour
1 (4⅛-ounce) package ROYAL® Instant Dark 'n' Sweet Chocolate Pudding & Pie Filling*
⅓ cup firmly packed brown sugar
2 teaspoons DAVIS® Baking Powder
1 teaspoon salt
1 cup chunky peanut butter
2 eggs
2 tablespoons semi-sweet mini chocolate chips

In medium bowl, dissolve baking soda in buttermilk, stirring well; set aside.

*Royal® Instant Chocolate Pudding & Pie Filling may be substituted.

In large bowl, combine flour, pudding mix, brown sugar, baking powder and salt; set aside.

In medium bowl, with electric mixer at low speed, beat peanut butter, eggs and buttermilk mixture until smooth. Add to dry ingredients with chocolate chips, stirring just until moistened. (Batter will be very stiff.) Spoon batter into greased 9×5×3-inch loaf pan.

Bake at 350°F for 60 minutes or until toothpick inserted in center comes out clean. Let stand in pan 10 minutes. Remove from pan; cool on wire rack.

Makes 1 loaf

Caramel Pecan Spice Cakes

Cake

    1 **package DUNCAN HINES® Moist Deluxe Spice Cake Mix**
    1 **package (4-serving size) vanilla instant pudding and pie filling mix**
    4 **eggs**
    1 **cup water**
    ⅓ **cup CRISCO® Oil or CRISCO® PURITAN® Oil**
    1½ **cups pecan pieces, toasted and finely chopped (see Tip)**

Caramel Glaze

    3 **tablespoons butter or margarine**
    3 **tablespoons granulated sugar**
    3 **tablespoons brown sugar**
    3 **tablespoons whipping cream**
    ½ **cup confectioners sugar**
    ¼ **teaspoon vanilla extract**
    Pecan halves, for garnish
    Maraschino cherry halves, for garnish

Caramel Pecan Spice Cakes

1. Preheat oven to 350°F. Grease and flour two 8½×4½×2½-inch loaf pans.

2. **For cake,** combine cake mix, pudding mix, eggs, water and oil in large bowl. Beat at medium speed with electric mixer for 2 minutes. Stir in toasted pecans. Pour into pans. Bake at 350°F for 55 to 60 minutes or until toothpick inserted in center comes out clean. Cool in pans 15 minutes. Loosen loaves from pans. Invert onto cooling racks. Turn right-side up. Cool completely.

3. **For caramel glaze,** combine butter, granulated sugar, brown sugar and whipping cream in small heavy saucepan. Bring to a boil on medium heat; boil 1 minute. Remove from heat; cool 20 minutes. Add confectioners sugar and vanilla extract; blend with wooden spoon until smooth and thick. Spread evenly on cooled loaves. Garnish with pecan halves and maraschino cherry halves before glaze sets.

Makes 2 loaves (24 slices)

Tip: To toast pecans, spread pecan pieces evenly on baking sheet. Toast in 350°F oven for 8 minutes or until fragrant. Cool completely.

Orange Cinnamon Swirl Bread

Bread

1 package DUNCAN HINES® Bakery
    Style Cinnamon Swirl Muffin Mix
1 egg
⅔ cup orange juice
1 tablespoon grated orange peel

Orange Glaze

½ cup confectioners sugar
2 to 3 teaspoons orange juice
1 teaspoon grated orange peel
    Quartered orange slices, for garnish
    (optional)

1. Preheat oven to 350°F. Grease and flour
8½×4½×2½-inch loaf pan.

2. **For bread,** combine muffin mix and
contents of topping packet from Mix in
large bowl. Break up any lumps. Add
egg, ⅔ cup orange juice and 1 tablespoon
orange peel. Stir until moistened, about
50 strokes. Knead swirl packet from Mix
for 10 seconds before opening. Squeeze
contents on top of batter. Swirl into batter
with knife or spatula, folding from
bottom of bowl to get an even swirl. (Do
not completely mix into batter.) Pour into
pan. Bake at 350°F for 55 to 60 minutes or
until toothpick inserted in center comes
out clean. Cool in pan 10 minutes. Loosen
loaf from pan. Invert onto cooling rack.
Turn right-side up. Cool completely.

3. **For orange glaze,** place confectioners
sugar in small bowl. Add orange juice, 1
teaspoon at a time, stirring until smooth
and desired consistency. Stir in 1
teaspoon orange peel. Drizzle over loaf.
Garnish with orange slices, if desired.

Makes 1 loaf (12 slices)

Tip: If glaze becomes too thin, add more
confectioners sugar. If glaze is too thick,
add more orange juice.

Orange Cinnamon Swirl Bread

Cocoa Banana-Nut Bread

2 extra-ripe, medium DOLE® Bananas,
    peeled
1½ cups all-purpose flour
1⅓ cups sugar
6 tablespoons unsweetened cocoa
1 teaspoon baking soda
½ teaspoon salt
¼ teaspoon baking powder
2 eggs
½ cup vegetable oil
⅓ cup DOLE® Chopped Almonds

Preheat oven to 350°F. Grease 9×5-inch
loaf pan.

Purée bananas in blender (1 cup).
Combine flour, sugar, cocoa, baking soda,
salt and baking powder in large bowl.
Add eggs, oil and puréed bananas; beat
just until well blended. Stir in almonds.
Pour into prepared pan.

Bake 55 to 60 minutes or until wooden
pick inserted in center comes out clean.
Cool in pan on wire rack 10 minutes.
Remove from pan. Cool completely on
wire rack. Loaf may be stored in
refrigerator, well wrapped, for 1 week.

Makes 1 loaf (16 servings)

For Muffins: Prepare batter as directed,
omitting almonds. Spoon scant ½ cup
batter into 10 greased 2½-inch muffin
cups. Bake in 350°F oven 20 to 22 minutes
or until wooden pick inserted in center
comes out clean. Cool in pan on wire rack
3 minutes. Sprinkle with powdered sugar,
if desired. Serve warm.

Makes 10 muffins

Quick Banana-Bran Bread

MAZOLA® No Stick cooking spray
1 package (7 ounces) bran muffin mix
⅓ cup chopped nuts
¼ cup flour
¼ teaspoon cinnamon
1 egg, lightly beaten
1 ripe banana, mashed (about ⅓ cup)
⅓ cup HELLMANN'S® or BEST
    FOODS® Real Mayonnaise or
    Light Reduced Calorie
    Mayonnaise Dressing
⅓ cup water

Preheat oven to 350°F. Spray
8½×4½×2½-inch loaf pan with
cooking spray.

In medium bowl combine muffin mix,
nuts, flour and cinnamon. In small bowl
combine egg, banana, mayonnaise and
water. Add to flour mixture, stirring just
until moistened. Pour into prepared pan.

Bake 35 to 40 minutes or until toothpick
inserted into center comes out clean. Cool
in pan on wire rack 10 minutes. Remove
from pan; cool completely on rack.

Makes 1 loaf

Peanut Butter Bread

2 cups flour
½ cup sugar
2 teaspoons baking powder
½ teaspoon baking soda
½ teaspoon salt
1 cup SKIPPY® SUPER CHUNK® or
    Creamy Peanut Butter
½ cup KARO® Light or Dark Corn
    Syrup
2 eggs
1 cup milk

Preheat oven to 350°F. Grease and flour
9×5×3-inch loaf pan.

In medium bowl combine flour, sugar,
baking powder, baking soda and salt. In
large bowl with mixer at medium speed,
beat peanut butter and corn syrup until
smooth. Beat in eggs 1 at a time.
Gradually beat in milk. Stir in flour
mixture just until moistened. Pour into
prepared pan.

Bake 50 to 55 minutes or until toothpick
inserted into center comes out clean. Cool
in pan 10 minutes. Remove from pan;
cool on wire rack.

Makes 1 loaf or 12 servings

Poppy Seed Quick Bread

1 can SOLO® *or* 1 jar BAKER® Poppy
    Filling
4 eggs
1 cup vegetable oil
1 can (12 ounces) evaporated milk
1½ cups sugar
1 teaspoon vanilla extract
4 cups all-purpose flour
5 teaspoons baking powder
½ teaspoon salt

Preheat oven to 350°F. Grease two 9×5-
inch loaf pans; set aside.

Beat poppy filling, eggs, oil, evaporated
milk, sugar and vanilla in large bowl with
electric mixer at low speed until well
blended. Combine flour, baking powder
and salt in medium bowl; add gradually
to poppy mixture, beating at medium
speed until blended. Beat 2 minutes. Pour
into prepared pans.

Bake 55 to 65 minutes or until wooden
pick inserted in center comes out clean.
Cool in pans on wire racks 10 minutes.
Remove from pans; cool completely on
racks. *Makes 2 loaves*

Golden Apple Boston Bread

⅓ cup honey
⅓ cup molasses
¼ cup butter (½ stick), softened
1 cup whole wheat flour
1 cup rye flour
1 cup yellow cornmeal
2 teaspoons baking soda
½ teaspoon salt
2 cups buttermilk
2 cups coarsely chopped Golden
   Delicious Apples

Preheat oven to 350°F. Grease two 8½×4½-inch loaf pans.

Beat honey, molasses and butter in large bowl with electric mixer until fluffy. Combine flours, cornmeal, baking soda and salt in medium bowl. Add dry ingredients to honey mixture alternately with buttermilk, stirring just until moistened. Stir in apples. Divide batter into prepared pans.

Bake 1 hour or until wooden pick inserted in center comes out clean. Cool breads in pans on wire rack 10 minutes. Serve warm. *Makes 2 loaves*

Favorite recipe from **Washington Apple Commission**

Golden Apple Boston Bread

Bran Cherry Bread

Bran Cherry Bread

2 cups all-purpose flour
¾ cup sugar, divided
1 tablespoon baking powder
1 teaspoon salt
½ teaspoon ground nutmeg
1½ cups KELLOGG'S® CRACKLIN'
   OAT BRAN® cereal
1¼ cups skim milk
1 egg
2 tablespoons vegetable oil
1 jar (10 ounces) maraschino cherries,
   drained and finely chopped
1 cup chopped walnuts, divided
1 tablespoon margarine

Combine flour, ½ cup sugar, baking
powder, salt and nutmeg. Set aside. In
large mixing bowl, combine Kellogg's®
Cracklin' Oat Bran® cereal and milk. Let
stand 10 minutes or until cereal is
softened. Add egg and oil. Beat well. Stir
in flour mixture. Set aside 2 tablespoons
chopped cherries. Fold remaining
cherries and ¾ cup nuts into batter.

Spread in 9×5×3-inch loaf pan coated
with nonstick cooking spray.

Melt margarine in small skillet until
bubbly. Remove from heat. Stir in
remaining ¼ cup sugar, ¼ cup nuts and
cherries. Sprinkle over batter.

Bake in 350°F oven about 1 hour. Cool in
pan on wire rack 10 minutes. Remove
from pan.   *Makes 1 loaf (15 slices)*

Sunday Morn Cranberry-Orange Bread

2 cups flour
1 cup fresh or frozen cranberries,
   coarsely chopped
¾ cup sugar
½ cup coarsely chopped walnuts
2 teaspoons baking powder
¼ teaspoon salt
1 egg, lightly beaten
1 teaspoon grated orange peel
½ cup orange juice
⅓ cup HELLMANN'S® or BEST
   FOODS® Real Mayonnaise or
   Light Reduced Calorie
   Mayonnaise Dressing

Preheat oven to 350°F. Grease and flour 2
(7½×3¾×2¼-inch) loaf pans.

In large bowl combine flour, cranberries,
sugar, walnuts, baking powder and salt.
In small bowl beat egg, orange peel,
orange juice and mayonnaise until
smooth; stir into flour mixture just until
moistened. Spoon into prepared pans.

Bake 60 to 70 minutes or until toothpick
inserted into center comes out clean. Cool
in pans on wire racks 10 minutes.
Remove from pans; cool completely on
racks.   *Makes 2 loaves*

Almond Loaf

1 can SOLO® Almond Paste
¾ cup butter or margarine, softened
¾ cup sugar
3 eggs
2 cups all-purpose flour
2 teaspoons baking powder
¼ cup milk
½ cup chopped almonds, raisins or candied cherries
⅓ cup SOLO® Toasted Almond Crunch Topping

Preheat oven to 350°F. Grease 9×5-inch loaf pan.

Break almond paste into small pieces and place in medium bowl. Add butter; beat with electric mixer until mixture is creamy and smooth. Add sugar and eggs; beat until thoroughly blended. Combine flour and baking powder in small bowl. Add to almond mixture alternately with milk, beating until blended. Fold in chopped almonds. Pour into prepared pan; sprinkle toasted almond crunch topping over batter.

Bake 60 to 70 minutes or until wooden pick inserted in center comes out clean. Cool in pan on wire rack 10 minutes. Remove from pan; cool completely on rack.   *Makes 1 loaf*

Food Processor Method: Break almond paste into small pieces and place in container of food processor. Add butter; process until mixture is creamy and smooth. Add sugar and eggs; process until thoroughly blended. Transfer mixture to medium bowl; continue as directed above.

Fig Chocolate Oatmeal Bread

3 cups all-purpose flour
One 12-oz. pkg. (2 cups) NESTLÉ® Toll House® Semi-Sweet Chocolate Morsels
2 cups quick oats, uncooked
2 tablespoons baking powder
1 teaspoon baking soda
1 teaspoon salt
2 teaspoons cinnamon
½ teaspoon nutmeg
1 cup chopped figs, dates or raisins
One 16-oz. jar (1¾ cups) applesauce
1 cup firmly packed brown sugar
⅔ cup vegetable oil
4 eggs

Preheat oven to 350°F. Grease two 9×5×3-inch loaf pans.*

In large bowl, combine flour, semi-sweet chocolate morsels, oats, baking powder, baking soda, salt, cinnamon and nutmeg. Add figs and stir to coat; set aside. In large bowl, blend applesauce, brown sugar, oil and eggs until smooth. Stir in flour mixture just until moistened. Pour into prepared pans.

Bake 1 hour or until skewer inserted into center comes out clean. Cool 10 to 15 minutes; remove from pans. Cool completely.   *Makes 2 loaves*

*To make gift-size loaves, pour batter into three greased 7½×3½-inch loaf pans. Bake 45 to 55 minutes.

Blueberry Oat Bread

2 cups flour
1 cup uncooked quick or old-fashioned oats
1 tablespoon baking powder
1 teaspoon salt
½ teaspoon baking soda
½ teaspoon cinnamon
2 eggs
1 cup milk
½ cup sugar
⅓ cup KARO® Light Corn Syrup
¼ cup MAZOLA® Corn Oil
1½ cups fresh or frozen blueberries*

Preheat oven to 350°F. Grease and flour 9×5×3-inch loaf pan.

In large bowl combine flour, oats, baking powder, salt, baking soda and cinnamon. In small bowl combine eggs, milk, sugar, corn syrup and corn oil until blended; set aside. Toss blueberries in flour mixture. Stir in egg mixture until well blended. Pour batter into prepared pan.

Bake 60 to 70 minutes or until toothpick inserted into center comes out clean. Cool in pan 10 minutes. Remove from pan; cool on wire rack.

Makes 1 loaf or 12 servings

*If using frozen blueberries, do not thaw before adding to flour mixture.

Piña Colada Bread

2½ cups flour
½ cup sugar
2 teaspoons baking powder
½ teaspoon baking soda
½ teaspoon salt
2 eggs
½ cup KARO® Light Corn Syrup
⅓ cup MAZOLA® Corn Oil
¼ cup rum
1 can (8 ounces) crushed pineapple in unsweetened juice, undrained
1 cup flaked coconut

Preheat oven to 350°F. Grease and flour 9×5×3-inch loaf pan.

In medium bowl combine flour, sugar, baking powder, baking soda and salt. In large bowl with mixer at medium speed, beat eggs, corn syrup, corn oil and rum until blended. Gradually stir in flour mixture just until moistened. Stir in pineapple and coconut. Pour into prepared pan.

Bake 60 to 65 minutes or until toothpick inserted into center comes out clean. Cool in pan 10 minutes. Remove from pan; cool on wire rack.

Makes 1 loaf or 12 servings

Top to bottom: Blueberry Oat Bread, Peanut Butter Bread (page 192) and Piña Colada Bread

Banana Macadamia Nut Bread

  2 cups all-purpose flour
¾ cup sugar
½ cup LAND O LAKES® Butter,
     softened
  2 eggs
  1 teaspoon baking soda
½ teaspoon salt
  1 tablespoon grated orange peel
  1 teaspoon vanilla
  1 cup mashed ripe bananas (2 medium)
¼ cup orange juice
  1 cup flaked coconut
  1 jar (3½ ounces) coarsely chopped
     macadamia nuts *or* walnuts
     (¾ cup)

Heat oven to 350°F.

In large mixer bowl combine flour, sugar, butter, eggs, baking soda, salt, orange peel and vanilla. Beat at low speed, scraping bowl often, until well mixed, 2 to 3 minutes. Add bananas and orange juice. Continue beating, scraping bowl often, until well mixed, 1 minute. By hand, stir in coconut and nuts. (Batter will be thick.) Spread into 1 greased 9×5-inch loaf pan or 3 greased 5½×3-inch mini-loaf pans.

Banana Macadamia Nut Bread

Bake 9×5-inch loaf for 60 to 65 minutes or mini loaves for 35 to 45 minutes, or until wooden pick inserted in center comes out clean. Cool 10 minutes; remove from pans.
     Makes 1 (9×5-inch) loaf or 3 mini loaves

Apple Raisin Loaf

  2 eggs
  3 tablespoons vegetable oil
⅔ cup sugar
  1 can SOLO® *or* 1 jar BAKER® Apple
     Filling
¾ cup lemon-flavored or plain yogurt
  2 cups all-purpose flour
  2 teaspoons baking powder
  1 teaspoon baking soda
  1 teaspoon ground cinnamon
  1 teaspoon ground nutmeg
½ teaspoon salt
¼ teaspoon ground cloves
½ cup raisins

Preheat oven to 350°F. Grease 9×5-inch loaf pan; set aside.

Beat eggs, oil and sugar in large bowl with electric mixer until blended. Stir in apple filling and yogurt. Combine flour, baking powder, baking soda, cinnamon, nutmeg, salt and cloves in medium bowl until mixed. Add to apple mixture and stir until blended. Fold in raisins; pour into prepared pan.

Bake 65 to 70 minutes or until wooden pick inserted in center comes out clean. Cool in pan on wire rack 10 minutes. Remove from pan; cool completely on rack.   *Makes 1 loaf*

Blueberry Tea Bread

1 package DUNCAN HINES® Bakery
   Style Blueberry Muffin Mix
1 egg
⅔ cup water
1 tablespoon grated lemon peel
   Orange Cream Cheese
   (recipe follows)
   Lemon Cream Cheese
   (recipe follows)

1. Preheat oven to 350°F. Grease and flour
8½ × 4½ × 2½-inch loaf pan.

2. Rinse blueberries from Mix with cold
water and drain.

3. Combine muffin mix and contents of
topping packet from Mix in medium
bowl. Break up any lumps. Add egg and
water. Stir until moistened, about 50
strokes. Fold blueberries and lemon peel
gently into batter. Pour into pan. Bake at
350°F for about 1 hour or until toothpick
inserted in center comes out clean. Cool
in pan 10 minutes. Invert onto cooling
rack. Turn right-side up. Cool completely.

4. To serve, cut bread into thin slices. Cut
each slice in half or into fancy shapes, if
desired. Spread with Orange Cream
Cheese or Lemon Cream Cheese.

Makes 1 loaf (18 slices)

Orange Cream Cheese

1 package (8 ounces) cream cheese,
   softened
3 tablespoons grated orange peel
¼ teaspoon paprika
   Orange peel strips, for garnish

Combine cream cheese, grated orange
peel and paprika in small bowl. Stir with
wooden spoon until thoroughly blended.
Spread on bread slices. Garnish with
strips of orange peel.

Makes 1 cup spread

Blueberry Tea Bread

Lemon Cream Cheese

1 package (8 ounces) cream cheese,
   softened
2 tablespoons milk
2 tablespoons grated lemon peel
1 tablespoon confectioners sugar
   Lemon peel strips, for garnish

Combine cream cheese, milk, grated
lemon peel and confectioners sugar in
small bowl. Stir with wooden spoon until
thoroughly blended. Spread on bread
slices. Garnish with strips of lemon peel.

Makes 1 cup spread

Tip: To make long strips of lemon and
orange peel use a citrus zester. This
handy gadget is available at kitchen
specialty shops.

Apple Bran Loaf

1½ cups all-purpose flour
 ½ cup sugar
 1 teaspoon DAVIS® Baking Powder
 1 teaspoon baking soda
 1 teaspoon ground cinnamon
1½ cups NABISCO® 100% Bran™
 1 cup seedless raisins
 ¼ cup FLEISCHMANN'S® Margarine, melted
 ⅔ cup hot water
 1 cup MOTT'S® Regular Apple Sauce
 1 egg, slightly beaten
 1 teaspoon vanilla extract

In medium bowl, mix flour, sugar, baking powder, baking soda and cinnamon; set aside.

In separate bowl, mix bran, raisins, margarine and hot water; let stand 5 minutes. Add apple sauce, egg and vanilla. With mixer at medium speed, beat for 2 minutes. Stir in flour mixture just until blended. Spread in greased 9×5×3-inch loaf pan.

Bake at 350°F for 55 minutes or until toothpick inserted in center comes out clean. Cool in pan 10 minutes. Remove from pan; cool on wire rack.

Makes 1 loaf

Apple Bran Loaf

Banana Date Bread

 2 cups flour
1½ teaspoons baking powder
 ¼ teaspoon salt
 2 eggs
 ⅔ cup KARO® Light or Dark Corn Syrup
 ½ cup MAZOLA® Corn Oil
 1 cup mashed ripe bananas (about 2 medium)
 1 cup chopped dates
 1 cup chopped walnuts

Preheat oven to 375°F. Grease and flour 9×5×3-inch loaf pan.

In medium bowl combine flour, baking powder and salt. In large bowl with mixer at medium speed, beat eggs, corn syrup and corn oil until blended. Beat in bananas. Gradually stir in flour mixture just until moistened. Stir in dates and walnuts. Pour into prepared pan.

Bake 60 to 70 minutes or until toothpick inserted into center comes out clean. Cool in pan 10 minutes. Remove from pan; cool on wire rack.

Makes 1 loaf or 12 servings

Cranberry Nut Bread

 2 cups all-purpose flour
 1 cup sugar
1½ teaspoons baking powder
 ½ teaspoon salt
 ½ teaspoon baking soda
 ¼ cup butter or margarine, cold, cut into 4 pieces
 ¾ cup orange juice
 1 egg, beaten
 1 tablespoon grated orange peel
1½ cups fresh cranberries, coarsely chopped
 1 cup pecan or walnut halves, coarsely chopped

Preheat oven to 350°F. Grease 9×5-inch loaf pan.

Combine flour, sugar, baking powder, salt and baking soda in medium bowl. Cut in butter until mixture resembles coarse crumbs. Combine orange juice, egg and orange peel in small bowl; mix well. Add egg mixture to flour mixture; stir just until moistened. (Batter will be lumpy; do not overmix.) Fold in cranberries and pecans. Pour into prepared pan.

Bake 60 to 70 minutes or until wooden pick inserted in center comes out clean. Let cool in pan on wire rack 15 minutes. Loosen edges; remove from pan. Cool completely on wire rack.   *Makes 1 loaf*

Streusel Lemon Bread

½ cup finely chopped nuts
¼ cup firmly packed light brown sugar
½ teaspoon ground nutmeg
 2 cups unsifted flour
 1 teaspoon baking powder
½ teaspoon baking soda
1¼ cups granulated sugar
½ cup margarine or butter, softened
 3 eggs
½ cup REALEMON® Lemon Juice from
      Concentrate
½ cup BORDEN® or MEADOW
      GOLD® Milk

Preheat oven to 350°F.

In small bowl, combine nuts, brown sugar and nutmeg; set aside. Stir together flour, baking powder and baking soda; set aside. In large mixer bowl, beat granulated sugar and margarine until fluffy. Add eggs, 1 at a time; beat well. Gradually beat in ReaLemon® brand. Add milk alternately with flour mixture; stir well. Spoon half of batter into greased and floured 9×5-inch loaf pan. Sprinkle half of nut mixture over batter; top with remaining batter, spreading to pan edge. Top with remaining nut mixture.

Bake 50 to 55 minutes or until wooden pick inserted near center comes out clean. Cool 15 minutes; remove from pan. Cool completely. Store tightly wrapped.
    Makes one 9×5-inch loaf

Pumpkin Bread

1¾ cups all-purpose flour
1½ cups sugar
 1 teaspoon baking soda
 1 teaspoon cinnamon
¼ teaspoon baking powder
¼ teaspoon salt
⅛ teaspoon nutmeg
 1 cup (half of 12-oz. pkg.) NESTLÉ®
      Toll House® Semi-Sweet Chocolate
      Mini Morsels
½ cup raisins, optional
 1 cup LIBBY'S® Canned Solid Pack
      Pumpkin
 2 eggs
½ cup vegetable oil
⅓ cup water

Preheat oven to 350°F. Grease 9×5-inch loaf pan.

In large bowl, combine flour, sugar, baking soda, cinnamon, baking powder, salt and nutmeg; stir in mini morsels and raisins. Set aside. In small bowl, blend pumpkin, eggs, oil and water; stir into flour mixture just until moistened. Pour into prepared pan.

Bake 70 to 75 minutes until skewer inserted into center comes out clean. Cool 10 minutes; remove from pan. Cool completely. To store, wrap in plastic wrap.   *Makes 1 loaf*

Holiday Cranberry Bread

2 cups all-purpose flour
½ cup granulated sugar
1½ teaspoons baking powder
½ teaspoon baking soda
½ teaspoon salt
¾ cup milk
⅓ cup vegetable oil
2 teaspoons white vinegar
1 teaspoon grated orange rind
1 egg
One 6-oz. pkg. (1 cup) NESTLÉ® Toll
    House® Semi-Sweet Chocolate
    Morsels
½ cup walnuts, chopped
2 cups cranberries, chopped
    Confectioners' sugar, optional

Preheat oven to 350°F. Grease 9×5×3-inch loaf pan.

In large bowl, combine flour, granulated sugar, baking powder, baking soda and salt. In small bowl, blend milk, oil, vinegar, orange rind and egg. Stir milk mixture, semi-sweet chocolate morsels and nuts into flour mixture just until flour mixture is moistened and ingredients are evenly mixed. Fold in cranberries. Spoon into prepared pan.

Bake 55 to 60 minutes until skewer inserted into center comes out clean. Cool 10 minutes; remove from pan. Cool completely. Sprinkle confectioners' sugar on top. *Makes 1 loaf*

Carrot Bread

2 cups finely shredded carrots
½ cup granulated sugar
½ cup packed brown sugar
1 teaspoon baking soda
¾ cup vegetable oil
2 eggs, lightly beaten
1½ cups all-purpose flour
½ cup whole wheat flour
2 teaspoons baking powder
½ teaspoon salt
1 teaspoon ground cinnamon
½ teaspoon ground nutmeg
¾ cup chopped walnuts

Preheat oven to 350°F. Grease 9×5-inch loaf pan.

Combine carrots, sugars, baking soda and oil in large bowl; mix well. Add eggs; mix well. Combine flours, baking powder, salt cinnamon and nutmeg in medium bowl until blended; stir into carrot mixture. Stir in walnuts. Pour into prepared pan; let stand 5 minutes.

Bake 50 to 60 minutes or until wooden pick inserted in center comes out clean. Cool on wire rack. Wrap in foil or plastic wrap. Let stand at room temperature overnight before slicing.
Makes 1 loaf (12 slices)

Tip: Most carrots are sold in film bags with the tops removed. When you buy carrots, look to see that the bag contains fresh-looking, smooth and well-shaped carrots of good orange color. If you buy carrots that are not packaged, look for those with fresh green tops and well-shaped, brightly-colored roots.

Top to bottom: Holiday Cranberry Bread and Fig Chocolate Oatmeal Bread (page 195)

Chocolate Raisin Bread

One 12-oz. pkg. (2 cups) NESTLÉ® Toll
House® Semi-Sweet Chocolate
Morsels, divided
6 tablespoons butter
2 cups all-purpose flour
1 teaspoon baking powder
1 teaspoon baking soda
1 teaspoon salt
1 egg
1½ cups milk
½ cup sugar
1 teaspoon vanilla extract
1 cup coarsely chopped nuts
½ cup raisins

Preheat oven to 350°F. Grease 9×5×3-inch loaf pan. Combine in top of double boiler over hot (not boiling) water, 1 cup semi-sweet chocolate morsels and butter. Stir until morsels are melted and mixture is smooth. Set aside.

In small bowl, combine flour, baking powder, baking soda and salt; set aside. In large bowl, combine egg, milk, sugar and vanilla extract; mix well. Add melted morsels; mix until well blended. Gradually stir in flour mixture until dry ingredients are just moistened. Stir in remaining 1 cup semi-sweet chocolate morsels, nuts and raisins. Pour into prepared pan.

Bake 65 to 70 minutes until skewer inserted into center comes out clean. Cool 10 minutes; remove from pan. Cool completely on wire rack. *Makes 1 loaf*

Cinnamon Nut Tea Bread

1 package DUNCAN HINES® Bakery
Style Cinnamon Swirl Muffin Mix
¾ cup toasted pecans, finely chopped
(see Tip)
2 tablespoons all-purpose flour
½ teaspoon baking powder
1 egg
⅔ cup water
Cranberry-Orange Cream Cheese
(recipe follows)
Honey Butter (recipe follows)

1. Preheat oven to 350°F. Grease and flour 8½×4½×2½-inch loaf pan.

2. Combine muffin mix, contents of topping packet from Mix, chopped pecans, flour and baking powder in medium bowl. Stir until blended. Knead swirl packet from Mix for 10 seconds. Squeeze contents onto dry ingredients. Add egg and water. Stir until thoroughly blended, about 50 strokes. Pour into pan. Bake at 350°F for 65 to 70 minutes or until toothpick inserted in center comes out clean. Cool in pan 10 minutes. Invert onto cooling rack. Turn right-side up. Cool completely.

3. To serve, cut bread into thin slices. Cut each slice in half or into fancy shapes, if desired. Spread with Cranberry-Orange Cream Cheese or Honey Butter.
Makes 1 loaf (18 slices)

Cranberry-Orange Cream Cheese

1 package (8 ounces) cream cheese,
softened
1 container (12 ounces) cranberry-orange sauce, divided
2 to 3 drops red food coloring

Combine cream cheese and ¼ cup cranberry-orange sauce in small bowl.

Stir with wooden spoon until thoroughly blended. Stir in red food coloring. Spread on bread slices. Garnish with remaining cranberry-orange sauce.

Makes 1 cup spread

Honey Butter

½ cup butter, softened
¼ cup honey
   Pecan halves, for garnish

Combine butter and honey in small bowl. Stir with wooden spoon until thoroughly blended. Spread on bread slices. Garnish with pecan halves.   *Makes ¾ cup spread*

Tip: To toast pecans, spread in a single layer on baking sheet. Toast in 350°F oven for 5 to 7 minutes or until fragrant. Cool completely.

Caramel Banana Nut Loaves

Cake
1 package DUNCAN HINES® Moist Deluxe Banana Supreme Cake Mix
1 package (4-serving size) banana cream instant pudding and pie filling mix
4 eggs
1 cup mashed bananas (about 2 medium-size ripe bananas)
½ cup water
½ cup CRISCO® Oil or CRISCO® PURITAN® Oil
1 cup toasted chopped walnuts

Caramel Frosting
¼ cup butter or margarine
2 tablespoons dark brown sugar
1 teaspoon water
1 container (16 ounces) DUNCAN HINES® Vanilla Layer Cake Frosting
   Walnut halves, for garnish

Caramel Banana Nut Loaves

1. Preheat oven to 350°F. Grease and flour two 9×5×3-inch loaf pans.

2. **For cake,** combine cake mix, pudding mix, eggs, mashed bananas, ½ cup water and oil in large bowl. Beat at medium speed with electric mixer for 2 minutes. Stir in chopped walnuts. Pour into pans. Bake at 350°F for 50 to 55 minutes or until toothpick inserted in center comes out clean. Cool in pans 15 minutes. Loosen loaves from pans. Invert onto cooling racks. Turn right-side up. Cool completely.

3. **For caramel frosting,** place butter, brown sugar and 1 teaspoon water in small saucepan. Bring to a boil on medium heat; boil 1 minute, stirring constantly. Place Vanilla frosting in medium bowl. Stir in caramel mixture until thoroughly blended. Frost sides and tops of loaves. Garnish with walnut halves.   *Makes 2 loaves (24 slices)*

Tip: To toast walnuts, spread chopped walnuts evenly on baking sheet. Toast in 350°F oven for 6 to 8 minutes or until fragrant. Cool completely.

Blueberry Orange Loaf

Blueberry Orange Loaf

1 package DUNCAN HINES® Bakery
    Style Blueberry Muffin Mix
½ teaspoon baking powder
2 egg whites
⅔ cup orange juice
1 teaspoon grated orange peel

1. Preheat oven to 350°F. Grease
8½×4½×2½-inch or 9×5×3-inch
loaf pan.

2. Rinse blueberries from Mix with cold
water and drain.

3. Empty muffin mix into bowl. Add
baking powder; stir to combine. Break up
any lumps. Add egg whites and orange
juice. Stir until moistened, about 50
strokes. Fold in blueberries and orange
peel. Pour into pan. Sprinkle contents of
topping packet from Mix over batter.
Bake at 350°F for 45 to 55 minutes or until
toothpick inserted in center comes out
clean. Cool in pan 10 minutes. Loosen
loaf from pan. Invert onto cooling rack.
Turn right-side up. Cool completely.

Makes 1 loaf (12 slices)

Tip: Freeze extra grated orange peel for
future use.

Almond & Poppy Seed Loaf

¾ cup all-purpose flour
¾ cup whole wheat flour
2 teaspoons poppy seed
1½ teaspoons baking powder
½ teaspoon baking soda
½ teaspoon salt
¾ cup milk
⅓ cup honey
2 eggs
¼ cup vegetable oil
1 cup shreds of wheat bran cereal
1 teaspoon vanilla extract
¼ teaspoon almond extract
½ cup toasted diced almonds

Preheat oven to 350°F. Grease
8½×4½×2½-inch loaf pan.

Combine flours, poppy seed, baking
powder, baking soda and salt in large
bowl. Beat milk, honey, eggs, oil, cereal,
vanilla and almond extract in medium
bowl until well mixed. Let stand 2
minutes or until cereal is softened. Stir in
almonds. Add liquid mixture to flour
mixture; stir just until moistened. (Batter
will be lumpy; do not overmix.) Pour into
prepared pan.

Bake 45 to 55 minutes or until wooden
pick inserted in center comes out clean.
(If loaf browns too quickly, cover loosely
with aluminum foil during baking.) Let
cool in pan on wire rack 10 minutes.
Loosen edges; remove from pan. Cool
completely on wire rack. *Makes 1 loaf*

*Favorite recipe from **Almond Board of California***

Lemony Banana-Walnut Bread

⅔ cup shortening
1 cup granulated sugar
2 eggs
1½ cups mashed ripe bananas
    (about 3 medium bananas)
7 tablespoons fresh lemon juice,
    divided (about 3 lemons)
2 cups all-purpose flour
1 teaspoon baking soda
½ teaspoon salt
½ cup chopped walnuts
1 tablespoon grated lemon peel
½ cup powdered sugar

Preheat oven to 325°F. Grease two
8½×4½-inch loaf pans.

Beat shortening and granulated sugar in
large bowl with electric mixer at medium
speed until well blended. Add eggs, one
at a time, mixing well after each addition.
Blend in bananas and 6 tablespoons
lemon juice. Combine flour, baking soda
and salt in small bowl; add to banana
mixture, mixing until blended. Stir in
walnuts and lemon peel. Pour evenly into
prepared pans.

Lemony Banana-Walnut Bread

Bake 50 to 60 minutes or until wooden
pick inserted in center comes out clean.
Remove from pans; cool completely on
wire racks. Combine powdered sugar
and remaining 1 tablespoon lemon juice
in small bowl; stir until smooth. Drizzle
over loaves. *Makes 2 loaves*

Tip: If you buy bananas tinged with
green, let them ripen at room
temperature. You can keep fully ripe
bananas in the refrigerator for a few
days—the skin will darken but the
banana inside will taste great.

Apple-Chocolate Quick Bread

3 cups all-purpose flour
One 12-oz. pkg. (2 cups) NESTLÉ® Toll
    House® Semi-Sweet Chocolate
    Morsels
1½ cups sugar
4½ teaspoons baking powder
1 teaspoon cinnamon
½ teaspoon salt
4 eggs
⅔ cup vegetable oil
2 tablespoons milk
3 cups chopped apples

Preheat oven to 350°F. Grease two
8½×4½×2½-inch loaf pans.

In large bowl, combine flour, semi-sweet
chocolate morsels, sugar, baking powder,
cinnamon and salt. In medium bowl,
blend eggs, oil and milk. Stir into flour
mixture just until dry ingredients are
moistened. Fold in apples. Spoon into
prepared pans.

Bake 60 to 70 minutes until skewer
inserted into center comes out clean. Cool
10 minutes; remove from pans. Cool
completely. *Makes 2 loaves*

Brandied Fruit Loaf

2 cups raisins
1 cup currants
½ cup chopped pitted dates
¼ cup chopped mixed candied citrus
    peel
1 cup packed brown sugar
¾ cup strong tea, cooled
¼ cup brandy
3 tablespoons butter or margarine,
    melted, cooled
1 egg, slightly beaten
2 cups all-purpose flour
1 teaspoon baking powder
½ teaspoon salt
½ teaspoon ground nutmeg
½ teaspoon ground cinnamon
½ cup chopped walnuts

Preheat oven to 325°F. Grease 9×5×3-inch loaf pan; line with waxed paper and grease again. Combine raisins, currants, dates, citrus peel, brown sugar, tea and brandy in large glass bowl; stir until sugar dissolves. Cover; let stand 8 hours or overnight at room temperature.

Stir butter and egg into fruit mixture. Combine flour, baking powder, salt, nutmeg and cinnamon in small bowl; stir in walnuts. Add flour mixture to fruit mixture, stirring just until blended. Pour into prepared pan.

Bake 1½ hours or until wooden pick inserted in center comes out clean. Let cool in pan on wire rack 15 minutes. Loosen edges; remove from pan. Peel off waxed paper. Cool completely on wire rack. *Makes 1 loaf*

Chocolate Chunk Banana Bread

2 eggs, lightly beaten
1 cup mashed ripe bananas
    (about 3 medium bananas)
⅓ cup vegetable oil
¼ cup milk
2 cups all-purpose flour
1 cup sugar
2 teaspoons CALUMET® Baking
    Powder
¼ teaspoon salt
1 package (4 ounces) BAKER'S®
    GERMAN'S® Sweet Chocolate,
    coarsely chopped
½ cup chopped nuts

HEAT oven to 350°F.

STIR eggs, bananas, oil and milk until well blended. Add flour, sugar, baking powder and salt; stir until just moistened. Stir in chocolate and nuts. Pour into greased 9×5-inch loaf pan.

BAKE for 55 minutes or until toothpick inserted in center comes out clean. Cool in pan 10 minutes. Remove from pan to cool on wire rack. *Makes 1 loaf*

Prep time: 20 minutes
Baking time: 55 minutes

Left to right: Chocolate Chunk Banana Bread and Chocolate Chunk Sour Cream Muffins (page 140)

Glazed Triple Chocolate Bread

Glazed Triple Chocolate Bread

Bread

⅔ cup firmly packed brown sugar
½ cup LAND O LAKES® Butter, softened
1 cup semi-sweet miniature real chocolate chips, melted
2 eggs
2½ cups all-purpose flour
1½ cups applesauce
1 teaspoon baking powder
1 teaspoon baking soda
2 teaspoons vanilla
½ cup semi-sweet miniature real chocolate chips

Glaze

½ cup semi-sweet miniature real chocolate chips
1 tablespoon LAND O LAKES® Butter
5 teaspoons water
½ cup powdered sugar
¼ teaspoon vanilla
Dash salt

Heat oven to 350°F.

For bread, in large mixer bowl combine brown sugar and ½ cup butter. Beat at medium speed, scraping bowl often, until creamy, 1 to 2 minutes. Add 1 cup melted chocolate chips and eggs; continue beating until well mixed, 1 to 2 minutes. Add flour, applesauce, baking powder, baking soda and 2 teaspoons vanilla. Reduce speed to low; continue beating, scraping bowl often, until creamy, 1 to 2 minutes. By hand, stir in ½ cup chocolate chips. Spoon batter into 5 greased 5½×3-inch mini-loaf pans.

Bake for 35 to 42 minutes or until top is dry when touched. Cool 10 minutes. Remove from pans. (Bread can be frozen unglazed. Remove from freezer; bring to room temperature before glazing.)

For glaze, in 2-quart saucepan combine ½ cup chocolate chips, 1 tablespoon butter and water. Cook over low heat, stirring constantly, until melted and smooth. Remove from heat. Stir in powdered sugar, ¼ teaspoon vanilla and salt until smooth and creamy. Drizzle *each* warm loaf with glaze. Cool completely.
Makes 5 mini loaves

Lemon Cranberry Loaves

1¼ cups finely chopped fresh
    cranberries
½ cup finely chopped walnuts
¼ cup granulated sugar
1 package DUNCAN HINES® Moist
    Deluxe Lemon Supreme Cake Mix
1 package (3 ounces) cream cheese,
    softened
¾ cup milk
4 eggs
    Confectioners sugar

1. Preheat oven to 350°F. Grease and flour two 8½×4½×2½-inch loaf pans.

2. Stir together cranberries, walnuts and granulated sugar in large bowl; set aside.

3. Combine cake mix, cream cheese and milk in large bowl. Beat at medium speed with electric mixer for 2 minutes. Add eggs, one at a time, beating well after each addition. Fold in cranberry mixture. Pour into pans. Bake at 350°F for 45 to 50 minutes or until toothpick inserted in center comes out clean. Cool in pans 15 minutes. Loosen loaves from pans. Invert onto cooling racks. Turn right-side up. Cool completely. Dust with confectioners sugar. *Makes 2 loaves (24 slices)*

Tip: To quickly chop cranberries or walnuts, use a food processor.

Golden Pumpkin Bread

1½ cups all-purpose flour
1 cup firmly packed brown sugar
1 cup cooked mashed pumpkin*
½ cup LAND O LAKES® Butter,
    softened
2 eggs
1½ teaspoons ground cinnamon
1 teaspoon baking powder
1 teaspoon baking soda
1 teaspoon salt
½ teaspoon ground ginger
¼ teaspoon ground cloves

Heat oven to 350°F.

In large mixer bowl combine all ingredients. Beat at medium speed, scraping bowl often, until well mixed, 2 to 3 minutes. Pour into greased 9×5-inch loaf pan or 3 greased 5½×3-inch mini-loaf pans.

Bake for 45 to 55 minutes for 9×5-inch loaf or 30 to 35 minutes for mini loaves, or until wooden pick inserted in center comes out clean. Cool 10 minutes; remove from pan. Cool completely; store refrigerated.
    Makes 1 (9×5-inch) loaf or 3 mini loaves

*You may substitute 1 cup canned pumpkin for 1 cup cooked pumpkin.

Lemon Cranberry Loaf

Banana Nut Bread

**2 extra-ripe, large DOLE® Bananas,
   peeled**
⅓ cup margarine
⅔ cup sugar
2 eggs
2 cups all-purpose flour
2 teaspoons baking powder
½ teaspoon baking soda
½ cup buttermilk
¾ cup chopped nuts

Preheat oven to 350°F. Grease 9×5-inch loaf pan.

Purée bananas in blender (1¼ cups). Beat margarine and sugar in large bowl until light and fluffy. Beat in puréed bananas and eggs. Combine flour, baking powder and baking soda in small bowl; add to banana mixture alternately with buttermilk, blending well after each addition. Stir in nuts. Pour into prepared pan.

Bake 50 to 60 minutes or until wooden pick inserted in center comes out clean. Cool in pan on rack 10 minutes. Turn out onto rack; cool completely.

Makes 1 loaf

Lemon Blueberry Poppy Seed Bread

Bread

**1 package DUNCAN HINES® Bakery
   Style Blueberry Muffin Mix**
2 tablespoons poppy seed
1 egg
¾ cup water
1 tablespoon grated lemon peel

Drizzle

½ cup confectioners sugar
1 tablespoon lemon juice

1. Preheat oven to 350°F. Grease and flour 8½×4½×2½-inch loaf pan.

2. Rinse blueberries from Mix with cold water and drain.

3. **For bread,** combine muffin mix and poppy seed in medium bowl. Break up any lumps. Add egg and water. Stir until moistened, about 50 strokes. Fold in blueberries and lemon peel. Pour into pan. Sprinkle with contents of topping packet from Mix. Bake at 350°F for 1 hour or until toothpick inserted in center comes out clean. Cool in pan 10 minutes. Loosen loaf from pan. Invert onto cooling rack. Turn right-side up. Cool completely.

4. **For drizzle,** combine confectioners sugar and lemon juice in small bowl. Stir until smooth. Drizzle over loaf.

Makes 1 loaf (12 slices)

Tip: To help keep topping intact when removing loaf from pan, place aluminum foil over top.

Lemon Blueberry Poppy Seed Bread

Chocolate Nut Loaves

2¼ cups all-purpose flour
1 teaspoon baking soda
¼ teaspoon salt
1 cup (2 sticks) margarine or butter,
  softened
2 cups sugar
5 eggs
3 squares BAKER'S® Unsweetened
  Chocolate, melted, cooled slightly
1 cup buttermilk or sour milk*
2 teaspoons vanilla
1 cup finely chopped nuts
  Powdered sugar (optional)
  Chopped nuts (optional)

HEAT oven to 350°F.

MIX flour, baking soda and salt; set aside. Beat margarine and sugar in large bowl until light and fluffy. Add eggs, one at a time, beating well after each addition. Stir in chocolate.

ADD flour mixture alternately with buttermilk, beating after each addition until smooth. Mix in vanilla and 1 cup nuts. Pour into 5 greased and floured 5×3-inch loaf pans.

BAKE about 50 minutes or until toothpick inserted into centers comes out clean. Cool in pans 10 minutes. Remove from pans to cool on wire racks. Sprinkle with powdered sugar; garnish with chopped nuts, if desired.

Makes 5 loaves

Prep time: 30 minutes
Baking time: 50 minutes

*To make sour milk, add 1 tablespoon vinegar to 1 cup milk; let stand 5 minutes.

Tip: Loaves may also be baked in 2 (9×5-inch) loaf pans. Bake 1 hour.

Old-Fashioned Apple Loaf

2 cups all-purpose flour
2 teaspoons baking powder
1 teaspoon apple pie spice*
½ teaspoon salt
¼ teaspoon baking soda
⅔ cup chunky apple sauce
½ cup granulated sugar
2 eggs
¼ cup CRISCO® Oil
2 tablespoons milk
2 tablespoons chopped walnuts
2 teaspoons butter or margarine
1 teaspoon packed brown sugar

Preheat oven to 350°F. Oil and flour 8×4-inch loaf pan.

Mix flour, baking powder, apple pie spice, salt and baking soda in medium mixing bowl. Set aside. Combine apple sauce, granulated sugar, eggs, Crisco® Oil and milk in large mixing bowl. Mix well. Add flour mixture. Beat at medium speed with electric mixer just until combined, scraping bowl occasionally. Pour into prepared pan. Combine walnuts, butter and brown sugar in small mixing bowl. Mix with fork until crumbly. Sprinkle down center of loaf.

Bake at 350°F for 35 to 45 minutes or until golden brown and wooden pick inserted in center comes out clean. Immediately remove from pan. Cool on wire rack.

Makes 1 loaf

*Substitute ¾ teaspoon ground cinnamon, dash ground nutmeg and dash ground cloves for apple pie spice, if desired.

Acknowledgments

The publishers would like to thank the companies and organizations listed below for the use of their recipes in this book.

Almond Board of California
American Dairy Association
American Egg Board
Arm & Hammer Division, Church & Dwight Co., Inc.
Armour Swift-Eckrich
Best Foods, a Division of CPC International Inc.
Borden Kitchens, Borden, Inc.
California Apricot Advisory Board
California Table Grape Commission
California Tree Fruit Agreement
Canned Fruit Promotion Service
Checkerboard Kitchens, Ralston Purina Company
Del Monte Foods
Diamond Walnut Growers, Inc.
Dole Food Company, Inc.
Hershey Chocolate U.S.A.
The HVR Company
Kellogg Company
The Kingsford Products Company
Kraft General Foods, Inc.
Land O' Lakes, Inc.
Libby's, Nestlé Food Company
Thomas J. Lipton Co.

McIlhenny Company
Michigan Blueberry Growers Association
Mott's U.S.A., A Division of Cadbury Beverages Inc.
Nabisco Foods Group
National Cherry Foundation
Nestlé Food Company
Ocean Spray Cranberries, Inc.
Oklahoma Peanut Commission
Oregon-Washington-California Pear Bureau
Pet Incorporated
The Procter & Gamble Company, Inc.
The Quaker Oats Company
Roman Meal Company
Sokol and Company
The Sugar Association, Inc.
Sun·Maid Growers of California
USA Rice Council
Washington Apple Commission
Western New York Apple Growers Association, Inc.
Wisconsin Milk Marketing Board

Photo Credits

The publishers would like to thank the companies and organizations listed below for the use of their photographs in this book.

Almond Board of California
Armour Swift-Eckrich
Best Foods, a Division of CPC International Inc.
Borden Kitchens, Borden, Inc.
California Apricot Advisory Board
California Tree Fruit Agreement
Checkerboard Kitchens, Ralston Purina Company
Del Monte Foods
Dole Food Company, Inc.
Hershey Chocolate U.S.A.

The HVR Company
Kellogg Company
Kraft General Foods, Inc.
Libby's, Nestlé Food Company
Mott's U.S.A., A Division of Cadbury Beverages Inc.
Nabisco Foods Group
Nestlé Food Company
Pet Incorporated
The Procter & Gamble Company, Inc.
USA Rice Council
Washington Apple Commission

INDEX

METRIC CONVERSION CHART

VOLUME MEASUREMENT (dry)

⅛ teaspoon = .5 mL
¼ teaspoon = 1 mL
½ teaspoon = 2 mL
¾ teaspoon = 4 mL
1 teaspoon = 5 mL
1 tablespoon = 15 mL
2 tablespoons = 25 mL
¼ cup = 50 mL
⅓ cup = 75 mL
⅔ cup = 150 mL
¾ cup = 175 mL
1 cup = 250 mL
2 cups = 1 pint = 500 mL
3 cups = 750 mL
4 cups = 1 quart = 1 L

VOLUME MEASUREMENT (fluid)

1 fluid ounce (2 tablespoons) = 30 mL
4 fluid ounces (½ cup) = 125 mL
8 fluid ounces (1 cup) = 250 mL
12 fluid ounces (1½ cups) = 375 mL
16 fluid ounces (2 cups) = 500 mL

WEIGHT (MASS)

½ ounce = 15 g
1 ounce = 30 g
3 ounces = 85 g
3.75 ounces = 100 g
4 ounces = 115 g
8 ounces = 225 g
12 ounces = 340 g
16 ounces = 1 pound = 450 g

DIMENSION

¹⁄₁₆ inch = 2 mm
⅛ inch = 3 mm
¼ inch = 6 mm
½ inch = 1.5 cm
¾ inch = 2 cm
1 inch = 2.5 cm

OVEN TEMPERATURES

250°F = 120°C
275°F = 140°C
300°F = 150°C
325°F = 160°C
350°F = 180°C
375°F = 190°C
400°F = 200°C
425°F = 220°C
450°F = 230°C

BAKING PAN SIZES

Utensil	Size in Inches/Quarts	Metric Volume	Size in Centimeters
Baking or	8×8×2	2 L	20×20×5
Cake pan	9×9×2	2.5 L	22×22×5
(square or	12×8×2	3 L	30×20×5
rectangular)	13×9×2	3.5 L	33×23×5
Loaf Pan	8×4×3	1.5 L	20×10×7
	9×5×3	2 L	23×13×7
Round Layer	8×1½	1.2 L	20×4
Cake Pan	9×1½	1.5 L	23×4
Pie Plate	8×1¼	750 mL	20×3
	9×1¼	1 L	23×3
Baking Dish	1 quart	1 L	
or Casserole	1½ quart	1.5 L	
	2 quart	2 L	